Imagining the African American West

RACE AND ETHNICITY IN THE AMERICAN WEST

Series editors:
Albert S. Broussard
Maria Raquel Casas
Dudley Gardner
Margaret Jacobs
Delphine Red Shirt
Benson Tong

Blake Allmendinger

Imagining the African American West

University of Nebraska Press
Lincoln and London

∞

Set in New Caledonia by Bob Reitz.
Printed by Thomson-Shore, Inc.

Library of Congress Cataloging-in-Publication Data
Allmendinger, Blake.
Imagining the African American West / Blake Allmendinger.
p.   cm.—(Race and ethnicity in the American West)
Includes bibliographical references and index.
ISBN-13: 978-0-8032-1067-7 (cloth: alk. paper)
ISBN-10: 0-8032-1067-1 (cloth: alk. paper)
1. American literature—West (U.S.)—History and criticism.
2. American literature—African American authors—History and criticism.
3. African Americans—West (U.S.)—Biography—History and criticism.
4. African Americans—West (U.S.)—Intellectual life.   5. African Americans—
West (U.S.)—Historiography.   6. African Americans—West (U.S.)—History.
7. Frontier and pioneer life in literature.   8. West (U.S.)—Intellectual life.
9. African Americans in literature.   10. West (U.S.)—Historiography.
11. West (U.S.)—In literature.   I. Title.   II. Series.
PS271.A434   2005
810.9'3278—dc22
2005010261

Contents

Illustrations

Acknowledgments

I would like to thank the National Endowment for the Humanities and the American Council of Learned Societies for supporting my research in 2000 and 2001 while I was working in residence at the Huntington Library.

I would also like to thank Lars Larson, my graduate research assistant, colleague, and friend, for helping to make this book possible.

A version of chapter 2 first appeared in the September 2003 issue of *American Literature*.

Bill Pickett bites a steer's lip in a rodeo staged near the turn of the century. (Author's collection)

Introduction

Did you know that an African American[1] cowboy invented the sport known as steer wrestling? Bill Pickett introduced the sport while performing in rodeos in the early twentieth century. After wrestling a steer to the ground, he would bite the animal's lip, paralyzing the steer and forcing it to surrender to his control.[2]

Did you know that "The Yellow Rose of Texas" was written by a Texas plantation owner who was in love with one of his slaves? In the mid-nineteenth century, Colonel James Morgan composed the ballad in honor of Emily West, a "high yellow" woman with "golden-skinned" charms.[3]

Did you know that not all of the Okies who left Oklahoma during the Dust Bowl and who moved to California were white? There were also a number of African American immigrants. Some of them, who are now almost one hundred years old, still live in the small town of Teviston.[4]

Although whites represent the majority of the population, other races and ethnic groups live in the West. In Westerns, minorities often play subordinate and stereotypical roles. But in reality, non-whites have made major contributions to the West throughout history.

Like other racial and ethnic groups, African Americans have been visible in the region for centuries. But scholars did not begin to study the West and its inhabitants until fairly recently. In "The Significance of the Frontier in American History," published in 1893, Frederick Jackson Turner complained that nineteenth-century American historians paid too much attention to the North and the South. While focusing on tensions between the two regions, scholars neglected the West. According to Turner, the Civil War was merely a sectional "incident" and a brief affair compared to westward migration, which was a national movement that continued throughout most of the century.[5]

Martha Williams, one of the original black Okies, lives with her son Clay in a shack in Teviston, California. (Photograph by Matt Black © 2000)

Turner overemphasized the importance of the frontier in order to compensate for the previous lack of attention the West had received. In some fields, such as African American history, the West has continued to play a peripheral role until recently. For example, historians of the nineteenth century have concentrated on African Americans who were slaves in the South and who moved to the North after escaping or receiving their freedom. But what about the African Americans who journeyed to the West during the same period?

Since the early sixteenth century, people of African origin have inhabited the western part of the continent. African slaves accompanied early Spanish explorers and later Lewis and Clark. They intermingled with other races, settled throughout the region, and worked in many professions. However, until the twentieth century, people of African heritage, including African Americans, were less numerous in the West than other racial and ethnic minorities. In the nineteenth century, for example, whites were more attuned to the presence of Mexicans and Native Americans because large numbers of indigenous peoples posed a greater threat to American empire than a few thousand African American slaves or freedmen and -women.[6] In the states, "the color line" referred to invisible barriers and social and legal distinctions between blacks and whites.[7] The term was not used in the West. But Turner's phrase "the frontier line" had a similar meaning.[8] It referred to the border between "civilization" and "savagery," represented by whites and indigenous peoples, respectively. Mexicans and Native Americans constituted the "other," the presence that stood in the way of westering "civilization." Until the frontier was secured and territories and states were created, there were no laws or social codes governing black-white relations. African Americans on the early frontier were perceived as relatively nonthreatening entities.

Today, people associate the West with sepia-tinged memories of a rural frontier, even though most of its residents now live in large and increasingly sprawling metropolitan areas. Thus, another reason why we tend to forget that there is an African American West is because African Americans did not begin migrating to the region in large numbers until the twentieth century. When they did so, like many other Americans, they moved to urban locales. Since the West is not urban, in the minds of people who cling to the notion of a mythic frontier, the concept of a modern multicultural West is not very popular.

Until recently, the only books on the African American West were specialized histories that documented the roles played by African Americans in the preindustrial West. *The Negro Cowboys* (1965), by Philip Durham and Everett L. Jones, claims that approximately five thousand cowboys on the frontier were of African origin. *The Buffalo Soldiers* (1967), by William H. Leckie, tells the story of the U.S. Army's nineteenth-century African American cavalry regiments. *Exodusters* (1976), by Nell Irvin Painter, chronicles the migration of African American homesteaders to Kansas in the late 1870s. *Blacks in Gold Rush California* (1977), by Rudolph M. Lapp, documents the presence of African American miners in the mid-nineteenth century. Several general histories of the African American West have appeared more recently. *The Black West*, published by William Loren Katz in 1987 and revised many times over the years, is an accessible history aimed at nonspecialists. *In Search of the Racial Frontier* (1998), by Quintard Taylor, provides a comprehensive survey of African Americans in the American West. It spans almost five hundred years and serves as an indispensable guide for scholars in African American and western American history. *African Americans in the West* (1998), a bibliography of secondary sources compiled by Bruce A. Glasrud, is designed to help scholars interested in conducting further research.

There are few literary studies of the African American West, for the obvious reason that not every historical personage leaves a literary record for the sake of posterity. Some early African Americans, including slaves and

Mary Ellen Pleasant, nineteenth-century San Francisco entrepreneur. (Author's collection)

ex-slaves, were illiterate. Others were too busy homesteading, prospecting, ranching, serving in the military, or running small businesses to keep journals, compose fiction and poetry, or write autobiographies. For instance, Mary Ellen Pleasant came to San Francisco during the gold rush, worked as a cook, invested her wages, and eventually became a wealthy real estate maven and entrepreneur. She owned three laundries and a boardinghouse, speculated in mining, and became notorious for harboring a fugitive slave. If ever a life deserved to be chronicled, it was certainly hers.[9]

Other African Americans, prominent as well as obscure, narrated their personal histories. But they lived in the West for a short time and their experiences there made up only a small portion of their autobiographies. *The Life and Adventures of James Williams, a Fugitive Slave* was published in 1873. But only five of the fifty-six chapters cover the author's career as a miner and businessman on the early frontier. In 1902, Mifflin Wistar Gibbs published *Shadow and Light*. A brief portion of the autobiography covers a period in the mid-nineteenth century when Gibbs was a San Francisco merchant, newspaper founder, and community activist. The remainder documents his travels to Canada, to the American South, and to lands overseas. The first work in African American literature dealing extensively with the American West is *The Life and Adventures of James P. Beckwourth* (1856), the autobiography of a mulatto who worked in the fur industry and lived with a tribe of Crow Indians. However, Beckwourth does not identify himself as a person of color; instead, he attempts to pass as white in his autobiography.

Beckwourth's book raises the following question: To what extent can a work offer insights into the African American western experience when its author denies having had a "racial" experience? The question that arises most frequently in this study is that of representation. In the nineteenth century, for example, African Americans in the West were a diverse group of people. They were slaves, ex-slaves, and freedmen and -women. They lived in segregated towns and farming communities, with whites, and among indigenous tribes. Some had pure African blood. Others had white antecedents, Spanish and Mexican ancestors, and relationships to Native Americans. They pioneered the Great Plains, crossed the southwestern desert, and discovered routes through the Rockies. Can a few literary works by a handful of writers, not all of whom identified as people of color, speak for the thousands of African Americans living in the region prior to the twentieth century? Probably not. For this reason their works are even more valuable. Such documents, including Beckwourth's autobiography, a trilogy of homesteading novels by Oscar Micheaux, and racial melodramas by Pauline Hopkins and Sutton E. Griggs, were published at a time when accounts of African Americans in the region were rare.

In the twentieth century, as the number of African Americans in the region increased, so did the volume of literature about the African American western experience. Where there was once a scarcity there is now an abundance of artistic works to consider, including futuristic fiction and historical novels, Westerns and mysteries, contemporary urban dramas and regional autobiographies, not to mention music and film. Again, there is the problem of representation. Since it is impossible to consider each of these works, which ones should a critic select for analysis in a representative study? In the first three chapters of this book I evaluate works by individual authors, such as James P. Beckwourth, Oscar Micheaux, Pauline Hopkins, and Sutton E. Griggs, among the few African Americans writing on the West in the nineteenth and early twentieth centuries. In the remaining five chapters I sift through the material that has accumulated over the last one hundred years, attempting to group together works that are products of cultural movements, such as the Harlem Renaissance; examples of genres, such as Westerns, detective fiction, and historical novels; and literature that examines similar themes, such as women's rights and urban unrest.

In the process of researching and writing this book I came to realize that there is no such thing as a "representative" African American western experience. Although James P. Beckwourth attempted to pass as white in his autobiography, other African Americans were not only proud of their heritage but militant in their support of minority rights. The South Dakota homesteader Oscar Micheaux was a conservative who admired Booker T. Washington. But his contemporary, Sutton E. Griggs, a Baptist preacher from Texas, was more politically radical. In a novel he published at the turn of the century, Griggs debated whether African Americans should secede from the nation and form their own government. He anticipated a black nationalist movement that would become more influential in the decades to come.

There are many different impressions of place, just as there are many different types of racial experience. For Pauline Hopkins, the West is Kansas Territory in the mid-nineteenth century. In her historical novel, published in 1902, the African American characters fight to make Kansas a free state when it enters the Union. They join John Brown's brigade and fight to abolish the institution of slavery. Langston Hughes remembers Kansas differently in his fictional autobiography, published in 1930. Here, Kansas is portrayed as a midwestern state populated by small towns and neighborhoods where African Americans lead mostly peaceful if not trouble-free lives.

Kansas is either the West or the Midwest, depending on its position at a particular time. Similarly, Texas and Oklahoma are part of the South as well as the West. In *Shadow and Act* (1953), Oklahoma native Ralph Ellison notes that the state, like the Deep South, has a history of slavery and racism. But he also suggests that Oklahoma was a frontier during his youth, to the extent that it offered greater freedom and more opportunities for racial minorities. Although California is geographically part of the West, in some ways it seems to be an exceptional place, a land of extremes. But the West has never been one thing in particular. It has represented different things to various people living in numerous places over hundreds of years.

For some African American writers, the West is an uncivilized territory. For others, it is a cultivated farm or a rural community. For many, however, the West is a city, sometimes more dangerous than the early frontier. Jewell Parker Rhodes sets her historical novel *Magic City* in Tulsa in 1921, during one of the largest race riots of the twentieth century. In *Twilight: Los Angeles*, Anna Deavere Smith dramatizes the "uprising" that happened in 1992 in Los Angeles. Although many African American westerners live in urban locations, not all of them view urban experience in a negative light. Even those writers and artists who explore racial unrest and social apocalypse often believe that regeneration and redemption are possible. *Magic City* concludes with the hero's decision to build a new Tulsa out of the ashes. *Twilight* refers to that moment right before darkness, to a time of hope, not despair.

African Americans disagree about whether or not the West is a place of promise. Over the last several centuries they have migrated to the region in order to establish segregated townships and farming cooperatives as well as experimental racial utopias. But Toni Morrison, Pearl Cleage, and Octavia Butler suggest that these "ideal" communities were sometimes imperfect, impractical, or conceptually flawed. Some individuals embraced the West while others rejected it. James P. Beckwourth left St. Louis at an early age. He spent most of the rest of his life in the Rocky Mountains, in the Southwest, and in the Sierra Nevada, working successfully as a fur trader, scout, and self-employed businessman. However, Oscar Micheaux lost his farm in South Dakota, became disillusioned, and went back to Chicago. Other African Americans had mixed emotions about the region. Several members of the Harlem Renaissance grew up in the West. Langston Hughes, Wallace Thurman, and Taylor Gordon were raised in Kansas, Utah, and Montana, respectively. They left the West in order to pursue artistic careers in New York. Yet during the Renaissance they wrote about their experiences growing up in the West, revealing various feelings, ranging from nostalgia to bitterness.

Many African American writers, artists, and filmmakers work within genres while expanding the boundaries or resisting the limitations that those genres impose. For example, "black" Westerns obey the same formulas as traditional Westerns. At the same time, they depart from tradition by introducing racial themes and prominent minority characters. Similarly, "black" detective novelists, such as Chester Himes and Walter Mosley, have noir sensibilities. Like other writers in the noir detective tradition, they set many of their works in western cities such as Los Angeles. However, unlike their white counterparts, Himes and Mosley frequently examine racism and the role it plays in society.

Some African Americans reinvent genres such as Westerns and noir. Others use literature as a means of rewriting history. For example, African American women have become increasingly visible in western American literature. In *Flyin' West* (1992), Pearl Cleage reimagines the Exoduster migration that occurred in the late 1870s. African American women play significant roles in her drama, though they tend to be overlooked by historians. Toni Morrison was inspired to write *Paradise* (1997) after reading about a forgotten chapter in African American history: the founding of African American townships on the western frontier. Her novel also includes a group of mysterious women who challenge a patriarchal African American rural community. Few African Americans wrote about the West in the nineteenth century, and most of those who did were men. However, contemporary African American writers, including a large percentage of women, have recently written historical novels and plays situated in the early American West, told from the perspectives of women and racial minorities.

Frederick Jackson Turner was never more readable than when he was writing about the presence of Americans on the western frontier. Unlike some other historians, who write in unimaginative prose, Turner loved vivid metaphors and colorful imagery. In his essay, for example, he alternately refers to the influx of immigrants and the advancement of "civilization" as a "frontier line," as a "tide" (36), and as a "series of waves" (44). Some of these phrases have received critical scrutiny. [10] But one of my favorites has gone overlooked. At one point in his essay, Turner describes westward movement as "an uneven advance," with "tongues of settlement" protruding into the American "wilderness" (42). I love this phrase even though I have no idea what it means. Like most metaphors, it evokes poetic associations instead of defining something concrete. Maybe the "tongues" are peninsulas, extensions of human society. Or maybe Turner is referring to the protruding part of a wagon or trailer known as the "tongue," which attaches to the hitch of a vehicle. But if this is the case, then what is the "hitch" and what is the "vehicle" that pulls the wagon of "civilization"? At this point, my mental process, like the metaphor, begins to break down.

On a literal level—the one level on which Turner may not have intended it—the phrase "tongues of settlement" suggests the articulation of a presence in the American West. Ironically, Turner never acknowledged the existence of African Americans on the early frontier. Yet they have asserted their presence in the region over the course of the last several centuries, speaking in various "tongues," including the oral tradition, literature, music, and film.

Since the 1960s, the field of western American literature has expanded to include works by Chicanos, Native Americans, and Asian Americans. Scholars have become more interested in the experiences of western Jews, Mormons, and other religious minorities. Environmentalists and feminists have helped to redefine what used to be a politically conservative field. Yet within this increasingly diversified discipline, African American writers remain almost invisible. [11]

This book offers the first comprehensive study of African American literature about the American West. The only other book on this subject is Michael K. Johnson's *Black Masculinity and the Frontier Myth in American Literature* (2002). Because he writes on the subject of black masculinity, Johnson focuses almost exclusively on writings by African American men. In this book, however, I explore a variety of issues that pertain to African American women and men, on the early frontier and in the urban American West. I write primarily about literature, although I discuss other works, such as Western films and West Coast rap music, to the extent that they share with the literature certain generic affinities and thematic concerns.

This is an inclusive and representative study, but it is not an encyclopedic survey of works in the field. I have chosen examples of literary genres, movements, or trends, leaving out other examples that might have served just as well. I have excluded works such as *American Daughter* (1946), by Era Bell Thompson, simply because I could not find a way to incorporate it into my study. I limit myself to considering works by African Americans who represent the experience of living in the American West. I do not write about African Americans who were born or raised in the West unless they portray the West in their work. In addition, I do not include depictions of African Americans by white western writers and filmmakers. In many such novels and films, African Americans play secondary or stereotypical roles. [12] While it might be useful to contrast black and white representations of the African American West, it would also result in privileging, to some extent, these white representations, many of which have already been widely disseminated by the popular media. I have chosen to redress this situation by giving priority to works in which African Americans tell their own stories and take center stage. Doing so not only adds to our appreciation of African American literature but contributes to our understanding of the American West.

CHAPTER ONE

Beckwourth's Pass

In 1528, Esteban, a slave owned by a Spanish explorer, became the first person of African heritage to enter what would later become known as the American West. Over the course of the next three hundred years, other people of African heritage would come to the region, arriving by various routes, and some would play historically significant roles. Pío Pico, a politician of Mexican and African ancestry, twice served as governor of California during the period of Mexican rule. He wrote his memoirs in 1877.[1] William Leidesdorff, a merchant seaman of Danish and African ancestry, settled in California in the mid-1840s. He became a Mexican citizen and later worked for the United States government, serving under President James K. Polk, who was unaware of his African heritage.[2]

Americans of African ancestry also played prominent roles in the region in the early and mid-nineteenth century. In 1856, James P. Beckwourth published his autobiography, in which he recounted his experiences as a mountain man, trapper, and scout and as an honorary member of a Native American tribe. *The Life and Adventures of James P. Beckwourth*—as told to Thomas D. Bonner, a white man—was the first work in American literature to relay the story of an African American on the western frontier. Beckwourth was born in Virginia, sometime around the turn of the century, to a slave owned by Sir Jennings Beckwith, a descendant of minor Irish aristocrats (the name was altered to Beckwourth in the autobiography). In 1810, Beckwith and his family, including "twenty-two negroes," moved to St. Louis, Missouri.[3] One biographer believes that Beckwith may have manumitted his son during this period, noting that Beckwourth's subsequent jobs—as a blacksmith's apprentice, lead miner, and itinerant worker—"indicate that he was regarded as a *free* black man, because he was able to move as he pleased."[4] Between 1824 and 1828, Beckwourth worked for the Rocky Mountain Fur Company, first as a blacksmith, servant, and groom, then as a trapper. From approximately 1828 until 1834 he lived with a tribe of Crow Indians, during which time he was employed by the American Fur Company. Between 1837 and 1866, when he died, he held a variety of jobs and traveled extensively. He was recruited to fight in Florida against the Seminole Indians; became a trader on the Santa Fe Trail; served as a guide in California before the Mexican-American War; ran a saloon; discovered a route through the Sierra Mountains that was later named Beckwourth Pass; moved to Colorado, where he was tried and acquitted on charges of killing a man; and finally returned to the Montana Territory to live with the Crow.

Not all of this information appears in the autobiography. The book was published ten years before the end of his life and focused primarily on the time Beckwourth spent in the Rocky Mountains, working for the fur trade and living with Native Americans. In addition, *The Life and Adventures* conveys the impression that Beckwourth was white. The book fails to mention that his mother was a slave or that he was the son of a slave. No one knows who made the decision to disguise Beckwourth's racial identity—Beckwourth, Bonner, or the two men working in collaboration on the autobiography— or why that decision was made. However, the majority of readers at the time would have been white, and those readers would have been acquainted mostly with white trappers and scouts, both real and fictitious (such as Daniel Boone, Davy Crockett, and Natty Bumppo), in the mid-nineteenth century. The collaborators may have decided to portray Beckwourth as white in order to create a readily identifiable character and to appeal to conventional expectations and popular tastes.

Although Beckwourth may have passed as white in order to win acceptance with readers who lived in the states, he was relatively welcome as an African American on the western frontier. He became integrated into white and Native American frontier communities. He independently contracted his services to several fur companies, owned a hotel, became a self-employed merchant and guide, and was able to pursue various entrepreneurial schemes. For forty years he was free "to move as he pleased." By comparison, an African American man who lived in the states, even a manumitted slave, undoubtedly would have been more confined. Typically, he would not have been granted the same human agency—geographic mobility, social acceptance, and professional options—as a white man in antebellum society. The autobiography suggests that the treatment of African Americans differed according to region in the mid-nineteenth century. Although Beckwourth played a significant role on the western frontier, only a "white" man could be expected to play that role in the "civilized" world where people were reading his autobiography.

African Americans such as Beckwourth experienced only relative freedom in the early American West. In Texas, California, and Kansas, the territories with the largest African American populations in the early and mid-nineteenth century,[5] freedom was by no means guaranteed. Most African Americans in Texas Territory were slaves. When Texas became a state in 1845, it legalized the institution of slavery. California outlawed the practice in its state constitution, but it continued to allow slaveholders to enter the state. Kansas was contested terrain. African Americans and white abolitionists fought a long, bitter battle to ensure that Kansas was a "free" state when it entered the Union.

In other territories, African Americans were neither the subject of political debate nor the object of intense social scrutiny. In the Rocky Mountain region, where they were a statistically insignificant presence, they enjoyed greater freedom of movement and surprisingly diverse opportunities. The region had been sparsely populated by African Americans since the Louisiana Purchase in 1803. Fewer than two hundred "negroes" lived in the Montana Territory in 1870, when the first U.S. census was taken.[6] Throughout the nineteenth century, African Americans in the region represented an extremely small racial minority. Instead, Native Americans were the focus of U.S. economic and political policy, especially in the early decades of the century, when the American fur trade relied on tribes such as the Crow to provide them with beaver and otter pelts and animal hides. Beckwourth and other African American men were employed by U.S. companies to facilitate trade with Native Americans. For example, Edward Rose began working for the Missouri Fur Company in 1807 and later lived with various tribes, including the Crow. Moses "Black" Harris, who came west in 1832, joined the Rocky Mountain Fur Company and spoke the Snake language fluently.[7] Although African Americans were outnumbered by whites and Native Americans, they were vital to the success of the frontier economy. Some whites believed that Native Americans would rather do business with people of color, while one nineteenth-century ethnologist theorized that "negroes" had a "pacifying effect" on Native Americans.[8] In addition, Rose was believed to be part white and part Cherokee. His success as a trapper was partially attributed to his kinship with Native Americans.

Men such as Beckwourth, Harris, and Rose were able to move freely among races on the early frontier. Although they worked for the white-organized fur trade, some of them also lived with Native Americans. As representatives of American enterprise, they were perceived as agents of "civilization" (one writer describes Beckwourth as a "patriot" who supported westward expansion because he worked for the fur trade).[9] An African American trapper might even be referred to as "white" because he was affiliated with one of these companies. In his autobiography, Beckwourth recalls trapping along the Sage River and meeting his colleague, "Black" Harris (100). Beckwourth calls Harris a "white" man, placing the word in quotation marks. By the time Beckwourth published his autobiography, Harris was already well known to readers, having been celebrated in George Frederic Ruxton's *Life in the Far West* (1849), a sketchbook commemorating the Englishman's tour of America, and in Emerson Bennett's historical novels *The Prairie Flower* (1850) and *Leni Leoti* (1851). The nickname "Black" referred to the fact that Harris was not a Caucasian. Bennett explained that the trapper had a "dingy complexion" and "African" features.[10] Figuratively speaking, however, Harris was "white." Beckwourth used it as an honorary term to indicate that the trapper was not a Native or "savage" but a member of "civilization" who worked for one of the American companies.

If African Americans were indispensable to the white-organized fur trade, they were also useful to Native Americans. At times, Beckwourth and Rose lived with the Crow. They facilitated trade between whites and Native Americans, making it possible for the Crow to exchange pelts and hides for manufactured commodities, including guns and ammunition, certain foods, alcohol, wool blankets, glass beads, and other items that tribes could not produce for themselves.[11] One scholar claims that the Crow were an "ethnocentric people" who reluctantly admitted non–Native Americans into their tribe in order to foster better economic relations with fur traders.[12] In his autobiography, Beckwourth offers a different reason for why he lived with the Crow. He claims that a friend played a practical joke on the tribe, convincing the Crow that Beckwourth was a long-lost relation "who had been sold to the whites" as a young man and raised in captivity (140). An elderly Crow woman, after discovering "a mole over one of his eyes," allegedly identified Beckwourth as her son and welcomed him back into the tribe (146).

It is impossible to confirm whether Beckwourth's story is true or whether the tribe accepted the trapper because it wanted to strengthen its relationship with the American fur trade. One thing is certain, however. In the Rocky Mountain region in the early and mid-nineteenth century, race relations were based to some extent on economic necessity. White corporations, instead of discriminating against African American traders, trappers, scouts, and interpreters, frequently hired them to facilitate diplomatic and economic relations with Native Americans. Tribes adopted African Americans at least partly because of their valuable connections to trade.

In addition to necessitating flexible forms of economic exchange, the fur trade required negotiations among races on the Rocky Mountain frontier. The fur trade was based on a barter economy. Certain goods, such as pelts, were exchanged for different kinds of goods, usually manufactured commodities. There was no single currency and no standard rate of exchange. Representatives of the fur companies and Native Americans negotiated transactions, trading dissimilar items that had relative values for the different parties involved. Beckwourth enabled these transactions by claiming dual racial identities and maintaining simultaneous national and tribal allegiances. According to the autobiography, while working as an African American trapper for white corporations he passed as a Native American. He encouraged the Crow to produce raw goods and increased the tribe's power to purchase manufactured commodities. At the same time, he furthered the interests of American trade. Beckwourth—part white, part African American, and part "Native American"—successfully straddled the line between "civilization" and "savagery" in the Rocky Mountain region during this period.

After he entered the tribe, Beckwourth continued to negotiate for leverage with the Crow and to play multiple roles. In the autobiography, he soon realizes that the Crow have other interests besides trading with American companies. Occasionally, they attack other tribes, stealing horses and killing and scalping their enemies. Beckwourth disdains these activities. When tribes are at war, he comments pragmatically, "various branches of business are impoverished, and it becomes inconvenient for those engaged in them to make more than trifling purchases" (113). Beckwourth tries to persuade the Crow "to devote their undivided attention to trapping, not alone for their own benefit, but for the interest of [the American Fur Company] in whose service I was engaged" (214). He attempts to gain greater influence over the Crow by rising within the ranks of the tribe. Because the only way to achieve social standing or chieftainship is to demonstrate prowess in battle, Beckwourth decides to participate with the Crow in a series of raids.[13]

After each victory, Beckwourth receives a new name as a mark of respect. When he enters the tribe, the Crow call him Morning Star, meaning "the lost son" (149). Later he distinguishes himself as "the greatest man in the party" when he fights his first battle (153). In recognition for killing a Blackfoot, the

Crow name him Antelope (161). He becomes known as Big Bowl after he scalps several Cheyenne (169); Bull's Robe, after his next encounter with the same tribe of foes (177); and Enemy of Horses, after orchestrating a raid on an Arapaho herd (183). After scalping an "Indian," he receives "a still more ennobling appellation . . . the Bobtail Horse" (201). He also acquires the titles Red Fish (222) and Red Arm or Bloody Arm (262–64). Eventually, according to the autobiography, Beckwourth and Long Hair, another Crow warrior, become "head chief[s] of the nation" (267). Beckwourth earns this honor because of his military successes and leadership qualities, as his new name, Good War Road, suggests (269). His last name, Medicine Calf, refers to the good luck he has brought to the tribe (273).

The Life and Adventures does not reveal whether Beckwourth was able to use his increasing authority to convince the tribe to spend more time trapping and less time pursuing other activities. But it describes his brave deeds, his acceptance of numerous laurels, and his spreading fame within the tribal community. Beckwourth appears to be a mutable, indestructible figure. He survives a series of adventures and accidents, he seems to return from the dead on several occasions, and with each resurrection he reconfirms his reputation as a supernatural hero. When Beckwourth enters the tribe, pretending to be a long-lost relation, the Crow proclaim that he has come back from the "dead" (147). Later the tribe thinks that Beckwourth and his warriors have been killed by Cheyenne, "but when they saw us returning with twenty scalps, and only one of our party hurt, their grief gave way to admiration, and we were hailed with shouts of applause" (188). In the course of another battle, the Crow believe that Beckwourth has been killed by a bullet, though he has only been stunned by a ricochet. When he awakens, the tribe attributes his seemingly amazing recovery to powerful "medicine" (175). After presumably dying during another "fight with the Indians," Beckwourth revives once again. The Crow find "no bullet-wound on my body, and again it was proved that my broad-bladed hunting-knife (though not the same one) had averted the blow" (373). Periodically, whites hear rumors regarding Beckwourth's demise. On one occasion, when Beckwourth appears at Fort Clarke dressed as a Crow, he causes a dramatic sensation. "Good heavens!" exclaims one of the men at the fort. "I have heard your name mentioned a thousand times. You were supposed dead, and were so reported by Captain Sublet." Beckwourth boasts: "I am not dead, as you see; I still move and breathe" (178). Many months later, he almost dies in another battle with a tribe of Cheyenne. Afterward, when he appears at the fort, having recovered from near-fatal injuries, the traders again seem surprised: "I thought [one of

James P. Beckwourth appears dark-skinned in this photograph, taken in the mid-nineteenth century. (Nevada Historical Society)

them] would fall to the ground; it was some seconds before he could speak, his astonishment was so overwhelming." Others come running "to welcome one whom they had all long since supposed dead" (338).

The autobiography describes Beckwourth's exciting adventures, various forms of employment, different races and cultures with whom he came into contact, and places where he traveled or lived on the western frontier. The autobiography suggests that Beckwourth was able to do what he wanted, to define who he was, to adapt to any group or environment by reinventing himself, and to survive many calamities. In the autobiography, he has an ability to pass as a member of another race, to be resurrected, to change names and identities, and to enjoy physical freedom, social fluidity, and economic mobility.

Perhaps the most amazing feat that Beckwourth performed was passing as white in his autobiography. Photographs of Beckwourth reveal that he was not a Caucasian. People who knew him during his lifetime, as well as scholars who investigated his ancestry after his death, suspected that he may have been a mulatto, but they could never agree on the specific ingredients making up his racial identity. In *The Oregon Trail*, published seven years prior to the autobiography, Francis Parkman Jr. described Beckwourth as a "mongrel of French, American, and negro blood."[14] In his copy of the first edition of *The Life and Adventures*, Parkman wrote that the trapper was "a compound of white and black blood, though he represents otherwise."[15] In a work about mountain men that was published the year after *The Oregon Trail*, Lewis Garrard claimed that Beckwourth was half "black" and half French.[16] Biographers and western historians offer conflicting opinions as well. One believes that Beckwourth's mother was a full-blooded "negro"; others contend that she was one-quarter "black"; another maintains that Beckwourth was half "white," one-quarter "black," and one-quarter "Indian."[17]

In the autobiography, Beckwourth adds to this confusion by refusing to discuss his heritage. However, on several occasions he suggests a kinship with whites. He says that General William H. Ashley, the leader of the Rocky Mountain Fur Company expedition, treated Beckwourth like a "brother" (46). At times, Beckwourth even seems to be Ashley's superior. He allegedly saves Ashley's life when the general is attacked by a buffalo: "I, seeing the danger in which [Ashley] was placed, sent a ball into the beast just behind the shoulder, instantly dropping him dead" (57). Later, on the Green River, when their boat capsizes, Beckwourth demonstrates his impressive leadership qualities: " 'There is only one way I can possibly save you [from drowning],' " he remembers telling the general, " 'but you must follow my directions in the most minute degree.' " " 'Anything you say, James, I will follow,' said he" (59).

Beckwourth identifies himself as a representative of "civilization," which he defines as a white presence on the western frontier. He forges a trail through the wilderness, where "the white man" has never set foot (62). At first he doubts whether he can live with the Crow, but he decides that "civilized man can accustom himself to any mode of life when pelf is the governing principle" (120). "Many readers will doubtless wonder how a man who had been reared in civilized life could participate in such scenes of carnage," as Beckwourth describes (232). "But, in justification, it may be urged that the Crows had never shed the blood of the white man during my stay in their camp." They "were uniformly faithful in their obligations to my race," he maintains (198). A "white man can easily become an Indian" if he lives too long among "savages" (323). But Beckwourth never feels tempted to relinquish his ties to "civilization." At the end of the book he reassures readers regarding his loyalties, defining himself as "an American citizen" and "a friend of my race" (529).

Readers who were not aware of earlier claims that Beckwourth was a "mongrel" or a "compound" of several racial ingredients may have assumed that the trapper was white. Beckwourth never contradicts the claims made by Parkman and Garrard, but he uses such terms as "the white man," "my race," "civilized man," and "civilized life" to refer to groups or societies with which he identifies. At the same time, he puts a critical distance between himself and other African Americans who appear in the book, including a cowardly "negro" (339), a "velvet-headed scoundrel," and a "consummate villain" (249). These disreputable characters have nothing in common with the hero of the autobiography.

Beckwourth is articulate, erudite, at times sentimental, and poetic in temperament (the book concludes with a poetic tribute to one of his wives, "Pine Leaf, the Indian Heroine"). Allegedly, he dictated his story to Thomas D. Bonner, a justice of the peace who met Beckwourth in a California mining camp in the mid-nineteenth century.[18] Although Bonner claims in the preface that he "literally" transcribed the words that appear in the text (4), there are reasons to suspect that he may have contributed substantially to the production of the autobiography. On one hand, if Beckwourth had two years of schooling, as he says in the book (18), then he was not an "illiterate," as one critic has claimed.[19] On the other hand, it seems unlikely that a semi-educated mountain man would refer to hunting and fishing as "sylvan and piscatorial sports" (528). Whoever authored the autobiography wanted to stress that Beckwourth had lived among "savages" without losing his refinement or his gift for expressing his thoughts in felicitous prose and occasional poetry.

Some of the sketches that illustrated the first edition of the autobiography would have contributed to the reader's perception that Beckwourth was white (the pictures are unsigned, and the artist's name is unknown).[20] Chapter 36

Beckwourth seems lighter-skinned in this sketch, captioned "James P. Beckwourth in Citizen's Dress," which appeared in the first edition of his autobiography.

includes a portrait of the subject, captioned "James P. Beckwourth in Citizen's Dress." It shows a light-skinned man with a mustache and beard wearing a starched white shirt, bow tie, jacket, and vest. The chain from his pocket watch is draped across his chest like a banner proclaiming his elegance. In chapter 35, an illustration entitled "Attack of a Grizzly Bear" portrays Beckwourth as a man in the wilderness, seated on horseback, engaged in combat with an animal predator. The subject wears a buckskin jacket with fringe, leggings, and boots. A wide-brim hat casts a shadow over part of his face. But the features that remain visible are unmistakably white. In chapter 10, an illustration depicts Beckwourth punishing one of his "disobedient"

Indian wives. Here he has Caucasian facial characteristics but wears Native garb and has long, straight hair like the Crow.

In other sketches, however, Beckwourth's features are either hard to decipher or hidden from view. In chapter 30 the portrait of "Beckwourth as an Indian Warrior" depicts the subject on a prancing steed, holding a lance and shield. His face has been shaded an indeterminate gray. Beckwourth has a darker complexion in chapter 18, but he appears to be the same color as members of the Crow tribe who stand by his side. The picture seems to support Beckwourth's claim that he was able to pass as a Native American. Other illustrations make it impossible to determine Beckwourth's racial identity. In chapter 5, the picture of Beckwourth rescuing General Ashley from an attack by a buffalo shows the hero from a distance, in miniature, aiming his gun; his features are unrecognizable. In chapters 11 and 13 he is shown from the back, facing away from the viewer. As a whole, the sketches in the autobiography complicate and sometimes obscure, rather than clarify, Beckwourth's identity. They portray someone who is alternately light-skinned and dark-skinned, white and Native American. In different illustrations, Beckwourth resembles a warrior, a trapper, and an elegant gentleman. Sometimes he stands in the foreground and faces the viewer; sometimes he appears at a distance, blends into the background, or turns his back on the audience. Although most of the illustrations portray Beckwourth as white, they also show him playing various roles, striking multiple poses, and adopting different appearances.

Beckwourth was known as a "mountain man." However, the term was ambiguous. A mountain man might hunt in the mountains or trap along the rivers and streams. He might work for one of the fur companies but live with a tribe of Native Americans. He might trade with both groups but live independently. In *The Adventures of Captain Bonneville* (1837), Washington Irving described the typical mountain man as a semi-barbaric, semi-civilized creature who wore a "ruffled" calico shirt and rough leather breeches, moccasins "embroidered" with beads, and knives, ammunition, and other paraphernalia attached to a colorful sash that circled his waist. According to Irving, you could not "pay a fur trapper a greater compliment, than to persuade him you [had] mistaken him for an Indian brave."[21] After touring the region, Ruxton concluded that mountain men should be classified in the same "genus" as "primitive savage[s]," since both groups had instinctive hunting and trapping abilities and other "animal qualities."[22] In his novel, *The Scalp Hunter* (1856), Captain Mayne Reid portrays mountain men as a racially indeterminate, uncivilized breed. They have swarthy complexions; their faces are "greasy all over," "tanned by the sun, and smoked by the fire."

They wear deerskin, antelope hides, "mountain cat" pelts, and raccoon caps, which make them look like mongrel animals or members of a primitive race.[23]

Because mountain men wore coonskin caps, they were sometimes referred to as "coons." In the mountain man literature of the mid-nineteenth century, the term "coon" also had racial significance. Ruxton called mountain men both "niggurs" and "coons." So did Garrard. Bennett used the terms "nigger" and "coon" interchangeably.[24] These writers influenced the public's perception that mountain men were shape-shifting entities. People such as Beckwourth lived among animals and in human society. They moved freely among various social communities on the western frontier. They had cross-racial and polymorphous characteristics. This belief was consistent with Beckwourth's representation as a figure with many different personae in his autobiography.

Many white mountain men altered their corporeal and facial appearances, bore racial cognomens, and figuratively passed as "niggurs" or "coons." Beckwourth underwent a reverse transformation. The mulatto passed as a white man in his autobiography. The book reveals how Beckwourth allegedly fooled the Crow by claiming to be one of their tribe. But at the same time it presents inaccurate or ambiguous illustrations of Beckwourth, withholds information regarding his African heritage, and allows the audience to assume that he is white. The narrator gains the reader's trust by confiding how he masqueraded as a Native American. Yet in the process of making this deception transparently clear, he blinds the reader to yet another reality. The autobiography can be read as a history that documents the freedom of physical movement and self-transformation, the complex economic exchanges and intercultural contacts, and the racial mergers that were possible on the western frontier. It can also be read as a literary charade, as a fiction of passing that narrates an unconventional and adventurous life from a conventional (white) point of view. Beckwourth believed that his story would one day win him "renown" (418). But he and/or Bonner chose not to publicize the obvious feature that would have distinguished their work from other accounts of the nineteenth-century American West: the fact that Beckwourth was an African American man. Truth, in this case, was even stranger than autobiography.

CHAPTER TWO

The Pioneering Adventures
of Oscar Micheaux

Between 1919 and 1948, Oscar Micheaux produced, directed, and distributed more than forty feature-length films. Although his status as a pioneer in early African American cinema has been justly acknowledged, the films themselves, more often than not, have been damned with faint praise. Joseph A. Young, Micheaux's toughest critic, has written that "Micheaux was not an excellent filmmaker, nor even a good one. He turned out to be the best in a class of black filmmakers."[1] Donald Bogle, an authority on African American cinema, argues that Micheaux's films were "technically inferior" to Hollywood products because they were made in less time, with less money, and often with amateur casts and improvised crews. In addition, he addresses Micheaux's self-imposed limitations, claiming that Micheaux's body of work, for better or worse, "reflected the interests and outlooks of the black bourgeoisie." According to Bogle, Micheaux's films depicted "a fantasy world where blacks were just as affluent, just as educated, just as 'cultured,' just as well-mannered—in short, just as white"—as their Hollywood counterparts.[2]

Recently, critics have begun to reassess the few films by Micheaux that survive. In works that were once considered merely sensational and melodramatic, Micheaux now gets credit for dealing with such volatile and topical issues as rape, domestic abuse, lynching, and miscegenation. His focus on the African American bourgeoisie and his defense of Booker T. Washington have been re-understood as pleas for racial independence, self-education, and laissez-faire competition. Micheaux has been heralded as a "maverick stylist" and as a "model for the independent black cinema" whose once "technically inferior" films have been heralded in some quarters as examples of guerrilla, avant-garde filmmaking.[3] *Midnight Ramble*, a 1994 PBS documentary, has acknowledged Micheaux's contribution to race movies.[4] Since the mid-1990s, the Film and Video Program at Duke University has offered a web site and newsletter dedicated to educating readers about the once-forgotten African American filmmaker. Heading into the twenty-first century, the critical momentum propelling Micheaux to the front ranks among American artists has continued to build. In the fall of 2000, the Film Society of Lincoln Center, in conjunction with the New York Film Festival, screened a restored version of Micheaux's 1925 classic, *Body and Soul*, with a new jazz score composed by Wycliffe Gordon and conducted by Wynton Marsalis.

It is sometimes forgotten that before Micheaux became a pioneer in African American cinema he was a pioneer on the western frontier. Born in Illinois in 1884, the grandson of a slave, Micheaux moved to South Dakota in 1904, when parcels of land on the Rosebud Reservation were made available to settlers through an organized government lottery. In purchasing a quarter section and farming it, Micheaux became one of the earliest African American homesteaders on the U.S. frontier. After a drought in 1911, subsequent crop failures, foreclosure, and the collapse of his marriage, Micheaux turned to writing. He self-published *The Conquest: The Story of a Negro Pioneer*, an autobiographical novel, in 1913. Throughout the rest of his career, in fiction and film, Micheaux reworked this material. In 1917 he self-published *The Homesteader*, a longer, more complex, and less autobiographical work that also dealt with the hardships of pioneer life. In 1919 his adaptation of the novel became the first feature-length African American film. After filming *The Homesteader*, Micheaux stopped writing novels and began making movies full-time. During his most fertile period, between the early 1920s and the late 1930s, and during his resumed career as a writer in the following decade, Micheaux produced urban crime dramas, mysteries, melodramas, romances, and musicals. But he returned to the West periodically, directing *The Exile* (1931), a remake of *The Homesteader*, believed to be the first talking film in African American cinema.[5] In 1944 he self-published *The Wind from Nowhere*, the third literary account of his frontier experience. It served as the basis for his last film, *The Betrayal* (1948).

Although Micheaux's films have been resurrected and subjected to careful critical scrutiny, most of his writings remain out of print. Like his films, which were dismissed for decades, his books are still regarded as poorly crafted and ideologically conservative works. Joseph Young, the author of the first book devoted to the study of Micheaux's seven novels, claims that the fiction is marred by a crude grasp of language, a lack of artistic complexity, and an absence of "figurative imagery." More seriously, he alleges that as a member of the "assimilationist school" and as an apologist for Booker T. Washington, Micheaux accepted "a myth of black inferiority." Believing that he could succeed by imitating prosperous white pioneers, Micheaux, according to Young, embraced "Anglo-Saxon myths, Anglo-Saxon values, and Anglo-Saxon philosophy."[6] As another critic claims more succinctly and caustically, Micheaux, in his literature, "plays white as children play house."[7]

It is time to reopen the case against Oscar Micheaux and to reexamine this verdict. Like critics who have called for a reassessment of Micheaux's cinematic canon, I would argue that his writings have been simplistically treated. In my own study I have chosen to focus on three of Micheaux's seven novels—*The Conquest*, *The Homesteader*, and *The Wind from Nowhere*—which I have described as a trilogy. His four other novels, like most of his films, are not set in the West. But these loosely autobiographical works, and the film adaptations of Micheaux's western experience, reveal most about Micheaux's beliefs and how they intensified, changed, or evolved over time. The West becomes a testing ground for determining whether African Americans have a stake in the American dream, envisioned by Micheaux as a quest for personal freedom, respect by his peers, and economic success.

It has become commonplace to assume that Micheaux identified with the imperial enterprise of westward expansion, that he promoted farming and manual vocational skills, and that he tried to succeed as a pioneer by conservatively keeping his place in a segregated western farming community. Micheaux tends to be viewed, at best, as a dupe who was tricked by the promise of free enterprise and racial equality, and at worst, as an ideologue out of step with his times. Instead, *The Conquest*, the first work in the trilogy, refutes the notion that African Americans can translate the American dream into reality. *The Homesteader* and *The Wind from Nowhere* seem to contradict this conclusion. In these later novels, the heroes assimilate, prosper, and lift up the race. Yet because the sequels stray from Micheaux's own experience, they make success in the West seem like an entertaining mirage. As Micheaux's alter egos grow more heroic in stature, they become less representative of historic African American homesteaders.[8]

Micheaux was plagued by a profound double consciousness. Although he believed that African Americans could achieve economic success, he realized that whites underestimated his race's potential. Therefore he created fictional heroes who might inspire African American readers, while succeeding in terms that whites would respect, by conquering the frontier in the tradition of immigrant Anglo-Americans. But the myth of the frontier as a land of (equal) opportunity and as a place of renewal proved not to be viable. The triumphs of

Micheaux's western protagonists disguised his own failures as a homesteader, husband, and father. The contrast between negative personal experience and representations of an ideal reality created a tension that complemented and complicated Micheaux's double consciousness. With each artistic revision of his autobiography, the gap between experience and fantasy became increasingly harder to bridge.

His interest in western settlement and vocational enterprise puts Micheaux at odds with contemporary African American writers who migrated to cities in search of culturally and intellectually stimulating environments. In terms of subject matter and treatment, Micheaux has more in common with regional and Euro-American writers. Hamlin Garland's short-story collection *Main-Travelled Roads* (1891), like *The Conquest*, examines the conflict between romantic individualism and the forces of economic and social oppression that thwart the success of rural midwesterners.[9] Like *Giants in the Earth* (1927), the first novel in O. E. Rölvaag's trilogy about Norwegian American immigrants, Micheaux's three-volume chronicle examines the physical hardships and psychological disorientation experienced by characters who relate to the prairie as outsiders or foreigners.

At the same time, however, Micheaux signified within an African American artistic tradition. His frontier trilogy and his three western films illustrate a pattern of repetition and difference. By racializing the Anglo-national narrative of conquest and settlement and by retelling the story of an African American pioneer in more than one medium, Micheaux created a pattern that was "familiar and new."[10] Returning to the same material throughout his career was not a sign of creative exhaustion. It represented Micheaux's effort to resolve his early traumatic experience—farm failure, bankruptcy, and the loss of his wife—in works where the hero found cathartic redemption and therapeutic success. The fragmented self became reconstructed in fiction and film as Micheaux tried to reconcile regional tensions, racism, and economic constraints that prevented the African American man from making his frontier dreams a reality. In addition, he fashioned a new racial history as well as a fictional personal history. He embraced the frontier myth by celebrating westward migration, agrarian struggle, and the inevitable triumph of civilization. Yet he expanded the myth to include racial minorities as representative figures in the process of Manifest Destiny.

The Conquest marks an important departure from the traditional pathways of African American literature. Micheaux's alter ego heads west, unlike those members of his race who believed that urban industrial centers offered more advantages than rural southern or midwestern areas. He chooses wilderness over civilization, rejects most of his race, leaves behind his community, relocates his family, and attempts to reshape his destiny. Just as importantly, *The Conquest* challenges turn-of-the-century white frontier historiography. Whereas Frederick Jackson Turner's "The Significance of the Frontier in American History" (1893) defines the frontier as a "crucible"—as a land of equal opportunity that democratically forges Americans into a "mixed race" of citizens—*The Conquest* asks whether African Americans can participate in this forging of a multiethnic frontier society.[11]

Houston Baker has argued that when African Americans read Turner's essay they feel "no regret over the end of the western frontier." According to Baker, the West (as a place, as a myth) holds no promise for racial minorities and hence no significance.[12] At first *The Conquest* seems determined to disprove this hypothesis. Oscar Devereaux, Micheaux's thinly disguised alter ego, pursues his dream of becoming a homesteader. As the only minority farmer in Gregory County,[13] the lonely Oscar falls in love with a white woman who lives on a homestead nearby.[14] Determined to succeed on the prairie, but not wanting to offend the predominantly white local community that frowns on mixed marriages, Oscar renounces his sweetheart. Returning to Illinois in search of a wife, he meets Orlean McCraline, the daughter of a well-known African American minister. Having already sacrificed his true love in order to advance his career, the practical Oscar now views Orlean as a means to an end. He takes his fiancée out west, where she joins his sister and grandmother, also recent arrivals. The three women file claims on separate parcels of land that Oscar then cultivates, thereby increasing his empire and adding "to the wealth of the colored race in the state."[15]

Oscar internalizes white racism in the process of pursuing success. Accepting the unspoken premise that African Americans on the prairie can be separate yet equal, he practices self-segregation, marries within his race, and creates a black farming franchise. At the same time, he participates in the victimization of another racial minority, joining white settlers in displacing Native Americans by purchasing land on the Rosebud Reservation that once belonged to the Sioux.[16] Oscar identifies with the purpose of U.S. expansion and considers the Sioux lazy squatters. He contrasts their resistance to assimilation (to the peaceful relinquishment of their nomadic existence, to repatriation, and to agricultural reeducation) with his own ambition to farm as many acres as possible (178–81). As a "progressive" who believes in self-enterprise, Oscar admonishes his race for not "monopolizing more of the many million acres" that whites have seized for themselves (251–52).

Maintaining that African Americans can overcome racism by earning the good opinion of whites, he preaches the virtues of segregated schooling (248–50), manual industry (139), and bourgeois morality (193).

His behavior, however, fails to yield the predicted results. Although he studies experimental seeding and plowing techniques, Oscar cannot forecast the weather, which ultimately determines the fate of his crops. Nor can he persuade his wife to accept the hardships of farming. After their child is stillborn (262), Orlean leaves her husband, abandons her claim, and returns to her parents, precipitating an emotional and financial crisis that pushes Oscar deeper into despair. As one critic has observed, the death of Oscar's son represents the demise of his dream, for it disproves Turner's thesis that the West is a land of new beginnings and fresh opportunities or the site of symbolic rebirth. [17] The title of *The Conquest* is therefore ironic. [18] Instead of ruling his personal and professional destiny, the hero is conquered by the land, by social conventions, and by actions beyond his control.

Unlike the American Adam, who finds in the wilderness an ability to order the New World, Micheaux's pioneer loses his land, banishes hope, and retreats into exile at the end of the novel. In keeping with African American literary tradition, *The Conquest* critiques the Anglo-Saxon edenic myth. If white antebellum writers deployed the trope of the New World as paradise, ignoring the evils of slavery while stressing the "idyllic" qualities of southern plantation life, [19] so proponents of Manifest Destiny tended to discount the costs of western conquest and settlement, focusing instead on the divine right of Anglo-Saxon possession. Considering the genocide and enslavement of Native Americans and the persecution of Mormons and other religious minorities—both results of the process of frontier expansion—one might reasonably speculate whether minority homesteaders such as Oscar Micheaux could expect to receive unbiased treatment. Just as African American writers challenged representations of the plantation as pastoral, so Micheaux, in *The Conquest*, rejects the myth of the frontier as Eden.

The hero regains paradise in the final two works in the trilogy. *The Homesteader* and *The Wind from Nowhere* follow *The Conquest* in tracing the troubles of their respective protagonists, but they continue beyond the point where the first novel ends. Unlike *The Conquest*, *The Homesteader* features a hero whose fortunes improve. Jean Baptiste, Micheaux's alter ego, leaves Cairo, Illinois—referred to as "Egypt" because of its sizable African American population—and begins his own exodus. [20] Escaping from a rural ghetto that offers few opportunities, he exchanges bondage for freedom, migrating westward and staking a claim on the prairie. In South Dakota, the promised land, he loses his wife and son and almost forfeits the farm. But through a complicated series of plot twists, the protagonist avoids becoming a sacrificial victim, unlike his biblical namesake. He harvests a wheat crop and pays off his mortgage (515); gets revenge on the Reverend, who has sown dissent in his marriage (517–22); and marries his first love, a white woman, when he discovers that she has a trace of African blood (526). Just as Micheaux restores the farm to fertility, so he reunites Jean and Agnes Stewart (his "dream girl") in the "enchanted garden" where the lovers first met (139). Unlike contemporary African American writers who represented the vexed nature of interracial relationships by invoking Adam and Eve, their fall, and their expulsion from the Garden of Eden, Micheaux finds a solution that enables his hero to marry a "white" woman and simultaneously recapture paradise.[21]

In *The Wind from Nowhere* the author succeeds on even more grandiose terms, transforming the prelapsarian prairie into an agricultural utopia. At the end of the novel, Martin Eden, Micheaux's third alter ego, stands on top of Mt. Eden. The mountain has rich deposits of manganese that the hero will one day extract and sell in order to acquire more land and equipment, using the land to plant crops that will be successfully harvested "year after year." Micheaux envisions that Martin and his wife, Deborah, will use the profits from farming to lift up the race. They will pluck "worthy and industrious" minorities from the cities, settle them on ten-acre tracts, teach women to grow their own food, and hire men to work in "food product factories and manganese alloy plants" that Martin builds on the prairie.[22]

The Conquest is ironic because the hero suffers defeat. Although Micheaux's later heroes triumph over adversity, their success is ironic as well. For example, Martin's fortunes improve with the discovery of precious ore on his property. Accident plays the determining role in shaping his future, rather than planning, perseverance, and seasonal sacrifice. By transforming Martin's privately owned farm into a commune with factories, Micheaux suggests that an idealized urban industrial complex, superimposed upon an agrarian grid, offers African Americans a combination of the best opportunities. Success is based on contradiction as well as on compromise. Martin Eden is named after the hero of Jack London's novel, but London's protagonist triumphs professionally after years of hard work and struggle, then commits suicide after deciding that his achievements are hollow. Micheaux's Martin Eden finds fulfillment in enterprise, unlike Micheaux in real life or London's titular character. *The Wind from Nowhere* has to contradict its own literary and autobiographical sources in order to construct a myth of African American success in the West.

The Homesteader and *The Wind from Nowhere* seemingly affirm the place of African Americans in the national narrative of continental conquest and settlement. Micheaux not only saves his heroes from failure but rescues his heroines from the fate of the tragic mulatta. Once they discover their ancestry, Agnes and Deborah are able to marry the men they love and join their husbands in founding a new world on the prairie. [23] This discovery enables marriage to take place, leads to the founding of an agricultural dynasty, and results in the immigration of future minority homesteaders. Micheaux links a subplot involving the celebration of the heroines' African genealogy with the main plot concerning the African American heroes' reclamation of wilderness. He associates the recovery of racial roots with the placing of roots in the soil, narrating the story of African American settlement on the South Dakota frontier.

Micheaux erases his own failure as a minority homesteader, reproducing the West as a blank page and inscribing on it a fiction that makes success possible. In the process, however, his heroes become more and more passive, reactive, and dependent on others. *The Conquest* ends with Oscar watching helplessly as his wife reenters her father's house, closing "the door" on his dreams (311). In *The Homesteader*, Jean suffers further indignities. Orlean not only chooses to stay with her father; she beats her husband as well. "[With] a strength, born of excitement, she struck [Jean] in his face, in his eyes. . . . He reached out and caught her around the waist as he lost his footing and fell to his knees. As he lingered in this position his face was upturned. She struck him then with all the force in her body. He groaned, as he gradually loosened his hold upon her, and slowly sank to the floor" (383). In *The Wind from Nowhere*, Martin's wife, Linda, behaves even more violently. Seizing a gun from the symbolically impotent hero, she wounds him and makes him "sink to the floor with a groan" (294).

In all three novels, the pioneer's ability to master the prairie partially depends on his success in managing women. Because his worth is based on the amount of land that he owns—and because his wife, sister, and grandmother hold title to property that he farms and controls—the hero objectifies women, viewing them as a necessary means to an end ("I have always regarded matrimony as a business proposition," Oscar states in *The Homesteader* [183]). The hero becomes more reliant on women in the course of the trilogy: They become more instrumental, though not necessarily more sympathetic, as the hero becomes less effectual in shaping his fate. In *The Homesteader*, Orlean rebels against her father by stabbing him, then plunges the knife into her breast (521–22). In *The Wind from Nowhere*, after killing the Reverend,

Linda rushes out of the house, into oncoming traffic (349–51). When Jean becomes the prime suspect in the deaths of his wife and her father, Agnes comes to Chicago to rescue him (*The Homesteader*, 506). She hires a Pinkerton detective to solve the homicide-suicide and saves the hero from prison (508). In *The Wind from Nowhere*, Deborah also intervenes melodramatically. Traveling to Chicago, she lectures Linda on wifely disloyalty. When Linda tells her to mind her own business, Deborah says: " 'I'm *making* it my business, see!' and finishing, she smacked Linda hard on the cheek" (330). Then, taking a train, swimming across a river, and riding on horseback, she arrives home in time to prevent land-grabbers from seizing Linda's unoccupied farm (366–75).

The success of racial minorities in the West is an improbable fiction that relies increasingly on the positive outcome of such far-fetched scenarios. The melodramatic influences in *The Homesteader* and *The Wind from Nowhere* derive from western pulp fiction and African American literature. Like dime novels, the last two works in the trilogy feature villainous land speculators, evil railroad barons, and innocent farmers threatened with losing their mortgages.[24] The light and dark heroines play opposing roles in determining the fate of the hero. In the African American melodramatic tradition, they not only have different racial features but also symbolize positive and negative traits, respectively.[25] Marriage to the "white" heroine (Agnes or Deborah) guarantees assimilation, economic advancement, and progress for racial minorities. Marriage to the "black" anti-heroine (Orlean or Linda) necessitates a return to the city, dooms the hero to failure, and prevents upward racial mobility. Micheaux displaces onto the anti-heroine the hero's "dark" tendencies—his recurring habit of fantasizing about killing his wife and her father (*The Homesteader*, 484; *The Wind from Nowhere*, 276). By killing her father and taking her own life, the "dark" angel grants the hero's subconscious wish, removing the obstacles blocking his path to success. The "light" angel provides nonviolent solutions to the hero's problems by seeking divine inspiration. In *The Wind from Nowhere*, for instance, Deborah devises a plan for rescuing Martin while praying for guidance in church (357).

Tensions become increasingly noticeable in Micheaux's western trilogy. Irony suggests the presence of a double perspective. It forces the reader to question what conquest means and what price the minority homesteader pays for success. Paradoxically, as the hero becomes more triumphant, he becomes diminished as well. In addition, he develops psychological fantasies in which he imagines "acting out" in ways that society deems unacceptable. He is a latent misogynist who blames his wife for his troubles, a potential adulterer who desires an unattainable woman, and a would-be murderer who fantasizes about using violence to resolve his dilemma. In spite of his belief in the possibility of self-advancement, he reveals a secret racial self-loathing. He prefers a light-skinned wife who would facilitate his social assimilation and upward economic mobility. Although he begins his career as a homesteader, he ends it as an industrial-agrarian entrepreneur. The rural life that Micheaux depicts in his trilogy becomes more anachronistic and irrelevant with the passage of time. Whereas *The Conquest* and *The Homesteader* take place at the turn of the century, *The Wind from Nowhere*, published many years later, seems stuck in a time warp. It refers vaguely to an "economic depression" (14) that must have begun in the late 1920s. It mentions the existence of automobiles (20) but makes no further reference to modernization and industrialization, no allusion to world war, and no acknowledgment of progress that minorities have made since *The Homesteader*. Booker T. Washington, who died in 1915, no longer represents the views of a significant portion of the African American populace. He serves as a reminder of an earlier, more politically conservative period. Micheaux's prescription for ending unemployment and poverty, his allotment of "ten acres and a cow" to each western immigrant, seems like an "outdated" solution in the mid-twentieth century.[26] While African Americans in the 1940s migrated to large urban areas or went to fight overseas, Micheaux's characters remain on the prairie, staging the same battles their predecessors fought in *The Conquest* in 1913.

There is a "two-ness"—a double consciousness—and a tendency to encode contradictory messages in Micheaux's western trilogy. His novels can be read both as affirmations of faith in the ability of African Americans to participate in the development of the U.S. frontier and as fictions that subvert their ostensible purpose by inscribing minority success as a myth. Although Micheaux never systematically questions the process that results in the installation of whites in the region and in the removal or absence of racial minorities, he acknowledges that white farmers resent sharing land with a "squaw man" (*The Homesteader*, 86) or "nigger" (*The Conquest*, 87). Micheaux's alter egos show contempt for minorities who do not want to work hard, overcome society's low expectations, and lift up the race. But his heroes also resent whites who treat African Americans as second-class citizens and who attempt to prevent Micheaux's alter egos from achieving their fullest potential. As "exceptional" minorities who exhibit none of the negative stereotypical qualities seen in the rest of their race, Micheaux's heroes identify with white pioneers and entrepreneurs. However, as "representative" African American men who articulate the concerns of their people, the author's fictional surrogates also critique race relations, addressing racial prejudice, social double standards, and economic injustices, sometimes so subtly that critics fail to recognize the existence of a covert counternarrative. As a writer who solicited the patronage of his white rural neighbors as well as the following of an urban African American audience, Micheaux produced novels that members of his divided constituency were capable of interpreting differently.

For instance, although Micheaux has been criticized for embracing Booker T. Washington, who praised manual labor as a means of achieving prosperity, it has seldom been noted that Micheaux's alter egos often take shortcuts on the road to success.[27] While working as a Pullman porter, Oscar overhears passengers discussing the existence of cheap western land. After pumping a farmer for more information and learning that land costs more than eighty dollars per acre, the hero, who lacks investment capital, devises a scheme to raise funds (*The Conquest*, 51–53). By "knocking down" passengers—that is, by skimming money from travelers who pay for their accommodations in cash—Oscar acquires the money necessary to purchase land on the prairie. Defending his actions, the narrator claims that the Pullman Company exploits its "colored employees," paying them "starvation wages" and forcing them to steal in order to offset their "near-slave conditions" (50–51).

Elsewhere, when Oscar describes himself as a "radical" who supports the "progressive" platform of Booker T. Washington, he seems to be appealing to conservative readers, suggesting that African Americans should accommodate "obvious prejudice," accept the fact that they have few opportunities, and farm land as an alternative to working for "more equal rights" (251). Yet here the narrator takes advantage of his lowly position, revenges himself on a system that has forced African American men into servitude, and defends his actions without "regrets" or "apologies" (51). His lack of repentance indicates his awareness of a more radical audience, a second set of readers to whom he also appeals. Political liberals, and African Americans in particular, would have been sympathetic to the narrator's argument. Since the profession of Pullman porter was one of the few occupations open to African American men at the turn of the century, many of them would have recognized, as the narrator claims, that porters were treated as menial servants, paid inadequate wages, and subjected to harsh working conditions—that they were exploited by a company which repeatedly thwarted their efforts to unionize.[28] In the opinion of some readers, the narrator might have seemed justified in comparing his employment to slavery.

This episode suggests one reason why it is necessary to reread Micheaux. The author recommended patience with racial injustice, slow progress, and physical toil as a means of achieving success, but he practiced a more secular gospel than the one he preached. Both speculators and aspiring homesteaders participated in the South Dakota lottery in 1904. Those who drew winning numbers and qualified to purchase quarter-section tracts at affordable prices often turned around, sold their acreage to farmers, and made sizable profits. Others held onto their land, hoping that railroads would come west, bringing people and industry, thus driving up the cost of real estate and making their investments more valuable. [29] Micheaux's acknowledged distaste for farming and other forms of physical labor (*The Conquest*, 31–32) and his expressed admiration for white investors and businessmen (71–72) have led critics to wonder whether the author fancied himself as a "virtual slave" to the land (*The Wind from Nowhere*, 165) or rather as an entrepreneur. In later years, Micheaux's neighbors insisted that his "game was trying to outfox the railroad, and his farming efforts merely a front" that collapsed when the railroad decided to bypass his property.[30] Recently, critics have surmised that because negotiations involving the railroads and land speculators are "given such prominence in an otherwise 'personal' chronicle . . . one cannot help but wonder what role [Micheaux] had in the scheme."[31] To the extent that he admired (and may have conspired with) gamblers who bought and sold land for profit rather than farming it, Micheaux flirted with riskier and more radical methods of achieving success than those practiced by white homesteaders or by members of an African American bourgeoisie. [32]

Micheaux viewed writing as one of those radical methods—as a means to an end—whereby he could recoup his earlier financial losses. One of his alter egos, the debt-ridden Jean, claims in *The Homesteader* that he decided to "write his own story" when foreclosure on his mortgage seemed imminent (401). Likewise, Micheaux wrote *The Conquest* not just to chronicle his failure as a minority homesteader; he also self-published the novel in order to launch a new career as a writer. Writing was for Micheaux an entrepreneurial enterprise, the success of which depended initially on the support of a local white audience. Micheaux found a printer in Lincoln, Nebraska, who agreed to publish a thousand copies of the novel for seventy-five cents apiece but who demanded $250 before going to press. The aspiring writer went door-to-door seeking subscriptions from farmers, describing *The Conquest* as a book "about their lives as well as his own." Within two weeks he sold fifteen hundred copies for $1.50 apiece, cleared a respectable profit, and decided that writing, not farming, "offered the best hope for his continued financial health."[33]

The Conquest targeted two groups of readers. It appealed to white subscribers who invested in the novel as promotional literature. Because the novel extolled the availability of cheap land and the virtues of farming, and since it celebrated the arrival of railroads and the growth of racially tolerant frontier communities, it may have been expected to promote immigration. Doing so would have increased the value of prairie land, thus benefiting those who were already residents. But the novel also appealed to African American readers, whom Micheaux might have had a harder time pleasing, since the defeats suffered by the hero could be interpreted by minorities as discouraging news. *The Conquest* divides into two separate narratives. The novel's first half provides a social history of South Dakota at the turn of the century, focusing on Micheaux's alter ego and other thinly disguised historical figures who played pivotal roles in the frontier's development. The second half documents Oscar's return to the city, his critique of urban African American ghettos, his failure there to locate a suitable wife, his inability to find support for his pioneer enterprise within the community, and his final defeat. One critic complains that Micheaux did not "integrate" these two sections skillfully. Another believes that the "symbolic juxtaposition" between the two narratives—one situated on the prairie and featuring a predominantly white cast of characters, the other taking place among a metropolitan population of racial minorities—organizes a productive debate in Micheaux's work between region and race.[34]

One critic has commented on the "two-ness" reflected in Micheaux's sensibility. Jane Gaines writes that the artist saw "[the] Black culture through the eyes of the White culture," creating portraits of "an irredeemable Black underclass" that whites found believable.[35] If Micheaux courted white readers, however, he also curried favor with an African American audience. In 1915 he moved to Sioux City, Iowa, where he founded the Western Book Supply Company. In order to finance publication of *The Homesteader*, he sold stock in the company, mainly to white farmers in South Dakota, Nebraska, and Iowa.[36] He also attempted to expand his minority audience, launching "aggressive promotional tours" in "Black Belts" up north and down south, visiting schools, churches, and homes in efforts to publicize his endeavor.[37] In an advertising pamphlet he pitched the book to African American readers: "Consider it in the light of a gift to relatives or dear friends and let your order be for more than one copy."[38]

Similarly, in at least one scene in the novel, the narrator speaks to African American readers, shifting linguistic registers in order to address racial concerns. Visiting Chicago's South Side ("Darktown proper"), he discusses with a friend his search for a wife:

> "Well, how's Chicago?" he inquired irrelevantly.
> "Same old burg," she replied, drawing a chair up close.
> "And how's hubby?"
> "Fine!"
> "And the rest of the family?"
> "The same. Pearl, too."
> "Oh, Pearl. . . . How is Pearl?"
> "Still single. . . ."
> "Thought she was engaged to be married when I was here last year?"
> "Oh, that fellow was no good!"
> "What was the matter?"
> "What's the matter with lots of these nigga' men 'round Chicago? They can't keep a wife a posing on State Street."
> "Humph!"
> "It's the truth!"
> "And how about the women? They seem to be fond of passing along to be posed at. . . ."
> "Oh, you're mean," she pouted. Then: "Are you married yet?"
> "Oh, lordy! How could I get married? Not thirty minutes ago I saw the first colored girl I have seen in a year!" (149)

This passage contrasts with the rest of *The Homesteader*, revealing a textual tension between conventional European literary practice and African American oral tradition. Building on Henry Louis Gates's assumption that "the production of literature was taken to be the central arena in which persons of African descent could, or could not, establish and redefine their status within the human community," I would argue that Micheaux viewed the production of literature as such a means to an end.[39] The author wrote in order to demonstrate what he failed to prove as a farmer or land investor: that an African American man was capable, by means of hard work and self-education, of forging a successful career and, in the process, earning the admiration of whites. Likewise, the author's fictional surrogate speaks standardized English in order to indicate his erudition, his enhanced social status, and his will to assimilate.[40]

When Oscar enters the African American community, however, he changes personae. Although he remains chaste on the prairie, respecting the color line, in "Darktown" he trades innuendoes and flirts with a married African American woman. He becomes angry when white men pelt him with terms like "d—n nigger!" (125), but he takes no offense when a member of his own race refers to "nigga' men" playfully. Modulating from standardized English into salty vernacular, he participates in a companionable interchange characterized by unrestricted loose language and vocal inflections ("Oh, lordy!" "Humph!"). More to the point, Oscar promises his African American friend that he will not marry outside his race (151). The protagonist signifies his intention through the use of vernacular, reassuring African American readers that he has not lost touch with his ethnic identity even though he has moved to a predominantly white, rural community.[41]

Specific addresses to an African American audience occur seldom in Micheaux's frontier trilogy. The issue of split reception becomes more apparent when one considers the markets for film versus literature. Only a few stills remain of Micheaux's first film, *The Homesteader*. Archival records, however, indicate that the writer-director exploited the theme of miscegenation in order to attract more white viewers. In a letter to executives of the Lincoln Motion Picture Company, an African American corporation that considered producing a film version of Micheaux's novel in 1918, the author insisted that the subplot, concerning "the white girl who in the end turns out to be colored," would pique curiosity (according to rumor, a "white friend had told him that including the white girl . . . was one reason that many whites bought the book").[42] Like the novel, the film adaptation was pitched primarily to a white demographic. Micheaux wanted distribution rights to the picture west of Mississippi and north of Missouri, "among white people only." The producers, he wrote, could distribute *The Homesteader* in the remaining national markets, where "colored people" made up a greater share of the audience.[43] After negotiations fell through, Micheaux decided to produce the film independently, forming the Micheaux Book and Film Company (which later became the Micheaux Film Corporation) in 1918. Once again he waged a divided campaign, financing his film by selling stock in his new corporation to the same white investors who had purchased stakes in his novel, but promoting it in urban markets where there were more movie theaters. Realizing that race movies would appeal solely to African American viewers, he advertised the film in the *Chicago Defender* and other African American newspapers. By emphasizing the film's African American cast, he created an ethnic market for *The Homesteader*, which eventually grossed five thousand dollars.[44]

Movie still from *The Homesteader* (1919). No prints of the film exist. (Department of Special Collections, Charles E. Young Research Library, UCLA)

Having quit farming, and having abandoned his literary career in favor of filmmaking, Micheaux began spending more time in the East and Midwest, using such settings as New York and Chicago to film stories that featured African American middle-class professional or cosmopolitan characters. Although he continued to rely on whites for partial financial backing and never gave up hoping that his films would cross over, he gradually shifted his racial and geographical focus, targeting an urban African American audience. [45] Because the first adaptation of *The Homesteader* no longer survives, it is impossible to compare the film with the remake, *The Exile*, which appeared twelve years later. But the latter film differs significantly from the novel on which it was based, emphasizing city life rather than homesteading. The difference between the source novel and the film adaptation once again suggests Micheaux's awareness of audience, his alternating ability to satisfy white readers and viewers of race movies. As jazz music plays, the opening credits appear against a background of skyscrapers. A producer's note follows: "This is a story of Chicago—and the Negro," it claims. [46] The subsequent story adheres to the same basic outline as Micheaux's western novel, but it includes

Movie poster for *The Exile* (1931). (Courtesy of the Academy of Motion Picture Arts and Sciences)

more scenes set in the city. Orlean McCarthy, the hero's original romantic nemesis, is replaced by Edith Duval, the owner of a South Side speakeasy, who attempts to seduce Jean away from his wholesome life on the prairie. Although the film praises the virtues of the outdoors in passing and includes some brief footage of farming, it showcases scenes in the nightclub (including performances by an instrumental jazz orchestra, tap dancers, and chorus girls), narratively gratuitous but professionally choreographed sequences that are more entertaining than the ostensible story involving Jean's attempt to escape from his hostess's clutches.

Here, Micheaux seems less interested in privileging the West as a setting and less willing to portray whites as minority role models. The Micheaux Film Corporation had gone bankrupt in the late 1920s, and Micheaux had been forced to seek financial assistance from white investors who, in exchange, had demanded partial control of his company. This situation did not prevent the independently minded Micheaux from addressing white racism and from subtly satirizing white businessmen. In *The Exile* the audience learns that Edith's nightclub was once a mansion owned by a well-to-do meatpacker who abandoned his dwelling when migrating African Americans came to Chicago and infiltrated his neighborhood. Without seeking authorization, Micheaux filmed steel magnate Charles Schwab's home in New York, using the shots, tongue in cheek, to represent the juke joint's exterior.[47]

Micheaux's success—first as a farmer, then as a novelist, and last as a filmmaker—depended on the consumer loyalty and financial support of both races. Consequently, Micheaux's work was characterized by shifting self-interests and conflicting ideological messages. But his career as an artist was energized rather than paralyzed by such a profound double consciousness. Micheaux exploited his two-ness, his persona as an assimilated Negro and his reputation as a maverick African American filmmaker, attracting both white and minority followers. He emulated white entrepreneurs, aspired to membership in the African American bourgeoisie, and catered indiscriminately to any race, region, or industry that might advance his career. Joseph Young believes that Micheaux wrote novels and produced films in order to obtain "white support" and make money.[48] Elton Fax, an illustrator who knew Micheaux personally, offers a different perspective in *Midnight Ramble*, a 1994 PBS documentary. Micheaux liked to say that he made race movies in order to lift up "our people." "I'm sure he sincerely tried to do that because he felt it profitable to do so," Fax speculated. "After all, our people weren't going to theaters to see black people bring us down further." Although they disagree on his motives, the two men agree that Micheaux made success a priority.

Hoping to strike gold again, Micheaux returned to the subject of the West periodically. According to the author, *The Wind from Nowhere*, the final work in his trilogy, became a best-seller, appearing in at least nine editions.[49] The film version, however, flopped at the box office. Comparing it unfavorably to an amateur home movie, critics complained that *The Betrayal* suffered from poor production values, unprofessional acting, and ludicrous dialogue.[50] His final film, which no longer survives, apparently left the impression that Micheaux was a second-rate artist whose earlier efforts had broken new ground in African American cinema but whose technically inferior later productions remained fixated on the same subjects and themes.

Micheaux's return to familiar material, with disappointing results, may suggest that the writer and filmmaker ended his career in a state of creative exhaustion. However, rather than ranking his works in order of relative merit, it may be more useful to consider why Micheaux produced various versions of his autobiography. I believe that these retellings revise both the frontier myth and Micheaux's own experience in a manner that is consistent with the African American practice of repetition with difference. In psychological terms, his novels and films also enabled the subject to come to terms with his past by confronting and resolving that traumatic experience.

Psychoanalytic critics define accounts of trauma as mediated literary experiments. A subject's inability to forget a traumatic occurrence, combined with a psychological need to recollect the episode in a manner that the subject finds bearable, results in a literature of "double telling" that mixes dramatic distortion, and thus self-protection, with fact.[51] In Micheaux's case, a series of real-life traumatic events—including the failure of his farm, bankruptcy, the death of his son, and divorce—forced Micheaux to seek other forms of employment. Not only did writing autobiographical novels and screenplays provide him with necessary sources of income, but his art therapeutically helped him come to grips with his failure as a minority homesteader. In dramatic re-creations of his personal history, Micheaux blamed his defeats on forces beyond his control and imagined alternate outcomes that were more satisfactory. One expert, claiming that trauma is not just a pathology, insists that it is also "the story of a wound that cries out."[52] Through the artistic process, Micheaux reopened his own wounds and sought to heal them in repeated attempts to make sense of catastrophe.

Micheaux's novels and films illustrate how narratives about race and trauma sometimes converge. His works may be considered double tellings as well as retellings, cathartic artistic experiments in which the subject's personal failures come to stand for the traumatic historical experiences of African Americans—in particular, the obstacles faced by racial minorities on the western frontier. Repeatedly, Micheaux transforms the specifics of his life into representative art. In addition, his male protagonists, often the sole members of their race in the region, serve as test cases for determining whether equal opportunities exist for other racial minorities. In Micheaux's case, the reality of life on the prairie for an African American man at the turn of the century differed from the myth of the frontier as subscribed to by Anglo-Americans. The trauma engendered by his loss of faith in the myth was soothed somewhat by his subsequent artistic endeavors, in which he imagined a vibrant African American West as a real possibility. Micheaux's interpretations and revisions of history may be understood as attempts to bear witness to this possibility in fiction and film, for both whites and racial minorities, in rural and urban locations, over several decades of complex and productive creation.

CHAPTER THREE

Slavery, Secession, and Uncivil War

During the nineteenth century, many Americans settled on the western frontier. Although African Americans were part of this trend, they represented a minority in statistical terms. Those in the South were more likely to immigrate to the North or Midwest.[1] Others preferred leaving the states. Some started colonies, though not in western territories where opportunities beckoned and land was still plentiful. Before the Civil War, Henry and Mary Bibb journeyed to Canada, where there were four major race communities composed of expatriates. James T. Holly, a clergyman, resettled in Haiti and encouraged others to follow. At various times in his career, writer Martin Delany promoted sites in Africa, South America, and Central America. The West Indian missionary Edward W. Blyden favored Liberia, which had achieved independence as a republic in the mid-nineteenth century. So did Alexander Crummell, a missionary who worked in Liberia and Sierra Leone.[2]

Why did certain African Americans choose not to immigrate to the western frontier? In *The Conquest* (1913), a novel by former South Dakota homesteader Oscar Micheaux, a character who lives in Chicago claims that "colored people had been held in slavery for two hundred years and since they were free they did not want to go out into the wilderness and sit on a farm."[3] Some minorities may have preferred the convenience of living in cities, but others were willing to leave civilization, becoming cowboys and farmers, miners and merchants, members of the military, trappers and scouts.[4] Individuals and single families sometimes succeeded, whereas group migration and colonization movements did not fare as well. The Exodusters, a wave of African American southerners who came to Kansas to farm in the late 1870s, encountered white opposition and adverse weather conditions. Starting in the late 1880s, minority homesteaders founded dozens of townships in Oklahoma Territory, but within a few decades their populations decreased as inhabitants drifted to larger metropolitan areas.[5]

Two novelists who published around the turn of the century debated whether African American individuals or communities could thrive in the West. Sutton E. Griggs and Pauline Hopkins denounced racism and the institution of slavery, believing that African Americans could never achieve independence and equality as long as they remained in the states. However, on the frontier they might possibly establish a utopian society. In *Imperium in Imperio* (1899), Griggs debates whether African Americans should seize Texas, secede from the Union, and declare war on the states. Rather than contemplating a similar hypothetical scenario, in *Winona: A Tale of Negro Life in the South and Southwest* (1902), Hopkins situates her fictional character in a past historical struggle. Her heroine fights for Kansas to become a free state when it enters the Union after the war. *Winona* imagines a better America, where citizens in a new frontier state can vote to reject the institution of slavery, making it possible for African Americans to have full rights as citizens. *Imperium in Imperio* suggests that working within the political system to achieve independence, and assimilating within western society, may not be possible. But in spite of the reasons that some of his characters give for going to war with America, Griggs doubts whether outright rebellion is the best political strategy. And in spite of the fact that her heroine participates in a successful campaign to free Kansas from slavery, Hopkins questions whether Winona could find happiness if she stayed in the states. Both authors wrote at the turn of the century, at the approach of the millennium, during a period of historical reassessment and change, when concerns regarding the future of African Americans and the fate of the nation were invested with even greater significance.

Imperium in Imperio debates the political viewpoints of its two central characters. Belton, an African American, grows up in poverty. Although he believes that education and hard work will improve his situation, he encounters opposition by whites on the road to success. Bernard, his friend, is just as determined. As a mulatto, however, he has the support of a wealthy white father, a politician in Washington. Bernard attends Harvard, triumphs in his chosen profession, and moves among the eastern elite. Years later, he receives a summons from Belton inviting him to Texas, where Belton initiates Bernard into a secret organization composed of African American intellectuals, politicians, and businessmen called the Imperium. Although its members are com-

A. VIEW OF WACO

Waco, Texas, ca. 1865. (The Texas Collection, Baylor University, Waco, Texas)

mitted to fighting racism, they disagree on a method for doing so. Belton, the founder of the organization, favors peaceful negotiations with whites, like his role model, Booker T. Washington. However, Bernard believes in seceding from the nation and fighting oppression. Belton and Bernard address the Imperium, debating whether union or secession is the better alternative.

In the novel, the future of the nation is decided on the Texas frontier, a place associated with fluidity, possibility, violent rebellion, and change. Historically, Texas had been—in rapid succession—part of the Spanish colonial empire, an adjunct of Mexico, an independent republic, a state in the Union, and a member of the Confederacy. Suggesting that Texas might one day secede again, this time as an African nation-state, Griggs imagined another chapter in the state's checkered history. By transforming the state into a self-governing nation, African Americans would achieve the political sovereignty that they had long been denied. Both the Republic of Texas and the state in its first constitution had sanctioned slavery. Even after the war, the state had continued to disenfranchise free men and women and support segregation. Griggs located the Imperium in the real town of Waco, in the eastern third of the state, which was known as the "Black Belt" because of its plantation economy, living conditions reminiscent of slavery, and intense racial prejudice.[6] In addition, Waco was known as "Six Shooter Junction" because of its reputation for lawlessness in the late nineteenth century.[7] In making Waco the headquarters for a group of African American militants, Griggs played on the town's historical reputation for vigilante activity, but he cast racial minorities, rather than whites, as the new vigilantes.

Hopkins chose an equally unruly locale, the Kansas frontier. In *Winona*, the mulatta heroine and her brother are runaway slaves. After being captured, returned to their owners, and sold to a farmer who lives in Missouri, the siblings are rescued by Warren Maxwell, an Englishman who has fallen in love with Winona. The three go to Kansas, where they hide in a camp run by John Brown. The territory has become a political battleground since the passage of the Kansas-Nebraska Act several years earlier. Abolitionists such as Brown are fighting proponents of slavery to ensure that Kansas becomes a free state when it enters the Union. Winona, her brother, and Maxwell side with Brown in his bloody campaign. After getting kidnapped by slaveholders, transported back to Missouri, and rescued once more, they join Brown in a deadly raid on his foes. Brown leaves Kansas to avoid prosecution for murder. Winona, in a timely reversal of fortune, inherits an English estate, marries Maxwell, and moves overseas.

Kansas, like Texas, had a troublesome history. Although the Exodusters would later envision Kansas as the biblical promised land, the territory in the 1850s was hostile to racial minorities. Many white residents opposed the introduction of slavery because they wanted to prevent African Americans from coming to Kansas, not because they favored racial equality. At one constitutional gathering, legislators and delegates "simultaneously demanded the prohibition of slavery" and "the exclusion of free Negroes."[8] At the turn of the century, when Hopkins was writing *Winona*, the state still had a poor record on equal rights. One year before the novel appeared in the *Colored American Magazine*, where it was serialized in 1902, the magazine published an article on Kansas documenting its treatment of criminals. Unlike whites, who were sentenced to prison for crimes they committed, African Americans were sometimes lynched or burned at the stake.[9] Hopkins was an editor at the *Colored American Magazine* in addition to being one of the journal's frequent contributors. Familiar with the information in this article, she would have known that the free state had failed to fulfill its promise as a racial utopia. Hopkins may have been influenced by this knowledge when she decided to have her characters leave Kansas at the end of the novel. If Winona and her brother had stayed in the West, instead of moving to England, they would have continued to face persecution.

Griggs and Hopkins portray the frontier as a region of conflict and instability, not as the site of an ideal civilization. Although Belton and Bernard reunite in the West, they soon become separated by ideological differences. They destroy their friendship and divide the Imperium in the process of debating whether to secede from the Union. Winona is unsettled by the volatility of the early frontier. For the African American heroine, the West is not a safe haven but a place where kidnappings, rescues, hidings, abductions, border crossings, ambushes, and raids occur constantly. Although Winona is mobile, she is never technically free—from pursuit by her enemies, assaults on her virtue, or fears for her future. The novel charts her path as she moves from the North to the South, from Missouri to Kansas, and from the United States to England, seeking refuge and happiness.

Griggs relates racial crisis to geographic upheaval. Bernard wants to separate the races and secede from the Union. The formation of a new nation-state would result in a reconfiguration of the North American map. [10] For Hopkins, the question is not whether a state will secede but whether it will be free when it enters the Union. *Winona* shares certain characteristics with the western dime novel. [11] It dramatizes the conflict between "civilization" and "savagery"—between forces of freedom and proponents of slavery. The ratification of Kansas as a free state represents the triumph of civilization. It justifies westward expansion by associating territorial conquest with political freedom. Each crisis in the conflict erupts during a geographic disturbance, emphasizing the threat to civilization in an unsettled region. Because *Winona* was published as a magazine serial, like many western dime novels, every episode ended suspensefully. Each "cliffhanger" occurred at a narrative juncture that coincided with a geographic change or transition. At the end of chapter 3, Winona and her brother are kidnapped from their home in the North, returned to the South, sold to new owners, and sent to work on a farm in Missouri. [12] At the end of chapter 7, Winona and Judah escape from the farm and cross into Kansas (344–45). At the end of chapter 9, a southern mob is about to burn Maxwell on a stake at the "crossroads" of a small southern town. At the beginning of chapter 10, Free-Soilers rescue him, smuggle him back into Kansas, and leave him with Brown (368–73). In the cliffhanger at the end of the penultimate episode, Judah and his former kidnapper confront each other on the brink of a precipice (416–17). Although Kansas is part of the plains region, Hopkins changes the topography for the sake of suspense. She creates a mountainous setting to symbolize the dangers and obstacles involved in Judah's fight to be free.

Ultimately, Griggs and Hopkins reject the idea that blacks can receive fair

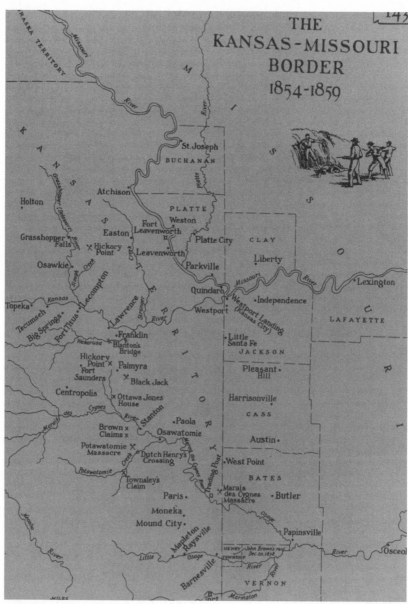

A map of the Kansas Territory and the state of Missouri. A drawing in the upper right corner commemorates the fight over slavery. (From *Atlas of American History Revised Edition*, by Charles Scribner's Sons, © 1978, Charles Scribner's Sons. Reprinted with permission of The Gale Group)

treatment or protection as minorities on the western frontier. Their characters have a hard time making their voices heard or manifesting their physical
presence. Throughout his career, Griggs promoted freedom of expression for
racial minorities. Unlike his contemporaries Charles W. Chesnutt and Paul
Laurence Dunbar, who relied on white patronage, Griggs founded his own
publishing company in 1908.[13] He believed that literature was an ideological
vehicle for disseminating political views and demanding social reforms.[14]
It was therefore necessary for African Americans to control the means of
production by governing the companies that published their literature.

In his fiction, Griggs suggested that the fight for freedom had not yet been
won. Early in his first novel, Belton loses his job as a journalist in Richmond,
Virginia, when he writes an editorial voicing his opposition to "fraud at the
polls."[15] Later, Bernard goes underground in order to publish a newspaper,
chronicling "every fresh discrimination, every new act of oppression, every
additional unlawful assault upon the property, the liberty or the lives" of
black citizens (201). Neither man can speak the truth without losing his job
or having to go underground. Griggs even questions the extent to which his
characters' ideas can be effectively represented by a sympathetic narrator.
Bernard sways the audience when he advises the members of the Imperium
to vote for secession. But the narrator cannot do justice to Bernard's oratorical
skills by merely reproducing the text of his speech. "Words can portray the
form of a speech, but the spirit, the life, are missing and we turn away disap-
pointed. . . . The following gives you but a faint idea of [Bernard's] masterly
effort" (206).

Griggs may have feared that print lacked the power to animate readers
since it immobilized language by fixing words on the page. Perhaps for that
reason, the speeches by Belton and Bernard seem dull and long-winded,
rehearsed, and lacking in urgency, even though both men are passionate and
highly articulate. In addition, the speeches have no effect on the outcome
of events in the novel. Because Belton and Bernard offer equally powerful
arguments—favoring union and secession, respectively—they divide their
constituents, creating a political stalemate that can only be broken by a third
party who intervenes at the end. One critic has suggested that the author's
"reliance on set formal speeches, oratorical contests, sermons, and political
debates" reflects a "polemical literary use of the oral tradition."[16] However,
in spite of the importance placed on verbal expression, the debate fails to
resolve the novel's central dilemma.

Like Griggs, Hopkins believed in the need for African American publica-
tions. She served on the editorial board of the *Colored American Magazine*,

one of the most popular early twentieth-century race periodicals. [17] In its first issue, published in May 1900, the "Race Journal" announced that it would "develop and intensify the bonds of that racial brotherhood, which alone can enable a people, to assert their racial rights as men, and demand their privileges as citizens." [18] Considering the magazine's mission to foster assertiveness, it is ironic that the titular character remains passive and silent throughout much of *Winona*. One critic blames this fact on the "imperial plot" of the western dime novel, which valorizes "white territorial and cultural expansion and dominance." Like the Western, *Winona* features white male protagonists and "an incredibly virtuous but almost invisible heroine." The novel becomes trapped in "self-contradiction." [19] The title refers to a female African American character, but the story centers on Maxwell, a male English aristocrat, and Brown, a white abolitionist.

As the novel progresses, Winona becomes increasingly reliant on Maxwell and Brown. The Englishman meets Winona shortly after the death of her father. "Poor child! Poor little thing!" he exclaims. "Heaven must have sent me here at this awful moment" (308). Maxwell becomes her informal guardian (311); a savior, who rescues Winona as well as her brother from slavery (336); and a lover, who is attracted to her because of her clinging and "childish" qualities (355). Throughout most of the novel, Winona is enslaved on a farm in Missouri, dependent on Maxwell for guidance, or made submissive to Brown. Although Brown believes in freedom for racial minorities, he treats women like second-class citizens. The women in his "patriarchal care" (373) "listened but did not intrude their opinions" when the men made their battle plans (380). [20]

On the one occasion when Winona plays a determining role, she assumes a male disguise, proving that she has "the pluck of a man" (348). [21] Dressed as "Allen Pinks," she enter a prison where Maxwell lies ill. The hero has suffered a serious shock, having witnessed the mistreatment of African Americans in prison, including possibly sodomy—"the shameful outrage, so denounced in the Scriptures, and which must not be described in the interests of decency" (385). Disguised as "Pinks," Winona nurses Maxwell, kisses him (388), and speaks in a caressing voice as "soft and low as a woman's" (389). After she helps him escape, Winona removes her disguise, much to the relief of the hero, who has begun to question the nature of his feelings for "Pinks" (392).

Although the West offers some freedom from convention and room for experimentation, ultimately it is not a liberating environment. [22] Winona temporarily assumes a different identity, but in the end she reverts back to type. After removing her disguise and becoming a woman once more, she never again plays a prominent role. She darkens her complexion in order to blend in with the prisoners (396), but when she takes off her makeup, the light-skinned Winona reassumes the part of the traditional heroine. (Although she and Maxwell have an interracial relationship, Winona has certain Caucasian traits that may have made their relationship seem more acceptable.) Maxwell is temporarily attracted to "Pinks," but Hopkins normalizes what would otherwise be a same-sex attraction by revealing Winona's identity, reinstating romantic convention, and marrying the heterosexual hero and heroine.[23]

Imperium in Imperio also features a scene in which Belton cross-dresses. He becomes a nurse in order to document how whites treat their servants (131–33). In each household where Belton works, the men make improper advances, assuming that African American women are fair sexual game. Belton discourages these advances, defending the integrity of his race and the virtue of the opposite sex. But one employer, becoming inflamed when "the nurse" resists, takes Belton by force (135). Although becoming a man empowers Winona, enabling her to free Maxwell from prison, becoming a woman renders Belton defenseless, leaving him prey to sexual victimization. One critic believes that Belton's rape symbolizes the emasculation of African American men in a racist society.[24] It serves as a metaphor, confirming Belton's suspicion before he went undercover that whites "felt that the Negro was easily ruled" (133). By equating female passivity with racial victimization, Griggs implicitly seems to suggest that the race can only be saved by aggressively dominant, heterosexual men. Griggs and Hopkins seem uncomfortable with men who deviate from the heterosexual norm. (Belton's rape and Maxwell's feelings for "Pinks" provoke equal anxiety.) They also view women as inessential participants in the fight for freedom on the western frontier. While Winona plays a subordinate role, the wives of Belton and Bernard play no role whatsoever. The men leave their wives when they join the Imperium, an exclusively male organization.[25] Griggs and Hopkins imagine the West as an unsettled region where social change and radical political action take place. To some extent, however, the frontier remains racist and sexist terrain.

Griggs and Hopkins published their novels at the turn of the century, in the shadow of the millennium. Because they shared a Protestant faith and certain evangelical tendencies, they viewed this historical turning point as a moment of reckoning. In their fiction, both writers suggested that the war on racism was a righteous endeavor, even though they predicted that it might lead to civil war, social apocalypse, or the coming of Judgment Day. Griggs was born in Texas in 1872, the son of a minister. At the age of eighteen he enrolled in a theological seminary in Richmond. Following graduation he was assigned to the local First Baptist Church. After serving in Memphis as president of the American Baptist Theological Seminary, in the mid-1920s he moved back to Texas, where he continued to preach.[26]

The African American Baptist Church was a potent force in the state. Because evangelical oratory appealed strongly to ex-slaves, the overwhelming majority belonged to either the Baptist or the Methodist Church. The Baptist Church was more popular because each congregation was granted religious autonomy.[27] African Americans could form their own congregations, separate from whites, if they chose. The Baptist Church was therefore more likely to appeal to African Americans who were activists.[28] Griggs was raised and educated within this religious community. Writing novels that one critic has described as "tractarian," he advocated political action as a means to achieve racial equality.[29] Aware that race relations had worsened at the end of the century, and inspired by evangelical fervor, Griggs warned of a potential racial apocalypse. *Imperium in Imperio* begins with "the sun of the Nineteenth Century" setting among "the blackest and thickest and ugliest clouds" (3). In a vision that takes the form of a biblical parable, Belton imagines "the awful carnage" that would result if African Americans declared war on society (43–45). Later, in Texas, Bernard moves to fulfill Belton's prophecy, issuing orders to arm African American militiamen, station troops at the border, and seize the state capitol (251–52). Only by sabotaging this plot does a member of the Imperium prevent Armageddon. He spares the nation a military conflict that would have "spread destruction, devastation and death all around" (262–63).

Like Griggs, Hopkins had a Protestant background, an interest in social reform, and concerns about race that peaked around the turn of the century. Two of her Baptist relations established churches in Boston, where Hopkins spent most of her life. In high school she wrote a prize-winning essay denouncing intemperance.[30] In *Winona* she deplores the "vile passions" of southerners who own slaves, gamble, and drink (343, 370). Yet she views violence favorably if it is associated with a righteous political cause. African Americans are justified in avenging an "eye for an eye" if they have been treated inhumanely as slaves (417). When Judah kills Thompson, a slaver, he feels "neither remorse nor commiseration for the deed just committed" (418). Sampson Steward, an abolitionist preacher, kills men from Missouri who burst into his church, looking for fugitive slaves: "I girded up my loins and taking a pistol in each hand, I led forth my elders and members against the Philistines; and I said to them: 'This day I will give the carcasses of your hosts unto the fowls of the air, and the wild beasts of the earth; that all the

earth may know that there is a God in Israel.' Verily, not one was spared"
(350). The preacher represents a punishing God. Like Sampson, his namesake, he slays his tormentors. So does Brown, who ambushes his enemies.
Hopkins seems to agree with W. E. B. DuBois, who writes in *John Brown*
(1909) that bloodshed in Kansas was "a disgrace to civilization but it was the
cost of freedom, and it was less than the price of repression."[31]

The conflict on the border results in vindication and freedom for the
forces of righteousness and death for the enemy. As he rides into battle,
the preacher shouts: "Blow ye the trumpet blow!" "Slay and spare not!"
(361). The omniscient narrator, warning that "justice cannot sleep forever"
(386), foresees a day when blacks will be free. After Winona escapes from
Missouri, Aunt Vinnie, a black woman, sings: "Dis is de year of Jubilee, /
Send dem angels down. / De Lord has come to set us free, / O, send dem
angels down" (437). (Originally, Hebrew slaves were emancipated during the
year of Jubilee, which occurred twice every century.)[32]

Such optimism proved not to be justified. In the decade before Hopkins
published her novel, segregation, civil rights violations, and lynchings were
common. The 1890s were ending, yet justice still slept. Hopkins worked for
the Massachusetts Bureau of Statistics until 1899, compiling information for
the census that appeared the following year.[33] She was trained to interpret
decades and centuries in terms of their historic significance. When considering why Winona leaves America at the end of the novel, it may be important
to remember two statistical facts. According to Frederick Jackson Turner,
the U.S. census of 1890 proved that the frontier was "closed."[34] From the
perspective of someone writing in 1902, the frontier was no longer viable.
By the early twentieth century, the prospect of a racial utopia would have
seemed beyond reach.

Nonetheless, Griggs and Hopkins believed that improved race relations
were possible. Unlike Belton, Griggs was unwilling to accommodate social injustice. But unlike Bernard, he could not imagine going to war with America.
At the end of the novel, a member of the Imperium leaks information to the
national government about the plot to secede. He justifies his act of "treason"
by claiming that Bernard is "a serious menace to the peace of the world"
(263). In *Winona*, although African Americans do not secede, the main characters move overseas. But while some find refuge in England, living among
the white aristocracy, others stay home preparing for a better society. At the
end of the novel, Aunt Vinnie, a working-class African American woman,
preaches a sermon: "White folks been ridin' a turrible hoss in this country, an'
dat hoss gwine to fro 'em you hyar me." Times are hard, she admits, but things

will improve. When an African American man in the audience testifies that a mule kicked him three times that morning, Aunt Vinnie says, "dat means good luck" (436).

Griggs and Hopkins were transitional figures, looking backward and forward at the turn of the century. Griggs created two heroes: one who reflected the earlier conservative views of Booker T. Washington and one who resembled modern African American nationalists and militant activists. One critic suggests that the author's "fanatical" ideas were tempered by a political outlook that was "essentially feudal."[35] Another claims that the novel's "strength and complexity derives from Griggs's failure to take a position."[36] A third calls Griggs an "integrationist" as well as a "militant,"[37] while a fourth says that after reading his novel, it is hard to determine what Griggs may have believed.[38]

Hopkins revealed similarly contradictory tendencies. Her white characters, such as Maxwell and Brown, were assertive and militant, but Winona was essentially passive. As a member of "the black genteel tradition," Hopkins created a light-skinned protagonist whose Caucasian characteristics and traditional female modesty made her appealing to the white bourgeoisie.[39] She wrote about controversial topics, such as racial rebellion and miscegenation, within the traditional confines of formula fiction.[40] At the same time, she experimented with genre, creating a work that combined the sentimental romance with the western dime novel. Finally, although *Winona* was set in the past, it was written with the future in mind. The abolitionist movement in *Winona* was an example of the kind of political activism that Hopkins wanted "to revive or encourage" at the turn of the century.[41] Although she believed in a millennial future, Hopkins was also aware of the historical record. The abolition of slavery on the western frontier had not resulted in the creation of a perfect society. In spite of her Protestant faith, Hopkins questioned the utopian premise of Manifest Destiny and the gospel of western conquest as providential design.

Prior to writing *Winona*, Hopkins became engaged in a similar debate about the appropriateness of U.S. military involvement in other parts of the world. In 1898, during the Spanish-American War, the nation sent troops to Cuba. During the Philippine-American War, which ended in 1902, the same year that Hopkins published *Winona*, it also stationed troops overseas. An article about African American soldiers fighting in Cuba graced the first issue of the *Colored American Magazine*, and an account by some of the "colored" men who served in the Philippines appeared in the same issue as part 1 of *Winona*.[42] Although the soldiers who were interviewed supported both wars, not all readers agreed. Some welcomed the opportunity to fight overseas in order to prove they were patriots, convinced that when they returned home they would be rewarded with newfound respect and treated as full-fledged American citizens. Others were skeptical, wondering whether they should intervene in the affairs of other countries and other people of color or stay home and fight for their own rights as minorities. [43] It is unclear whether Hopkins intended to comment on these contemporary political questions in her historical novel. However, Winona, like many other African Americans at the time, seems divided about what course of action to take. Although she fights for the forces of freedom on the nation's frontier, she then renounces her homeland after achieving political victory.

Griggs believed that U.S. military aggression was a form of racial oppression. In a letter to the editor published in the *Indianapolis World* on November 3, 1900, he predicted that the Philippine-American War would result in the enslavement of natives and worsen "the plight of black citizens." [44] In *Imperium in Imperio* he also argues that African American nationalism, like white imperialism, poses a threat to the world. Bernard wants to establish an empire within an empire, as the title of the novel suggests. He espouses a racial version of Manifest Destiny, claiming that the seizure of Texas and the war on whites is a justified cause. In the end, however, he becomes the reverse mirror image of his racist oppressor. He campaigns on a platform of African racial supremacy, divine right to the land, and military violence as a solution to political and racial disputes.

Although Griggs was born in Texas, he set only part of one novel there. Hopkins was raised in New England and never left home, and her descriptions of Kansas are vague and sometimes inaccurate. Neither Griggs nor Hopkins is a "regional" writer, concerned with portraying the West in realistic detail. Both of them view the frontier as abstract ideological ground—as a place where larger issues, relating to race, are sometimes decided. *Imperium in Imperio* and *Winona* are novels about region and race, but they are also products of a politically tumultuous era when African Americans were concerned with present as well as past racial injustices, with national and international political affairs as well as matters relating to the regional American West.

CHAPTER FOUR

The Significance of the Frontier in the New Negro Renaissance

The New Negro Renaissance refers to a flourishing movement of African American artistic expression that occurred in Harlem in the early decades of the twentieth century. Although the Renaissance was considered an eastern urban phenomenon, the movement included a significant number of artists who traced their roots back to the rural American West. In *The New Negro* (1925), Paul Kellogg claimed that the artists who immigrated to Harlem represented "another folk migration which in human significance can be compared only with [the] pushing back of the Western frontier."[1] This time, the "folk" were primarily African American rather than white, and they were moving in the opposite direction, relocating in a modern eastern metropolis. These "new Negro" residents, who resembled "the old pioneers" (273–74), were transforming Harlem into a vibrant artistic community.

Kellogg's comparison between nineteenth-century white frontier immigrants and twentieth-century urban African American artists is noteworthy because of the striking dissimilarities. Many white pioneers left "civilization" for sparsely populated western domains. African Americans, in "a reversal of that process" (275), journeyed mainly from southern rural locations to an industrial northeastern city. In "The Significance of the Frontier in American History" (1893), Frederick Jackson Turner argued that the exploration and clearing of wilderness had eventually led to the establishment of small frontier outposts, then larger communities, and finally urban centers of industry.[2] Like Turner, Kellogg imagined the city, in this case Harlem, as the final frontier. But unlike Turner, who predicted that successful urban entrepreneurs would be the new pioneers, Kellogg imagined ordinary citizens—struggling artists and racial minorities—filling these roles (275). Kellogg's "pioneers" were poor and socially marginal people of color. They were descendants of slaves who had been "sold or bartered" like chattel during an era when white pioneers were first making "their way into the New Territory and establish[ing] thriving communities."[3] Kellogg revised Turner's frontier thesis, focusing on the contributions and achievements made by racial minorities.[4]

The artists who pioneered new forms of expression were members of the New Negro Renaissance. The movement began at the end of World War I when a loss of faith in European civilization, combined with the increasing popularity of the Freudian notion that "primitive" peoples were free from the constraints of modern society, resulted in a growing interest in the American Negro and his African origins.[5] The bohemian artists in the New Negro Renaissance theoretically identified with a "primitive" African or non-Anglo culture. They were the opposites of white pioneers. Turner's archetypal frontiersmen entered the wilderness in order to conquer "savagery" and introduce "civilization." Renaissance artists pursued a different yet equally paradoxical goal. They went to the city and, instead of abolishing "savagery," practiced "primitivism" in a cosmopolitan setting.

Many works from the Renaissance have been described as examples of "primitive" art, including sculptures, paintings, and graphic designs influenced by American folk Negro or African sources; African American literature incorporating regional idioms or racial vernacular; jazz and blues; and anthropological representations of "black" rural practices. The term has been used to refer to works that are unsophisticated or "primitive" as well as those that are modern and highly refined. New York City, the home of the "primitive" during the New Negro Renaissance, was romanticized by African American writers as a mixture of the old world and new. In *A Long Way from Home* (1937), Claude McKay compared the city's skyscrapers to pyramids.[6] In *The Blacker the Berry . . .* (1929), Wallace Thurman referred to the people who lived in Harlem as "cliff dwellers."[7] Both Renaissance writers imagined the modern cosmopolitan American cityscape as an ancient, preindustrial, exotic locale. New York City had become a distant racial frontier, either desert Egyptian or southwest Native American, an early yet technologically superior and elaborately constructed society inhabited by dark-skinned precursors to Anglo-Saxon inhabitants.

Like the term "primitive," the word "frontier" had multiple meanings. The African American migration to Harlem after World War I inspired some writers to compare the influx of Negroes to a frontier military invasion. For example, in *Black Manhattan* (1930), James Weldon Johnson subtitled chapter 13: "The trek northward—the conquest of Harlem."[8] In another social history, *Harlem: Negro Metropolis* (1940), Claude McKay described the Negro campaign "to obtain and consolidate the new territory" of Upper Manhattan. Imagining New York City as a contested terrain partitioned by military and political borders, McKay mapped Negro Harlem's perimeters, claiming that Central Park in the 1920s formed its southern "frontier."[9] In *The New Negro*, Charles S. Johnson defined the "frontier" neither as a new territory to conquer nor as a border separating two hostile races. For Johnson, the editor of *Opportunity: A Journal of Negro Life*, Harlem was an experimental contact zone where Negroes and whites interacted: "[T]he new frontier of Negro life is flung out in a jagged, uneven . . . pattern," where contact with the Negro's surrounding culture "breeds quite uneven results."[10] An article that later appeared in his magazine, entitled "Interracial Frontiers: Extracts from the Annual Report of the National Urban League," recommended that social problems "made acute and aggravated by racial misunderstanding" be resolved by "representatives of the white and colored people coming together for a joint attack" on their differences.[11]

Harlem was not just a frontier in theory. Many artists in the New Negro Renaissance came from the West. Louise Thompson lived in several western states during her childhood, graduated from the University of California at Berkeley, and moved to New York City after winning a National Urban League fellowship. Claude McKay, a Jamaican, attended college in Kansas before being "gripped by the lust to wander and wonder."[12] Aaron Douglas, the best-known graphic artist of the New Negro Renaissance, was born in Topeka, Kansas, and educated in Lincoln, Nebraska, although his work was influenced by European modernist and early African art.[13] Sargent Johnson, a San Francisco sculptor, is frequently linked with the Renaissance even though he was inspired by Bay Area more than by East Coast aesthetics.[14] Arna Bontemps wrote three short stories about his life in Los Angeles.[15]

Some of the artists brought the West with them when they journeyed back east. In Harlem they remembered and wrote about the western frontier. Within a year of each other, three members of the Renaissance who were born and raised in the West published works that explored the region extensively. A fourth western writer, whose major novel appeared after the Renaissance, focused on the West to a lesser degree yet forged a subtle and complex connection between frontier myths and urban Negro reality. The writers registered a range of responses to the West and to Harlem as well. In *Born to Be* (1929), Taylor Gordon claimed that he preferred his hometown in rural Montana to Harlem. But in *The Blacker the Berry* . . . —a novel published the same year as Gordon's autobiography—Thurman suggested that there was little difference between Harlem and Rocky Mountain or Pacific Coast cities, all of which were equally racist. Interestingly, no western writer supported Kellogg's thesis that Harlem was the New Negro promised land. Langston Hughes, in *Not without Laughter* (1930), and Ralph Ellison, in *Invisible Man* (1952), hailed from Kansas and Oklahoma, respectively. Both men wrote about the urban frontier with ambivalence. Yet despite their lack of enthusiasm, all four writers shared an interest in the relationship between region and race, in the theme of flight from small towns to cities, and in the relative significance of Harlem to the twentieth-century Negro's development.

Of these four western writers, the least well known, Taylor Gordon, had the only true "frontier" pedigree. Born in 1893 in Montana, Gordon was raised by his mother, a laundress, in White Sulphur Springs, a colorful small town inhabited by sheep ranchers, miners, gamblers, and prostitutes. In 1910 Gordon left home, moved to the Midwest, and became a chauffeur. Later he met the renowned impresario John Ringling and traveled the country, employed as a railroad porter and cook in Ringling's deluxe private carriage. In New York City, where Ringling was based, Gordon met Rosamond Johnson, the brother of James Weldon Johnson. The revival of interest in Negro folk culture during the Renaissance had inspired the Johnson brothers to compile a collection of spirituals. In 1925, shortly after the book's publication, Rosamond Johnson invited Gordon to join him in performing some of these songs. In the process of doing so, Gordon met Muriel Draper, a wealthy New York hostess who ran a musical salon, and Carl Van Vechten, a patron of the Renaissance, who encouraged Gordon to write his autobiography.

Born to Be was published with a foreword by Van Vechten and an introduction by Draper. Although it was Gordon's success as a singer that led to his opportunity to write an autobiography, it was his account of his early years rather than his association with the New Negro Renaissance that attracted most notice. Numerous works about Harlem had appeared during the decade, but none had contrasted life in an eastern metropolis with Negro adventures on the western frontier. The book was a novelty because Gordon described what it was like growing up as a minority in a non-Negro society. Surprisingly, he claimed that he had never encountered racism while he lived in Montana. In the first section of his autobiography, he fondly remembers the multicultural residents of White Sulphur Springs: Anglo-European miners and ranchers, Chinese laborers, a Swedish undertaker, and a whorehouse madam of reputed English nobility. In such an eclectic society, Gordon writes, he "was

Taylor Gordon, far right, poses with classmates in White Sulphur Springs, Montana, ca. 1900. (Montana Historical Society)

accepted both high and low." [16] Looking back on his formative years, when he was "free to associate with many nationalities, colors and creeds," Gordon concludes that "the Race Question has never been the big ghost of my life!" (234).

Gordon claimed that he encountered racism for the first time while working as a driver in St. Paul, Minnesota. After being refused service in a restaurant because of his color, his mentor, an African American porter, tells Gordon, "Man, don't you know you's a niggah and can't do things heah like you did out home in Montana?" (69). In New York City he resolves to "learn all about niggahs, because I was one of them" (98). From this moment on he becomes an observer, noting racial attitudes in each place he visits. In parts of the South, including Oklahoma and Florida, where segregation is evident, Ringling's "nigger" can't even "*look* at a white woman" (126). Gordon learns about more subtle caste systems when he goes overseas: "In the U.S.A., a Nigger was a Nigger, as long as he had one drop of black blood. . . . But in the West Indies, they went according to shades" (154). While he is on a concert tour throughout England and Europe, audiences welcome the singer but treat him as a member of an exotic primitive species (205–7).

Assuming the role of the naive narrator, Gordon developed what one critic has called "an ingenious strategy for protesting prejudice." Posing as a

racially unmarked, innocent westerner, at home and abroad, enabled the author, apparently without bias, to critique individual, cultural, and institutional
bigotry.[17] According to *Born to Be*, Gordon lived in a state of prelapsarian
innocence in White Sulphur Springs, where he and his mother were the
only African American citizens. Only when he entered society, becoming
identified with an African American metropolitan populace, was he marked as
a "nigger."[18] Gordon seems to contradict Kellogg, who celebrates the benefits
of urban migration. Although the adolescent Gordon outgrows Montana and
dreams about going to "Big Cities" and becoming "an Easterner" (55), he
soon regrets his decision. Traveling by railroad makes him realize that he
misses his saddle horse (65). When the waiter in St. Paul refuses to serve
him, Gordon automatically reaches for his Colt .45, then remembers that he
no longer carries a gun like he did in Montana (68). As his train passes through
Pennsylvania on its way to New York, Gordon compares the Rocky Mountains
to the present "foot-hills—for that's what they were to me" (101). At the end
of his autobiography he claims that in spite of having met "the world's greatest
celebrities, artists, musicians, writers, bull-dikers, hoboes, faggots, bankers,
sweetbacks, hotspots, and royalty," he yearns "to go back to the mountains,
surround myself with wine, women and song, and spend the rest of my days"
(235).

Although he resolves to learn more about Negroes because he is "one
of them," the intellectually detached way in which Gordon studies his race
suggests that he feels no common bond with people of color. The Negro
spirituals strike no inner personal chord. The white audience's "reaction"
holds his "interests more than anything else" (191). Critics agree that Gordon
identifies more as a regional westerner than as a racial minority.[19] To be more
precise, Gordon associates with a particular place that embodies the best of
the region. The author has no particular affection for western locations except
for the idyllic White Sulphur Springs. Helena bores him (53), and Seattle
seems just like other big cities (86). His hometown, however, captures the
natural beauty of the rural frontier: "If God ever did spend any time here
on earth," he attests, it must have been in this edenic environment (4). In
winter, during "nature's grand opera season," the northern lights flash from
the western horizon. Gordon remembers, as a child, having had a "box seat" in
the valley, from which vantage point he watched "the Grand Mistress of Art"
produce a "kinetopic" display, starring the mountains as "actors and actresses"
and featuring a chorus of "coyotes and wolves [who] sang *a capella*" (10–11).

In this passage one sees the similarities between Gordon and Kellogg
instead of the differences. Kellogg portrays Harlem as the final frontier, while

Gordon imagines frontier Montana as having the same cultural advantages as the East Coast metropolis. The author compares the workings of primitive nature to an operatic performance that one might watch in the city. Although he is not stirred by the spirituals that have become associated with the cultural revival of the New Negro Renaissance, he is moved by the music of wolves and coyotes. For Gordon, White Sulphur Springs is not just an edenic retreat far from the maddening crowd; it is also a lively spot that rivals Harlem in its varied activities. The fin de siècle frontier (with its gambling saloon, Chinese opium den, brothel, and theater) and 1920s Harlem (with its numbers-running rackets, drag balls, and de rigueur rent parties) both satisfy primitive pleasures and cosmopolitan appetites. Gordon establishes Harlem as the complementary opposite of White Sulphur Springs, associating an urbane eastern environment with the western frontier through a set of reverse mirror images. Gordon, the westerner, squeezed into a formal tuxedo, singing "primitive" spirituals for the New York City elite, becomes the counterpart to Carl Van Vechten, Gordon's effete East Coast patron, comically dressed in a red cowboy shirt, sporting an orange-and-green bandanna handkerchief (229).

In reality, the residents of White Sulphur Springs were neither as innocent nor as sophisticated in their preference for social diversity as Gordon maintained. According to Gordon's biographer, the town at the turn of the century had "a record of bigotry." Only ten years before Gordon was born, four African American students had been expelled "to preserve the all-white local school." Gordon's sister was later prevented from singing Negro gospels in church.[20] One contemporary reviewer criticized Born to Be for not confronting the local racism that existed during this period. In an unsigned review in The Crisis, a journal affiliated with the NAACP and edited by W. E. B. DuBois, the reviewer mocked the idea that the West was a harmonious place, where seldom was heard a discouraging word. Revising the lyrics to "Home on the Range," the reviewer wrote mockingly: "of real life, in that drab western town, there must have been poignant tragedy. . . . But here there is scarce a serious word."[21]

For Gordon, race was a social construction. "Nigger" was a term that had no meaning for the boy from Montana. "Negro spiritual singer" was a persona he adopted during performances. Place was also an invention in Gordon's autobiography. Ignoring evidence to the contrary, the author portrayed White Sulphur Springs as a nonracist community. While Gordon idealized his hometown, preferring it to other locations, his counterpart in the Renaissance, Wallace Thurman, a fellow westerner, alleged that the West was as racist as other parts of America. Thurman was born in Salt Lake City in 1902. He lived in Chicago, Boise, and Omaha, then attended the University of Southern California for one semester before dropping out. After spending several years in Los Angeles, he moved to New York City in the mid-1920s. While he worked at *The Messenger* as a managing editor, the magazine published a series of essays on race and geography. "These 'Colored' United States" reported on a different state every month and rated each state from the perspective of African Americans. Most of the essays on western states dwelled on the positive, emphasizing progress in civil rights and economic opportunities for people of color, but Thurman's essay on Utah mocked the state's reputation as a refuge or promised land. In "Quoth Brigham Young: This Is the Place," Thurman had a bad word to say about everyone—Mormons, Gentiles, and racial minorities. Adopting a blasé perspective, he described Mormons as "dull," Gentiles as "more dull," and African Americans as "still more dull." But when he complained about racial segregation, lack of equal access to education, and the absence of an African American professional class, he sounded openly bitter. In Utah minorities were restricted to ghettos, ran nightclubs and "whorehouses" because they had no other job choices, and contributed nothing to the state but "sociological problems," he noted sarcastically.[22]

Gordon claims that his race was never an issue in White Sulphur Springs. However, Thurman portrays a West where racism exists in *The Blacker the Berry . . . .* Emma Lou Brown comes from Boise, a city where Thurman once lived.[23] As the only minority in her high school class, she feels like an "odd and conspicuous figure" (22). Uncle Joe insists "that as long as one was a Negro, one's specific color had little to do with one's life" (35), but experience teaches Emma Lou otherwise. The dark-skinned girl is rejected by whites and by light-skinned members of her race who make up Boise's "blue vein" society. If she had been a boy, "color of skin wouldn't have mattered so much," according to Emma Lou's mother, who says that boys have more freedom. "But she wasn't a boy," the narrator stresses, "and color did matter" (22). Unlike Uncle Joe, who believes that the individual controls his or her destiny, Emma Lou concludes that she is the victim of genetics and social conditioning. It is her fate to have been born a girl with dark "color chromosomes" (31) and to have been raised in an "environment" where her complexion is viewed as a curse (21).

Since she cannot alter biology, Emma Lou decides to change her physical setting. At the University of Southern California, where Thurman was also a student, she hopes to meet broad-minded minorities who will recognize her intrinsic worth rather than judge her because of her color. But the only student who befriends Emma Lou is another "primitive" girl from the rural West, a Texan named Hazel, with kinky hair, flattened nostrils, dark skin, a loud voice, a country vocabulary, and a penchant for wearing bright, vulgar colors (41–44). Emma Lou, who wants so desperately to be accepted by others, rejects Hazel's friendship because she herself has internalized the class prejudice and racial self-loathing—the preference for the "right sort of people"(50)—that exists among African Americans in Boise society. In turn, the university's light-skinned minorities, mulattoes, and blue-veined aristocrats, influenced by the same sort of thinking, shun Emma Lou. Thurman suggests that the parents of these students originally came to Los Angeles for the same reason that Emma Lou's family settled in Idaho, because the West theoretically offers "greater freedom and [more] opportunity" (59). But ironically, these color-conscious, upwardly mobile immigrant African Americans create an environment as racially oppressive as one in the North or the South. After one year in college, Emma Lou decides that "people in large cities were after all no different from people in small cities" (61) and that one region is the same as all others.

Eventually, however, Emma Lou changes her mind and convinces herself that the West is more provincial than other parts of America. Even Los Angeles has a small-town mentality: "It was no better than Boise. She was now determined to go East where life was more cosmopolitan" (70). But in Harlem her prospects are the same, if not worse. Employment agencies recommend her only for menial jobs, and African American men prefer dating lighter-skinned women. Emma Lou tries unsuccessfully to bleach her complexion and thinks that education will facilitate her upward mobility, but the courses she takes at City College only make her more aware of her worsening social position. "She had thought Harlem would be different, but things had seemed against her from the beginning, and she had continued to go down, down, down," the narrator notes fatalistically (189). Emma Lou had once dreamed that the cosmopolitan center of the New Negro Renaissance would be more enlightened than cities out west, but her "geographical flights"—from Boise to Los Angeles, from Los Angeles to Harlem—"had not solved her problems, and a further flight back to where her life had begun" was "too futile" for Emma Lou to consider (215). With no other alternatives, she remains in New York, where she resigns herself to fighting life's "future battles" (218).

One early review of *The Blacker the Berry . . .* criticized Thurman for suggesting that African American women were "doomed" to a "humdrum and sordid" existence. Offended by this pessimistic view and by descriptions of Emma Lou's squalid New York City environment, the reviewer criticized "this young man from the West" for having written a crude and "immature" novel. Unlike the best American literature, which had a "polished perfection," this work, produced by a youth from a primitive region, was "gauche" in its depiction of East Coast civilization. [24] More recently, a critic has disputed this charge by noting that Thurman was just as hard on the West as he was on the rest of America. However, the critic then contradicts himself by praising the West as a unique and positive place—by defining Thurman as a regional writer, with a western egalitarian, rural perspective, "who made urban Negroes squirm at their own pretentiousness and take greater pride in their heritage." [25]

For Thurman, the West was no better or worse than the rest of the nation. His contemporary Taylor Gordon found racism everywhere except in Montana, but Thurman refused to play favorites. In his essay on Utah he argued that there was "no state in the Union" where the "Negro" had been granted equal rights as a citizen. [26] The problem was not local or regional, he contended in The Blacker the Berry . . . . It was more complex and widespread. A combination of factors—including white discrimination, intraracial prejudice, restricted options for women, class repression, and snobbery—produced a caste system within a segregated African American community. Without a college degree or extensive career opportunities, Emma Lou has only one means of achieving upward mobility—marriage to a lighter-skinned man—a goal that remains unattainable.

Both writers celebrated the "primitive" during the New Negro Renaissance. For Gordon certain places were primitive, including White Sulphur Springs, a crude multicultural frontier community, and Harlem, its counterpart, a rowdy urban metropolis, the site of a folk Negro aesthetic. For Thurman the primitive impulse was racial, not regional. It was revealed in Hazel's preference for "low-down" blues music (55) and "circus-like," bright-colored clothes (44). It was responsible for Emma Lou's awakening sexual feelings, for the sensuous dances that stirred "her insides" (108), and for the mesmerizing performance of the Harlem piano player who looked like a "witch doctor" (151). Gordon romanticized the primitive, which appeared in danger of becoming extinct (with the closing of the frontier at the turn of the century and with the end of the Renaissance in the late 1920s). Thurman believed that the primitive was buried deep in the soul and that its instincts were often suppressed due to racial self-censorship and a bourgeois sense of propriety. The Negro's "heart of darkness" was an unexplored region, just as Gordon's spirit of place was ephemeral.

Langston Hughes and Wallace Thurman in California, date unknown. (Yale Collection of American Literature, Beinecke Rare Book and Manuscript Library. Reprinted with permission of Harold Ober Associates Incorporated)

In 1935, Langston Hughes published a short story with a striking thematic resemblance to *The Blacker the Berry . . . .* [27] "Flora Belle" chronicles an African American woman's unsuccessful search for a place to live happily. During her childhood, when a lynch mob forces her family to abandon their home, she and her parents move to Tall Rock, Montana. As the only African

American child in town, Flora Belle feels like a "stranger," an "outcast" (104). After her mother dies, she and her father move to Butte, which has a larger population of racial minorities. But Flora Belle, having been isolated from the rest of her race, considers the "Negroes" she meets "exceedingly strange" (105). As a woman, she drifts from one place to another, seeking a community in which she feels comfortable. The cities—Seattle, San Francisco, Monterey, Berkeley, San Jose, San Diego, and Marysville—become increasingly harder for the outcast to tolerate. Finally, in Fresno, Flora Belle buys a pistol and contemplates suicide. Rejected by whites as well as people of color, unable to marry because of her unattractive appearance, and forced to support herself by performing hard manual labor, Flora Belle sleeps with the gun under her pillow and dreams that it can take her "away—whenever she wanted to go. She felt sure it would not disappoint her—if she chose to leave Fresno" (108). Like the heroine in *The Blacker the Berry* . . . , Flora Belle discovers that the West offers no refuge for those who are racially ostracized. At the end of the story her future, like Emma Lou's, appears bleak and depressing.

"Flora Belle" tells a tale of unrelieved suffering, unlike Hughes's first novel, set in the West during the same historical period. *Not without Laughter*—a gentle account of African American life in a small Kansas town—offers a more balanced perspective. Aunt Hager and her family reside in an integrated, lower-middle-class neighborhood consisting of "Negroes" and "[g]ood white folks" as well as those who use "uncouth epithets" to refer to people of color. [28] Stanton, in the early twentieth century, is becoming progressively tolerant yet remains racist in certain respects. In fifth grade, racial minorities are allowed to study with whites but forced to sit in the back of the room (130). Anjee, Aunt Hager's daughter, represents Sweden in a color-blind pageant called the "Drill of All Nations" (70), yet Jimboy, her husband, loses his job because "white bricklayers said they couldn't lay bricks with a nigger" (71). Feelings about whites differ within the racial community. Recounting how southerners persecuted ex-slaves after the Civil War, a friend of the family concludes that white folks are "mean" (82). Harriet, another one of Aunt Hager's daughters, remembers how white children used to taunt her by calling her "Blackie," a memory that leaves an "unpleasantly lasting impression" (88). Aunt Hager, the voice of compassion, advises her family not to hold grudges. "[T]here ain't no room in de world fo' hate," she says. "There ain't no room in this world fo' nothin' but love" (184). Some characters, however, are unable to tolerate existing conditions. Jimboy jumps on a railroad car and leaves town; Harriet becomes an entertainer who travels the Midwest; Anjee and her son, Sandy, eventually move to Chicago. Only Aunt Hager and her third daughter, Tempy, stay put.

Like Taylor Gordon, Hughes in *Not without Laughter* created a picturesque portrait of western African Americans to please a largely white audience. In 1925, Carl Van Vechten advised Hughes, as he later encouraged Gordon, to pen his autobiography. Van Vechten assumed that Hughes's account of his childhood would be filled with soulful "nostalgia," colorful incidents, and "vivid descriptions" of Kansas.[29] Initially, Hughes attempted to craft such an autobiography. An early draft, "L'Histoire de ma vie," was influenced by the romantic literature that Hughes had read as a boy, in which people only "suffered in beautiful language, not in monosyllables, as we did in Kansas," he noted.[30] Later, with the financial support of Charlotte Mason, Hughes's white patron in the late 1920s, the author transformed his memoirs into a novel bearing even less resemblance to his own western experience.

In *Not without Laughter*, Aunt Hager—an uneducated African American laundress and a meek Christian Baptist—differs from Hughes's grandmother, Mary, who was part French and Native American, politically active, proud of her heritage, and somewhat more prosperous. Unlike Jimboy, an itinerant blues singer and likable ne'er-do-well, Hughes's father, James, was an emotionally distant, ambitious businessman, with no interest in music or poetry. Hughes's mother, Carrie, in addition to having a career of her own, established book clubs and cultural societies in the racial community. Anjee, however, works as a servant and has no time for hobbies.[31] In *Not without Laughter*, as Hughes later explained in an autobiography, he had chosen a "typical" family to represent the "Negro" experience.[32] With the exceptions of Tempy, who marries into the middle class, and Sandy, who pursues education, the members of Aunt Hager's family are financially struggling, sometimes unemployed, semi-literate people who speak in colorful dialect and periodically entertain themselves by singing the blues. Critics have both praised and faulted the author for associating the "typical Negro" with these "primitive" traits. In an early review in *The Nation*, one writer thanked Hughes for portraying the "real Negro"—the one who performs spirituals, labor songs, folklore, and jazz—as opposed to the one who conforms to "white norms."[33] Recently, a critic has described *Not without Laughter* as "an endearing coming-of-age novel noteworthy for its incorporation of blues and vernacular."[34] However, another critic has suggested that Hughes attempted to placate white readers by interspersing the novel with samples of "darky" wisdom and "minstrelsy."[35] Two of the book's most powerful scenes feature Jimboy's guitar-playing and the performance of "Benbow's wandering band"

Langston Hughes on horseback, 1932. (Yale Collection of American Literature, Beinecke Rare Book and Manuscript Library. Reprinted by permission of Harold Ober Associates Incorporated)

(59–69, 95–107)—proof, according to one critic, that *Not without Laughter* is paced by the "tom-tom rhythms" of a folk Negro tradition.[36]

Hughes, like Thurman, believed that the "primitive" essence resided in the soul, not in a particular geographic location. It found expression in Aunt Hager's spiritual hymns, in the sexually provocative dancing of Harriet, and in the music of Jimboy, the drifter who played his guitar as he traveled the country. Ancient impulses and traditions survived, even as the West became increasingly "civilized." Unlike Montana, which was still sparsely settled at the time Taylor Gordon published his autobiography, Kansas had lost much of its original regional character by the turn of the century. Two of Hughes's uncles had been Buffalo Soldiers, and Lewis Sheridan Leary, the first husband of Hughes's maternal grandmother, had fought with John Brown.[37] But the home of the Exodusters—the "free" state of Kansas, the favorite resettlement site for many black western immigrants—had become "a lost Eden" by the late nineteenth century.[38] The increase in population, both African American and white, had led first to the cultivation of Kansas as an agricultural area, then to the growth of small towns and cities. In the first two decades of the twentieth century, beginning with the publication of an article by Frederick Jackson Turner in 1901, the label "Middle West" or "Midwest" came into use. The term referred to the region located between "the sparsely settled Western mining, cattle-raising, and agricultural States," such as Taylor Gordon's Montana, and the wealthy industrial, manufacturing states in the East. Kansas was one of several transitional states, a former "pioneer province" in the process of becoming more "civilized."[39]

Increased racial tension was one of the by-products of civilization. Reflecting that fact in *Not without Laughter*, Hughes portrays a midwestern town that differs greatly from the conflict-free frontier of White Sulphur Springs. "I guess Kansas is getting like the South, isn't it, ma?" Sandy says to his grandmother. "They don't like us here either" (201). The old West, a mythical promised land for people of color, no longer exists, but escape to Harlem, the site of the New Negro Renaissance, is also impossible. The furthest away Sandy gets is Chicago. Like New York City, it has a densely populated community of racial minorities. But the South Side, unlike Harlem, has no artistic or intellectual movement, just the Monogram Theatre, which caters to an unsophisticated Black Belt vaudeville audience (291). Chicago, the hub of the Midwest, is less cosmopolitan than northeastern cities but less rough-and-tumble than the western frontier. When Sandy first arrives in Chicago, a homosexual African American man tries to pick him up on the street. When he learns that Sandy comes from a small town in Kansas, he attempts to sound out the boy's sexuality. "Oh, out west where the girls are raring to go! I know! Just like wild horses out there," he says, seeking confirmation or hesitation in Sandy's response (282). Sandy's confusion stems from the fact that he is neither a cowboy—a tamer of horses and women—nor a man of the world, accustomed to dealing with effeminate strangers whom he meets in Chicago. He is no more at home in the city than he is on Taylor Gordon's "frontier."

Like Kansas, Oklahoma was a "transition" state, although it occupied a different geographic position. As a southwestern border state, it resembled the South to the extent that it discriminated against racial minorities. However, like states in the West, it offered African Americans fewer restrictions and more opportunities. In *Shadow and Act* (1953), Oklahoma native and African American writer Ralph Ellison reminded the reader that the forty-sixth state, one of the last territories to enter the Union, had no tradition of slavery. Segregation existed, but "relationships between the races were more fluid" than they were in other parts of the region. A disregard for social conventions, a greater sense of personal freedom, and the right to "range widely" in an "unstructured latitude" were all "frontier attitudes," according to Ellison. In early Oklahoma, African Americans had more scope than they had in the South—or in "deceptively 'free' Harlem," for that matter.[40]

Ellison portrays the frontier as a state of mind, as a mythic construction, and as a series of "attitudes" in *Invisible Man*. Although the anonymous central character and first-person narrator has never lived in the West, he has a "frontier" mentality that affects the way he thinks about racial migration, interracial relations, and his chances for success as he moves from the rural South to the urban Northeast. He imagines that Harlem is the next "Negro" frontier, but he becomes "undeceived," to paraphrase Ellison. The narrator comes to New York in the 1940s, more than a decade after the end of the New Negro Renaissance. By now, Harlem has acquired a legendary reputation. The "stories which I had heard of the city-within-a-city leaped alive in my mind," says the narrator, who associates the place with "dreams," not "realities."[41] Harlem represents the landscape of fantasy, a stage upon which the narrator imaginarily acts out his manifest destiny. One night he goes to a movie—"a picture of frontier life," "an epic of wagon trains," a story of "settlers" who weather natural catastrophes and war with the Indians as they roll "ever westward" (170). As a recent arrival to Harlem who plans to conquer the city, the narrator roots for the immigrants and embraces their project uncritically.

Ellison, too, succumbed to "the intense spell" of the movies. In the introduction to *Shadow and Act* he describes how Hollywood, through "the vicarious identification and empathic adventuring which it encouraged," enabled him to relate to pioneers, cowboys, and other western heroes, in spite of his race.[42] Yet he was also aware that Oklahoma was not like the movies, that minorities in real life had precarious freedoms. Similarly, he realized that Harlem "[was] not Oklahoma."[43] Ellison's double vision accounts for the presentation of contradictory perspectives in the aforementioned scene. The narrator cheers for the film's presumably white western heroes, even though (as the reader learns in parentheses) "there was no one like me taking part" on the screen. "I forgot myself . . . and left the dark room in a lighter mood," says the African American narrator, unaware of the irony and unintentionally punning on his cross-racial identification. But his subconscious nags him that night while he sleeps. In the morning he has a hangover feeling, a suspicion that he is "playing a part in some scheme which [he] did not understand" (170).

In fact, the narrator becomes a pawn in two movements competing for political and territorial power. He is recruited by the Brotherhood, a predominantly white organization of political radicals, and by Ras the Destroyer, a West Indian immigrant and black nationalist leader who advocates the overthrow of the city's racial majority. Disillusioned by the Brotherhood, which has merely exploited him as a token minority, and unsympathetic to Ras the Destroyer, who strikes him as a dangerous fanatic, the narrator finds himself caught in the middle during a street riot. Having once identified with white western heroes in their fight against Indians, the narrator now finds himself unable even to determine which race is the enemy. At first the "white-helmeted policemen" (552), wearing their riot gear, patrolling on horseback, seem cast as the good guys, having been charged with the responsibility of maintaining order and upholding the peace. In the words of one bystander: "here comes the cops up the street, riding like cowboys, man" (563). Ras the Destroyer—dressed like an Abyssinian chief, "a fur cap upon his head, his arm bearing a shield, a cape made of the skin of some wild animal" (556)—is the West Indian leader of a group of primitive "savages" that goes on the warpath against Anglo-American "civilization." Then, in a reversal of roles, the policemen are cast as the villains and Ras the Destroyer becomes the Negro Lone Ranger. "Ride 'em, cowboy. Give 'em hell and bananas," shouts one of the rioters (562). The chieftain's horse bolts up the street, "leaping like Heigho, the goddam Silver!" accordingly (564).

If the protagonist no longer respects white authority, as evidenced by his rejection of the Brotherhood's nearly all-white fraternity and his fear of the cowboy-like New York City police, he also rejects the equally imperialist enterprise of Ras the Destroyer, who exhorts African Americans to take back America.[44] He no longer sees Harlem as space that one race can conquer; instead, he sees it as contested terrain. The story of westward expansion, over-simplified in the film he watches, pits whites against Indians and celebrates the triumph of Anglo-Americans, as depicted by Hollywood. The drama of Manifest Destiny differs from the reality of Harlem, where "civilization" and "savagery" are relative terms—where, instead of a clear victory for one side, there is only chaos and rioting. Ellison's novel illustrates that 1940s Harlem was a "racial frontier," a contact zone where blacks and whites met, not always in harmony.[45]

Unlike Wallace Thurman, who argued in *The Blacker the Berry . . .* that color was fate and that place was irrelevant, Ellison maintained throughout his career that the African American experience had been shaped by geography, for "the slaves had learned through the repetition of group experience that freedom was to be attained through geographical movement." In moving west, African Americans were repeating a pattern begun by runaway slaves and continued by freedmen and -women who had joined Indians in what was now Oklahoma.[46] By "going to the Nation (meaning the Indian Nation), [they] were trying to escape from slavery in a scene consisting of geographical space."[47] African Americans as well as whites associated the region with freedom. Yet whereas "Frederick Jackson Turner's theory of the frontier has been so influential in shaping our conception of American history," Ellison noted, "very little attention has been given to the role played by geography in shaping the fate of Afro-Americans."[48] This group also believed in the liberating or restorative powers of the western frontier. But according to Ellison, it could not assume that a change of scene would automatically make life less difficult. The partial restrictions imposed on African Americans in Oklahoma during Ellison's youth had made that much clear. Instead, it was the responsibility of "individuals who make their home in any given locality" to determine their destiny.[49]

Ellison was more hopeful than Thurman, but he was less optimistic than Gordon, who claimed that an African American in White Sulphur Springs enjoyed unrestricted freedom of movement and social equality. While white children were going to school, Gordon worked part-time in a brothel, lounged in the local saloon, and ran errands all over town. "I was accepted both high and low, never questioned why or what I was doing in conspicuous places" (17). Gordon understood this to mean that he was accepted by whites. Ellison might have suggested, ironically, that it proved just the opposite. Because he was a racial minority, no one cared enough to make sure that Gordon stayed in school and got a good education. In places where white children would never be found, he blended into the scenery, assuming a stereotypical place as a servant or errand boy. Instead of standing out as an African American resident, Gordon became the invisible man of White Sulphur Springs.

Ellison's unnamed protagonist is also invisible. His anonymity is characterized by an absence of place as well as by a lack of identity. After the riot he retreats underground, establishing an illegal residence in the basement of an apartment building on the "border" of Harlem (5). The invisible man has become a liminal figure on the fringe of society, and the location of his new home is fitting. According to Ellison, "Harlem is the scene and symbol of the Negro's perpetual alienation in the land of his birth." In the essay "Harlem Is Nowhere," Ellison laments that the once vibrant capital of the New Negro Renaissance has been transformed into a ghetto, a place of despair. But it is also the source of "transcendence," where minorities can triumph—through imagination, education, and hard work—over "sordid reality."[50] Correspondingly, at the end of the novel, the narrator decides to end his self-imposed hibernation. "I'm shaking off the old skin and I'll leave it here in the hole. I'm coming out, no less invisible without it, but coming out nevertheless" (581).

For Hughes and Ellison, the "frontier" was a historical memory or a cultural myth, not a habitable place in the early twentieth century. In *Not without Laughter*, Kansas has become part of midwestern civilization. Jimboy and Harriet preserve a "primitive" folk Negro tradition by performing the blues. But according to Harriet, the future depends on Sandy, the representative of the next generation, who leaves the midwestern provinces, goes to the city, and views education as a means "to help the black race" (298). Ellison's protagonist also moves to the city. As part of his education, he learns that the frontier of his imagination is a deceptive mirage. Harlem is the site of potential racial transcendence. But transcendence can be achieved only through synthesis: by revising the narrator's original thesis (a belief in his ability to conquer the city) without succumbing to the antithetical threat of despair (a feeling that life in Harlem offers minorities no hope at all). The "frontier" myth is a sustaining influence, but it is only one of many inspirations for African Americans, and one of many allusions in *Invisible Man*, which references a wide range of literary, folkloric, and musical sources.

A number of western African American writers contributed to the Harlem and post–Harlem Renaissance. But in spite of the fact that they shared a racial heritage and regional roots, they differed in the way they depicted the rural West and the urban metropolis (most notably Harlem) and in the way that they defined the "primitive" as a racial or regional trait. Gordon and Thurman were bookends, offering opposing views on the importance of biological identity and geographic environment. Hughes and Ellison were positioned between these two writers. It was the "middle" West and the frontier as "middle ground"—a place of interracial contact and compromise—that appeared in *Not without Laughter* and *Invisible Man*. Even so, these two works were almost as dissimilar as *Born to Be* and *The Blacker the Berry*. . . . *Not without Laughter*—with its gentle nostalgia, air of dignified resignation, and tentative faith in the future—was written during the height of the New Negro Renaissance and before the depression, with the support of a wealthy white patron whose social views were conservative. *Invisible Man*—with its cynical humor, subversive political content, and experimental technique— was darker, edgier, and more strident in tone. Ellison wrote in the aftermath of the Renaissance, having lived through the depression, the Harlem riots of the mid-1930s, and World War II. He was mentored by Richard Wright, a naturalist writer and African American political radical, a figure as different from Hughes's genteel white patron as possible.[51] The works produced by these writers were as diverse as their ideas about race and as wide-ranging as the geographic region from which they all came. The West was not only meaningful to African Americans who settled there. It was important to writers who left and who later explored the West in some of the most seminal works of the New Negro Renaissance.

CHAPTER FIVE

Hip Hopalong Cassidy
Cowboys and Rappers

The first fictional "black" western hero appears in *Deadwood Dick, the Prince of the Road; or, The Black Rider of the Black Hills* (1877). In this first installment in a series of dime novels written by Edward L. Wheeler, a young eastern gentleman is cheated out of his rightful inheritance. He moves to the frontier, becomes an outlaw, and vows to avenge other victims of crime. The Deadwood Dick series was enormously popular. Between 1877 and 1885, Wheeler wrote thirty-three Deadwood Dick novels for the publishing house of Beadle and Adams. The series was also innovative in several respects. Before Deadwood Dick, the dime-novel hero was a woodsman, plainsman, or scout, a figure of natural nobility and refined moral sentiments. Deadwood Dick was an exile from eastern civilization, an outlaw motivated by a thirst for revenge. He used violent and illegal tactics to defeat his opponents.[1]

In order to distinguish Deadwood Dick from earlier dime-novel heroes and to emphasize his moral ambiguity, Wheeler created for his character a symbolic disguise. The "black rider" wore a dark mask and costume to conceal his identity because he operated outside the law.[2] In *Deadwood Dick as Detective: A Story of the Great Carbonate Region* (1879), the hero disguises himself "in a suit of black knee-boots, black slouched hat, and a black mask," hiding everything "except a firm mouth, a jetty mustache, and a chin that bore signs of character."[3] In *Deadwood Dick's Doom; or, Calamity Jane's Last Adventure* (1881) he also sports a black beard.[4] Occasionally Wheeler attributed his hero's appearance to nature, not artifice. In *Deadwood Dick's Dream; or, The Rivals of the Road* (1881) he writes that the outlaw has "dark" eyes and weathered "brown" skin.[5] His robust complexion is a sign of good health. But elsewhere in the series his color suggests something sinister. In *Deadwood Dick's Device; or, The Sign of the Double Cross* (1879) his "swarthy" looks complement his "wild, dark nature."[6] Color becomes a regional marker as well as an indication of temperament. It associates Deadwood Dick with the rugged outdoors, reveals his tempestuous character, and suggests his affiliation with outcasts or underdogs. The hero identifies with the dispossessed, the working classes, and the economically vulnerable, who are victimized by claim jumpers, railroad corporations, and frontier real estate barons. There is no textual evidence, however, that Deadwood Dick is literally "black" or that he extends his protection to racial minorities. In his research on pulp fiction, one critic discovered that there were no nineteenth-century dime novels aimed at African American readers. Furthermore, "no narrative formulas were developed that could tell a racial story, as the few accounts of race in the dime novels show."[7]

Nevertheless, one African American cowboy implied in his autobiography that he was the inspiration for Wheeler's protagonist. In the preface to *The Life and Adventures of Nat Love, Better Known in the Cattle Country as "Deadwood Dick"* (1907), the author claimed that his book would interest readers "who prefer facts to fiction."[8] According to Love, he received the nickname "Deadwood Dick" in 1876 at a Fourth of July celebration in Deadwood, Dakota, where he won contests in riding, roping, and shooting (97). Although he became a local celebrity and later demonstrated his bravery in many encounters with Native Americans, he insists: "I was not the wild blood thirsty savage and all around bad man many writers have pictured me" (70). At least one critic has accepted the likelihood that Nat Love was the "real" Deadwood Dick.[9] But Love never explicitly makes such a claim. He coyly alludes to works of "fiction" that have distorted the facts of his life without referring to the Deadwood Dick novels by name. It is chronologically possible that Love was the model for the fictional hero. The cowboy acquired his honorary alias a year before Wheeler published the first installment in the Deadwood Dick series. However, Wheeler lived in Pennsylvania and upstate New York. Like many writers of pulp Westerns, he never visited the region where his novels were set. Is it likely that Wheeler would have known about Love, who was nothing more than a local frontier celebrity?

If Love inspired the Deadwood Dick series, then his failure to receive proper credit reflects an unfortunate historical tendency to overlook the role that African American cowboys played in the West. Revisionist historians estimate that several thousand such cowboys worked on the frontier in the late nineteenth century.[10] Yet only a few (including Isom Dart and Bill Pickett) have received much attention, and only Nat Love immortalized his story in an autobiography. Love may or may not have inspired a series of dime novels aimed at white readers, but he was the first in a series of African American writers, musicians, and filmmakers to represent the cowboy experience from the perspective of racial minorities.

In the late 1930s, Herb Jeffries starred in four musical Westerns. During his early career as a jazz singer, while performing in the South, Jeffries had noticed segregated movie theaters showing Westerns featuring white Hollywood stars. Realizing that there was a market for Westerns aimed at racial minorities, he determined to meet that demand. Unable to raise financing among African American businessmen, Jeffries turned to Jed Buell, a producer of Hollywood B-movies and novelty Westerns, such as *The Terror in Tiny Town* (1938), which featured an all-midget cast. Buell found a distributor who believed that "race" Westerns might be a profitable novelty. Working with a limited budget, Jeffries cast himself in the lead, wrote all the songs, and performed his own stunts. He hired Spencer Williams, who later portrayed Andy on television in *Amos 'n' Andy*, to write the screenplay, play Jeffries's sidekick, and provide comic relief. He cast actors from *Tarzan* pictures in many supporting roles and gave them a crash course in horseback riding and roping before filming began.[11]

Harlem on the Prairie (1937) and the three sequels that followed in some ways resembled white musical Westerns. Like Gene Autry and Roy Rogers, Herb Jeffries played a cowboy who did not drink, smoke, or consort with loose women. His character, Bob Blake, rescued a heroine whose homestead was mortgaged to a lecherous villain, protected a farmer from a rancher who wanted his property, or helped a prospector discover uranium. Periodically he burst into song while he played his guitar, accompanied by his backup singers, the Four Tones. The movies, produced on minuscule budgets, were marred by amateur editing, poor lighting and sound quality, and grainy cinematography, but these "C-minus westerns" were generically similar to B-movie serials.[12] Even the casting deemphasized the fact that these were "black" vehicles. The hero was light-skinned, wore a white hat, and rode a palomino. The comic sidekick and the villains had darker complexions. One critic faults these Westerns for failing to address "the black urban experience,"[13] while another one claims that they pandered to the genteel, color-conscious, African American bourgeoisie.[14]

No prints of the first film survive, but *Two-Gun Man from Harlem* (1938), the second film in the series, contrary to critical opinion, tries to make the formula Western relevant to an urban African American audience.[15] In the

Movie still from *Harlem on the Prairie* (1937). Herb Jeffries does not appear in this scene, and no prints of the film now exist. (Photographs and Prints Division, Schomburg Center for Research in Black Culture, The New York Public Library, Astor, Lenox and Tilden Foundations)

film, Bob Blake plays a cowboy who works on a ranch. While riding the fence line one day, he meets Sally and her young brother Jimmy. Blake learns that their mother has recently died, that their father has mortgaged the property, and that a man named Barker will repossess their home if the family cannot pay its debt. Blake falls in love with Sally and offers to help. Meanwhile, back at the ranch, Blake's boss discovers his wife and Barker in flagrante delicto. Barker shoots the husband and then runs away, leaving his gun at the scene of the crime. Blake returns to the ranch house and discovers the body. When the sheriff arrives, the wife plants the gun in Blake's holster, accuses the cowboy of attempting to rape her, and says that Blake murdered her husband. The lights go out suddenly, allowing Blake to escape.

The cowboy hitchhikes to Harlem. There, in a nightclub, Blake meets the Deacon, a preacher-turned-gangster who bears a strong resemblance to Blake. The hero assumes the Deacon's identity and returns home, transformed from an innocent murder suspect into a notorious criminal. As the gangster Deacon, he steals two thousand dollars and gives the money to Sally. He infiltrates Barker's gang and discovers that Barker murdered Blake's boss. In the end, he brings Barker to justice, saves Sally's family from bankruptcy, restores his good name, and inspires Jimmy to become a heroic cowboy like Blake.

Although the film has a certain wholesomeness, in keeping with white musical Westerns, it also has an edgier quality—a certain duality, as the title, *Two-Gun Man from Harlem*, suggests. As the opening credits roll, Blake rides across the screen singing "I'm a Happy Cowboy," his signature tune. By the end of the film, he has captured the villains without resorting to violence. But in spite of the fact that the conflict is fairly mild, the film hints at a darker side of humanity. The scenes in which Barker commits murder, the boss's wife frames Blake as the killer, and Blake escapes in the night echo scenes from gangster films and film noir. "You dirty rat!" says the boss when he catches Barker making love to his wife. Blake, unlike the characteristically chivalrous cowboy, refuses to play the fall guy when the gun is found in his holster. Suspecting that the boss's wife has something to do with the murder, he threatens to "choke" the truth out of her. She responds by mocking him, calling him "big boy" in the tradition of screen femmes fatales.

The film further establishes a connection between the Western and the black urban crime drama when Blake goes to Harlem. The fact that Blake and the Deacon are doubles suggests that there is little to distinguish between the cowboy-as-tough-guy and the preacher-turned-criminal. The men meet in a New York nightclub that resembles a western saloon. Arguing over a girl who dances like a "heifer on loco weed," they both draw their guns. In the scene, Harlem appears as an urban equivalent for the western frontier, a setting in which Blake and the Deacon are well matched as rivals. In turn, the frontier is a place where gangsters roam free. There, disguised as the Deacon, Blake enters Barker's gang, claiming that he used to be "an Eleventh Avenue cowboy, but now I practice the gun gospel." The two-gun man from Harlem is known for his ambidextrous skill as a gunslinger (he shoots "too straight, too fast, with both hands"). As played by Herb Jeffries, he also has alternately heroic and villainous qualities. In his dual roles as Blake and the Deacon, Jeffries combines aspects of the cowboy, the gangster, and the hard-boiled detective—types that were popular in films and pulp fiction in the late 1930s. He injects the Western with a grittier, more profane, urban black sensibility.

The following film in the series, *The Bronze Buckaroo* (1938), appears more conventional.[16] In this installment, Blake receives a letter from a former cowboy, Joe Jackson, who owns a ranch in Arizona. When Blake pays a visit, he learns that Joe's father has died and that Joe has since disappeared. Blake offers to investigate the case for Joe's sister, Betty. He discovers that Buck Thorn, a neighbor, wants to seize Jackson's property because there is gold underground. Thorn's henchmen have already murdered Joe's father. Now they have taken Joe hostage and have threatened to torture him unless he signs a deed giving Thorn ownership of the property. Blake tracks down the kidnappers, but while rescuing Joe he allows Thorn's men to escape. Blake and his posse follow the bad guys to their canyon hideout and force the men to surrender. Happily, Joe keeps the ranch and Betty rewards Blake with her love.

The Bronze Buckaroo more closely resembles white musical Westerns. Unlike Two-Gun Man from Harlem, it features no eastern locations and no urban characters. However, it acknowledges its imitative tendencies, devoting one of its subplots to the subject of racial impersonation and mimicry. In the film, Bob's dim-witted sidekick, Dusty, buys a "talking" mule from a cowboy who works at Joe's ranch. Later he realizes that he has been cheated when he finds a ventriloquist's manual explaining how the cowboy made the animal "speak." Dusty studies the manual, becomes a ventriloquist, and earns back his money by charging other cowboys to hear the mule "read" poetry. The cover of the manual shows a white ventriloquist holding a black doll on his lap, thus encouraging viewers to equate vocal impersonation with minstrelsy. But the film reverses the white-black relationship, granting the dim-witted Dusty (the dummy) the power to speak for Gable, the mule. The inarticulate animal becomes a puppet that the African American cowboy manipulates. Dusty not only stands in for Clark Gable but also quotes Greta Garbo ("I want to be alone" are the mule's first words). Dusty impersonates Hollywood movie stars, just as The Bronze Buckaroo puts a black face on white musical Westerns.

Harlem Rides the Range (1939), the final film in the series, lacks even these sly racial nuances.[17] In what by now was a familiar recycling of story lines from earlier episodes, Blake saves a rancher in danger of losing his property. A greedy villain wants to foreclose on the ranch when he discovers uranium, but Blake, with the assistance of the rancher's beautiful daughter, finds the money to pay off the mortgage and exposes the villain's scheme. With the exception of one song, "The Cowboy's Life Is the Only Life for Me," which includes a tap-dancing sequence, there is little trace of African American artistry. While it is impossible to say for sure why successive installments became more conventional, it may be that the assembly-line process of producing new episodes in rapid succession forced the filmmakers to rely increasingly on well-tested Hollywood formulas.

Movie poster for *Harlem Rides the Range* (1939). Herb Jeffries, who was billed as Herbert Jeffrey, appears in the upper left corner. (Courtesy of the Academy of Motion Picture Arts and Sciences)

No subsequent race Westerns pushed the boundaries as far as the Herb Jeffries series did, as the few surviving examples attest. *Look-Out Sister* (1946) imagines that an African American West exists, but only in fantasy.[18] When singer Louis Jordan becomes burned out performing, he goes to a sanatorium in order to rest. There he meets a young African American patient who likes to play cowboy. Inspired by the boy, Jordan dreams about an African

Movie poster for *Look-Out Sister* (1946). (Photographs and Prints Division, Schomburg Center for Research in Black Culture, The New York Public Library, Astor, Lenox and Tilden Foundations)

American dude ranch in Look-Out, Arizona, that hires him and his band. What ensues is predictable. Jordan saves the ranch from a passel of creditors and wins the heroine's undying gratitude by staging a concert that raises enough money to rescue the ranch from foreclosure. (Long on music and short on plot, the film appears to be mainly a vehicle for showcasing Jordan, a singer and bandleader of the mid-1940s.) But the cosmopolitan urbanite is a fish out of water. The scene in which Jordan tries to ride a horse is played strictly for laughs, and when he wakes up from his dream at the end of the film, the figure of the African American cowboy is a dim comic memory.

The Western attracted and at the same time challenged early African American filmmakers. Typically, it featured a hero who is alienated from civilization. Sometimes he is a victim of unjust persecution (Deadwood Dick is swindled out of his fortune, Bob Blake is framed for first-degree murder), yet he draws strength from his inner moral convictions and defends other victims (using violence, if needed), thereby regaining the respect of society. Racial minorities could identify with the cowboy-as-outcast while taking pride in a hero who was self-reliant, aggressive, and strong. However, in order to make race Westerns relevant to a predominantly urban African American audience, filmmakers incorporated elements that strayed from the formula. They added eastern locales, gangsters, and ethnic music and dance, sometimes creating fascinating regional juxtapositions, complex new characters, and an amalgamation of various artistic influences. But sometimes the experiments resulted in cinematic non sequiturs, such as tap-dancing cowboys; in conventional comedies starring predictable characters, such as Louis Jordan, a racial variation on the traditional tenderfoot; and in stereotypical moves, such as the casting of dark-skinned actors in subordinate roles.

Early African American films sometimes reproduced and sometimes revised the conventions of white musical Westerns. *Yellow Back Radio Broke-Down* (1969) has similar dualistic tendencies, typical of western African American literature. Ishmael Reed's novel incorporates elements of western pulp fiction and traditional African American narrative. *Yellow Back Radio Broke-Down* can be "broken down" into several components. Like dime novels, which were often called "yellow backs," it is set in the West. Like "radio," it is a "talking book" that signifies within the African American oral tradition.[19] The story of the Loop Garoo Kid, a cowboy who uses Haitian hoodoo to defeat a white cattleman, is an innovative retelling as well as a racial revision of popular western mythology.

The novel takes more liberties with generic conventions than its contemporary counterpart, the film *Blazing Saddles* (1974). In the Mel Brooks parody, the sheriff functions like most western heroes (in this instance, he saves the town from corrupt politicians who want to make way for a railroad by eliminating the local inhabitants). The humor derives simply from the fact that the sheriff is black—a circumstance that discomfits the townspeople and disarms his antagonists.[20] However, the Loop Garoo Kid not only represents a new kind of hero but inspires a new kind of narrative. Instead of protecting the townspeople, he pursues a personal, violent vendetta. At the end of the novel he has failed to resolve his dispute with a cattleman, and he leaves the West without having established his dominance. Unlike "Black Bart," the sheriff in *Blazing Saddles*, who imposes justice and establishes order by enforcing the law, the Loop Garoo Kid uses illicit black magic, disrupts, western society, and offers no resolution at the end of the novel.

Reed revises the Western to such an extent that only the genre's main outlines remain recognizable. The author has said that his decision to write in the Western genre was a tactical strategy. He believed that he could most successfully convey his ideas by introducing them in a popular medium.[21] But as critics have noted, *Yellow Back Radio Broke-Down* is a "horse opera" in more ways than one. Although the Loop Garoo Kid is a "cowboy," he is also an "Indian." He comes from the West Indies and uses black magic to cast spells on his enemies (according to hoodoo, a deity who possesses a victim is said to be "riding a horse").[22] Thus, metaphorically, the Loop Garoo Kid, like the white Western hero, is an accomplished equestrian. In the same way that the hero comes to possess the cattleman's spirit, the author infuses the novel with his own ideology. *Yellow Back Radio Broke-Down* becomes a vehicle for discussing an assortment of topics, including nineteenth-century imperialism, twentieth-century technology, Catholicism, realism versus abstract expression in African American literature, homosexuality, politics, and racial identity.[23] It dispenses with stylistic, linguistic, and orthographic conventions, including chapter divisions, paragraph indentations, quotation marks, and most punctuation.

Paradoxically, the novel is most like a Western when it deviates from formula, according to Reed. "[W]e cowpokes make up language as we go along," insists one of his characters.[24] Referring to Frederick Jackson Turner's famous address, "The Significance of the Frontier in American History" (1893), the bartender suggests that pioneering is an American trait (54). American speech is also adventurous, unlikely to conform to grammatical rules, and representative of many linguistic influences. In the novel, Reed believes that African American and West Indian cowboys and Native Americans have distinct personalities which they express in their own unique idioms. Black cowboys riff on language, produce funky syntactical improvisations, and speak in "jive talking dada" (129). Native Americans have names "that didn't mean anything but sounded like music" (41). Linguistic innovation and, by extension, literary experimentation become hallmarks of multicultural western society.

Reed's characters are figures of speech. The cowboy, for example, is a literary creation. In an interview, the author acknowledged: "I've never rode a horse in my life. That's really rich because 'Yellow Back' writers were usually dudes from the East like me. The cowboy would read their books and begin to ape the exaggerations of themselves they read. A case of life imitating art."[25] Reed argues that the West was "invented" by writers who imagined the region from a geographical distance and that "real" cowboys modeled themselves after purely fictitious characters. Thus he can boast about his own lack of qualifications for writing a Western (in ungrammatical language, stating "I've never rode a horse in my life"), since Westerns require neither historical accuracy nor fidelity to grammatical rules. Instead of having an authentic identity, the "cowboy" constructs his persona. In addition, he functions as an anarchic force, like the outlaw who can never be assimilated within an ordered society.[26] In Reed's case, the black cowboy "breaks down" frontier apartheid, challenges racial hegemony, brings chaos to Western civilization, and disrupts narrative rules.

Not all African American writers are as experimental as Reed. In *Gabriel's Story* (2001), David Anthony Durham follows in the tradition of Cormac McCarthy and sticks closer to history. Durham tells the story of Gabriel Lynch, an African American adolescent in Kansas who runs away from his family in the late nineteenth century. Joining a cattle drive, he participates in a series of violent adventures that lead to his coming-of-age. Along the way, Durham explores chapters in American history that previous writers have sometimes ignored: the African American homesteading movement in the mid-1870s, the government's persecution and abandonment of Native Americans, and the failure to honor Mexican landowners' rights after the Mexican-American War. Reed and Durham share a concern with race, creating African American characters who provide fresh perspectives on the frontier experience. Both writers examine the consequences of white conquest and settlement. Reed does this by subverting the formula Western for comic effect, whereas Durham more somberly exposes the fallacies of frontier mythology. He criticizes dime novels that romanticize history, writing a work that realistically addresses the plight of racial minorities.

Early in the novel, Gabriel makes friends with another African American boy. The newcomer, James, arrives in Kansas "talking of cowboys, outlaws, and hangings, with a dime novel shoved in his rear pocket. It was a gift that a recent immigrant had given him, as if that man, fresh from Waltham,

Massachusetts, had a manual on the West that had escaped those already living there." [27] Although the dime-novel writer has an uncertain grasp on history and western geography, he has a talent for describing "shady characters, broad-brimmed hats, and six-shooters" (38). Gabriel ironically refers to the book as a "manual," though it offers little useful information or advice for African American immigrants. Instead, the dime novel romanticizes the West and allegorizes Anglo-Saxon supremacy. It features a transplanted Englishman with blond hair who rides a white steed. In the climactic scene, the hero rescues a maiden by killing Mexican bandits who are attempting to ravish her.

A Native American rides past the boys as they finish reading the novel. Unlike the fictional Mexican bandits, who outnumber the Englishman, the lone rider wears a defeated expression and offers no apparent threat to his audience. Yet unlike the rest of his tribe, which has been "whipped and reserved," the Native American has the demeanor of a stoic survivor. "Gabriel entertained the thought that he was witnessing not a man of flesh and blood but an ethereal rider passed from the netherworld into this one on a mission of vengeance for his vanishing people" (40). For Anglo-Saxons, the progress of Western civilization is a triumphal narrative; for those who are destroyed in the process, it is a tragedy. James and Gabriel learn this lesson during a cross-country cattle drive. The white cowboys, their idols, rape a Mexican woman—unlike the dime-novel hero, who rescues a white woman from Mexican predators. As the journey continues, James and Gabriel become increasingly disillusioned. James, in particular, develops a sense of foreboding. "Why can't I tell a proper story that don't end in somebody dead or maimed?" he asks Gabriel (112). Later, having seen more death and destruction, one of the characters says in the book's final pages: "I think this is the end of it. It's not the end I would have written" (269).

Instead, Durham has written a revisionist Western that presents familiar frontier activities—such as homesteading, cattle roundups, and encounters with Native Americans—from the unfamiliar perspective of an African American youth. At the same time, "Gabriel's story" features a passive and silent protagonist. Marshall, a charismatic white cowboy, horse thief, and murderer, orchestrates the cattle drive, the rape of a Mexican woman, and the killing of innocent victims, all of which Gabriel witnesses. Like Caleb, the African American mute who takes orders from Marshall, the hero in this case is a subservient character. Although he features in each of the episodes, he seldom determines their outcome, and although he experiences personal changes, he can never fully convey their significance. He recounts his adventures when he returns to his family at the end of the novel. "It was difficult, but manageable, to tell of those things. It was another thing altogether to find the right words to form the images that haunted him still" (253). Durham filters Gabriel's story through a third-person narrator, elliptically paraphrasing dramatic events while simultaneously emphasizing that this bare-bones account is inadequate. "[Gabriel] felt a whole host of words tumbling around within him. He wanted to let them out. He wanted to shout and make it clear how much he wanted to stay, how he'd learned from this journey and come back different and would prove it with time. He wanted them all to understand him completely, to read him like a slate before them so they could know the things he'd been through while permitting him never to say them out loud" (258).

To what extent can the Western be revised to accommodate a minority consciousness? On one hand, Durham writes a novel in which African American cowboys and homesteaders play significant and historically overlooked roles. On the other hand, in order to be faithful to history, he must also acknowledge that African Americans were denied equal rights and freedom of expression in a predominantly white frontier society. Gabriel's status as unwilling participant and silent observer emphasizes his lack of autonomy as well as a lack of access to language that would allow him to author an interpretation of events in which he participated involuntarily. Thus the novel is forced to displace its central African American character by silencing his voice and restricting his field of activities. In addition, *Gabriel's Story* endorses some of western fiction's most troubling characteristics. Although the novel suggests that it is wrong for whites to use violence to intimidate Mexicans, Native Americans, and other minorities, at the same time it claims that the African American hero is justified in using violence to fight his racist attackers. Durham emulates other novelists in the western tradition, from James Fenimore Cooper to Cormac McCarthy, who defend violence as part of the process of western expansion and part of the ritual of the hero's coming-of-age.

To some extent, black Westerns mimic white Westerns; to some extent, they differ dramatically. While Herb Jeffries's earliest extant Western reflected a unique black sensibility, his later films became more formulaic and eventually lost their distinctiveness. Ishmael Reed's novel is so profoundly original that his indebtedness to the Western seems minimal, whereas *Gabriel's Story*, published more recently, shows a return to traditional patterns in American literature. Finally, rap music, like fiction and film, incorporates elements of frontier mythology. It establishes provocative and sometimes problematic connections between the old West and the contemporary black inner city.

The similarities between Westerns and rap music are broadly superficial as well as highly specific. Both genres typically feature male protagonists (gunslingers, urban "cowboys," or "gangstas"). These heroes—or anti-heroes— have uneasy relationships with frontier civilization and with contemporary urban society. They glorify violence and vigilante behavior (in Westerns, a "posse" is a deputized mob; in hip-hop it refers to a street gang or, more benignly, to a group of male associates). Both cowboys and "homeboys" tend to be territorial. Cowboys ride the unfenced range, protecting their turf from invading railroaders, farmers, and Native Americans. Gangs stake their claim to urban locations, challenging the authority of rival gangs, local police, and neighborhood residents.

Rappers do not sing about real cowboys, who work with livestock, earn low but respectable wages, and lead relatively mundane existences. Like most people, rappers prefer to imagine cowboys as romantic outcasts, bandits, and rebels. Rappers who call themselves "cowboys" identify as members of an anti-establishment. Yet the representation of cowboys as anti-establishment figures is a convention of Hollywood movies, white popular culture, and western mythology. The only thing radical about associating cowboys with rappers is transforming traditional white Western heroes into black urban characters. "Ghetto Cowboy" (1998), for example, describes an overly familiar scenario. In this song by Mo Thugs Family and Bone Thugs N Harmony, a sheriff tracks a group of outlaws out west. The only twist, in this case, is that the "cowboys" are African American men. Crucial Conflict, a Chicago-based group, uses "western" conceits metaphorically, sometimes for comic effect. *The Final Tic* (1996), their debut CD, features a song called "Hay," which is a tribute to "grass." "Ride the Rodeo" refers to a man who "mounts" women, traveling the circuit, or cruising the streets, looking for sport.

Punning gives certain words double significance. Sometimes transforming "westernese" into hip-hop "culture-speak" produces comic results, but sometimes it has serious ramifications. In "Westward Ho" (1996), by Westside Connection, Ice Cube tells his "ho" to come join his posse of "illegal amigos." The pun on "ho" establishes a comic, though offensive, connection: It reminds listeners that Westerns and rap music objectify women (in both genres, women are commonly typecast as prostitutes). But it also makes a satirical point by comparing nineteenth-century western imperialism with urban African American consumerism. "Westward Ho"—once the motto of Manifest Destiny, a justification for the conquest and exploitation of the continental frontier—now becomes a slogan for African American outlaws who have acquired wealth by illegal means. The song mockingly celebrates a commercial world in which African American men do their "shoppin' at Spiegels" and women are whores or commodities.[28]

West Coast rap, which became distinguished from East Coast rap in the late 1980s, most commonly celebrates the cowboy-gangsta persona.[29] In "California Love" (1995), Tupac Shakur compares West Coast rappers to cowboys and gangsters. "Now let me welcome everybody to the wild, wild west / A state that's untouchable like Elliot Ness." While many West Coast rappers posture as self-aggrandizing rebels, some artists consider the negative implications of such cross-cultural identification. In "Cowboys" (1996), the Fugees observe that rappers sometimes play the "Jesse James" character. They are poor minority role models who glorify crime. In reality, the Sundance Kid is merely "the everyday purse snatcher." Gang warfare, rather than being a heroic activity, actually destroys the inner-city community ("Covered in the grave cause you didn't know how to behave / Playin' cowboy, now you sleep with the slaves"). Encouraging rappers to stop playing the game, the Fugees facetiously quote Kenny Rogers, who says in "The Gambler": "You got to know when to hold 'em / Know when to fold 'em."

In two recent films, African American rappers and actors play versions of the "Jesse James" character. *Posse* (1993) and *Wild Wild West* (1999) revise the historical record by presenting racial minorities in prominent roles. At the same time, they exploit the market demand for African American popular culture. *Posse* refers to a gang of African American outlaws and vigilantes. The film stars actor-director Mario Van Peebles and rappers Tone Loc and Big Daddy Kane.[30] The men portray a group of ex-slaves who rebel against their racist commander by deserting their regiment in the Spanish-American War. They travel to Freemanville, a western African American township, where they encounter persecution once more. The sheriff of Cutterstown, a nearby all-white community, wants to evacuate members of the neighboring town. Scheming with speculators, he has concocted a plan to bring a railroad through Freemanville. Jessie Lee, the Van Peebles character, assembles his posse, rallies the African American settlers, and successfully defends against the hostile incursion of white civilization.

Posse begins with a prologue that establishes the presence of African Americans on the frontier in the late nineteenth century. While the camera surveys a montage of photographs, featuring such historical figures as Nat Love, Isom Dart, and Cherokee Bill, a narrator recites a list of statistics, including the fact that one-third of all cowboys were African American. Suggesting that "pictures don't lie," the narrator then introduces the fictional story of one such group of forgotten protagonists. As the film follows Jessie

Lee and his posse through a series of adventures, it explores contributions to American society made by racial minorities. It emphasizes the presence of African American troops in Cuba, the existence of African American townships on the western frontier, and the importance of minority education and political consciousness. During the course of the film, Jessie Lee falls in love with a teacher in Freemanville who believes that "education is freedom." As if to illustrate the point, a book recounting the story of the slave Nicodemus stops a bullet from killing one of the African American cowboys in battle. The film references future as well as historical struggles. When the citizens of Freemanville form a mob to retaliate against the people of Cutterstown, someone in the crowd yells: "No justice, no peace." The film encourages viewers to associate the rally cry of its fictional characters with contemporary movements to achieve racial equality.

However, *Posse* undermines its purpose as a revisionist Western and dilutes its political message by capitulating to formula.[31] Like a lynching, which the sheriff of Cutterstown calls a "demonstration of justice" but which onlookers witness as an entertaining event, Jessie Lee's retaliation against his white enemies, although morally justified, takes the form of a crowd-pleasing spectacle. In addition to graphic violence, *Posse*, like other Hollywood films, features gratuitous nudity. A love scene between Jessie Lee and the schoolmarm plays like a soft-core MTV video. There are many scatological references to one of the cowboys, who has a big penis, as well as frequent attempts to provide comic relief. The son of the independent filmmaker Melvin Van Peebles seems torn between making an original Western that might polarize viewers and creating a friendlier, more familiar product that offers something for everyone.[32] The plot acknowledges this dilemma by exploring the tension between racial and commercial imperatives. Although the sheriff is racist, he hates his African American neighbors primarily because they own land that the railroad requires. Personal ambition and corporate greed, rather than prejudice, motivate much of the plot.

Wild Wild West offers less social commentary than *Posse* and more Hollywood spectacle.[33] The film adaptation of the 1960s television series features charismatic stars and expensive special effects. James West (Will Smith) and Artemus Gordon (Kevin Kline) team up to stop a madman who has been kidnapping scientists. Dr. Loveless (Kenneth Branagh) has been working with these scientists to develop a weapons system that will enable him to create a military dictatorship. West, a captain in the U.S. Army (though everyone calls him a "cowboy"), provides traditional western heroics, demonstrating his skill as a horseman and gunslinger when confronting the enemy. Gordon, the sidekick-inventor, designs a series of gadgets to compete with the scientists' weapons. The most lethal device in the enemy's arsenal is an eighty-foot mechanical killing machine that resembles a giant tarantula. In the climactic scene, West and Gordon defeat this Goliath by using their quick wits and counter-technology.

In the series, white actors play the protagonists. In the film version, an African American actor plays West. No one seems to notice the change except the evil Dr. Loveless, who says to the captain, in a reference to his race: "How nice of you to add color to these monochromatic proceedings." The film tries to have it both ways. By not making an issue of race, it suggests that there is nothing remarkable about a Western with a central African American character. Only the villain, a white supremacist, despises the cowboy because of his color. At the same time, the filmmakers exploit race as a gimmick, reminding viewers that Will Smith, the "cowboy," has roots in African American rap. The title song, played at the end of the film, advertises Smith's cowboy-rapper persona. "Wild Wild West" is a remake of Stevie Wonder's "I Wish." In the original song, an African American man remembers his childhood, including associating with hoodlums he once used to idolize. New lyrics—by Will Smith, Dru Hill, and Kool Mo Dee—stress the singer's identification with frontier icons instead. Smith introduces himself in the song as James West: desperado, Rough Rider, and Buffalo Soldier. He calls himself the cowboy who outdraws the outlaws, the rapper J. W. G. ("James West Gangsta"), who outrhymes his competitors. Smith raps about "once upon a time" in a fictional West where outlaws, soldiers, African American cowboys, and rappers exist in the same cultural and temporal continuum.

By pairing Smith with an older, white co-star, the studio may have intended to broaden the film's demographic appeal. The African American singer-actor might have been expected to attract a younger, hipper, more racially diversified audience and to reanimate the Western, which had been out of fashion in Hollywood. The clean-cut, genial Smith might also have been considered more bankable than other rappers with "bad" reputations. By revising the original television series and casting an interracial pair of protagonists, the filmmakers added a new twist to the old Western formula. But by choosing a rapper whose music was noteworthy for its lack of anti-establishment rhetoric, they avoided alienating older, white, conservative, upper-middle-class viewers.

Successful African American Westerns are products of compromise. If they adhere too strictly to formula, they risk alienating part of their audience. How can African Americans appreciate chronicles of conquest and settlement when westward expansion often occurred at the expense of racial minorities? Works by Ishmael Reed and David Anthony Durham either satirize or soberly criticize the treatment of ethnic natives and immigrants. Given the fact that most African Americans live in urban locations, how can they be expected to identify with the "frontier" experience? Rap music suggests a solution. It transforms the inner city into a metaphorical wilderness populated by a cowboy-gangsta protagonist.

If African American Westerns stray too far from formula, they also risk losing part of their audience. On one hand, Nat Love never dwelled on his race in his autobiography, perhaps because he was afraid of making white readers uncomfortable. On the other hand, Herb Jeffries made Westerns in which all of the actors were African Americans. Consequently, his films had limited distribution and viewership. Recent filmmakers have tried to achieve greater commercial success by integrating their casts, by mixing traditional Western elements with aspects of African American popular culture, by featuring historical storylines with contemporarily relevant parallels, and by combining old-fashioned violence with advanced technological special effects. African American Westerns are a hybrid breed, the product of various artistic, ideological, and commercial influences.

CHAPTER SIX

Black Noir

Early African American literature explores the mystery of the human condition. In his autobiography, Frederick Douglass describes being taken from his mother in infancy, never meeting his father, and not knowing the date of his birth, "never having seen any authentic record containing it."[1] Douglass was born into ignorance, denied education, and prevented from having access to information that would have confirmed his humanity.

Though exposing the evils of slavery, some early African American writers maintained silence on certain subjects out of necessity. Douglass begins the final chapter of his autobiography by announcing his intention "not to state all the facts," fearing that he might betray the people who helped him escape via the underground railroad if he provided specific details.[2] Such narratives reveal the horrors of slavery while at the same time creating necessary veils of secrecy. For example, *Incidents in the Life of a Slave Girl* (1861) offers conflicting disclaimers. In an introduction, the editor writes that the author has presented the institution of slavery "with the veil withdrawn."[3] In a preface, however, Linda Brent admits that she has "concealed the names of places, and given persons fictitious names."[4] Like Douglass, she leaves the reader somewhat in ignorance. Just as the author assumes disguises and hides in the process of escaping from slavery, so she creates an intentional mystery, withholding information from the reader in order to protect her accomplices.

Three traditional story lines in eighteenth- and nineteenth-century African American literature involve mysteries relating to race: first, the escape of slaves, their pursuit, and their fear of detection; second, the separation of slave families, their reunion, and their discovery that they share biological ties; and third, the phenomenon of an African American passing as white until the discovery of his or her racial identity. The mystery genre in African American literature began to evolve in the early twentieth century. The first fictional African American detective appeared in 1901. *Hagar's Daughter*, by Pauline E. Hopkins, offered a minor character who was a cross-dressing sleuth. The first African American novel to feature an African American detective as the primary character was *The Conjure-Man Dies* (1932).[5] Rudolph Fisher's mystery takes place in Harlem at the end of the New Negro Renaissance. It follows a detective with the New York City police who investigates the murder of a deposed African king. The crime takes place in the king's private quarters, which are furnished with "gruesome black masks." Among the possible murder weapons are African artifacts: "misshapen statuettes of near-human creatures, . . . broad-bladed swords, slim arrows and jagged spear-heads of forbidding designs."[6] Like many other artists in the New Negro Renaissance, Fisher used literature, in this case the mystery genre, to explore African culture and "primitive" native traditions. At the same time, he represented Harlem as the site of modern-day African American creative activity. His detective uses his cerebral skills to solve a crime that challenges the greatest intelligence.

In *The Conjure-Man Dies*, Harlem is a place of "bright-lighted gaiety," the realm of "rhythm and laughter," the subject of "loud jest" and song.[7] The murder investigation is treated as an entertaining diversion, performed with elegant sophistication, in a spirit of merry festivity. Chester Himes, Fisher's successor, presents Harlem in much darker hues. In Himes's novels, written after the end of the Renaissance, the city is a depressing, violent, crime-ridden ghetto. Himes set his novels in Harlem in the mid-twentieth century because he believed that it symbolized the deteriorating social conditions of racial minorities in urban America.[8] In *Cotton Comes to Harlem* (1964) he claimed that the city which had once been associated with cultural enlightenment and economic prosperity was now known for poverty, high crime rates, unemployment, and homelessness.[9]

Himes began reading crime fiction in the mid-1920s while serving time for armed robbery in the Ohio State Penitentiary. He preferred Dashiell Hammett, Raymond Chandler, and other noir writers who depicted an existential world where hard-boiled heroes lived by their wits and their fists. During his seven-year sentence, Himes experienced dangerous situations in prison, where violence occurred among inmates "for the most nonsensical reasons."[10] Later, in his detective series, Harlem became an African American version of the existential noir world. It resembled the crowded, violent prison where

Himes had once been confined. Instead of merely imitating Hammett and Chandler, as he once claimed in an interview, Himes racialized noir. [11]

Unlike Sam Spade and Philip Marlowe, self-employed white private eyes, Himes's protagonists, Coffin Ed Johnson and Grave Digger Jones, are Harlem detectives employed by the New York City police. Representing the law in a crime-ridden neighborhood makes them unpopular, especially when duty forces them to side with whites against racial minorities. As Jones says to someone who ventures into a neighborhood nightclub in *The Real Cool Killers* (1959), "If you white people insist on coming up to Harlem where you force colored people to live in vice-and-crime-ridden slums, it's my job to see that you're safe." [12] Instead of having a single protagonist, Himes features a pair of cops who are opposites. [13] Johnson follows procedure and counsels his partner to play by the rules, whereas Jones frequently loses control, threatens suspects, and personally punishes criminals. During the course of the series, the tension between the two cops continues to grow, paralleling the increasing crime rate, worsening race relations, and more frequent conflicts between citizens and local police. [14] Like the place where Himes spent his youth, the Harlem ghetto resembles a prison where destructive acts are committed by a frustrated, confined population. Violence occurs for what Himes calls "nonsensical reasons." It is random, senseless, graphic, and sometimes cartoonish—the product of outrage, hopelessness, and comic despair. In treating life in an urban African American slum as absurd, Himes adopts the same attitude as early noir writers, who comment on the existential perversity of the human condition. As Raymond Chandler once wrote, "It is not funny that a man should be killed, but it is sometimes funny that he should be killed for so little, and that his death should be the coin of what we call civilization." [15]

Himes envisioned Harlem, like other twentieth-century American cities, as a microcosm of crime and corruption; as a manufacturer of capitalism, class conflict, and greed; as an impersonal space and alienating urban environment. Although he set his series in Harlem, he wrote his first book, an autobiographical novel, about his early years in Los Angeles. Like Chandler, he challenged the conventional myth that Los Angeles was a metropolitan paradise by exploiting the contrast between what Mike Davis calls "sunshine and *noir*." [16] For minorities in particular, California was not a land of opportunity but a region where racism existed, just as it did everywhere else in America. In his first novel, Himes invented a subgenre known as "black noir," in which a racist crime, an investigation of tense race relations, or a mystery surrounding someone's racial identity provides an excuse for exploring the urban western frontier and the enigmatic essence of the modern human condition.

If He Hollers Let Him Go (1945) covers four days in the life of Bob Jones, an African American who has moved from the Midwest to Los Angeles during World War II, seeking better social conditions and job opportunities. Jones is hired to work in the shipbuilding industry, but he is prevented from joining the union, segregated from white co-workers, and relegated to supervising an African American crew. He has a light-skinned, upwardly mobile girlfriend who wants him to pursue education and employment in a white-collar profession. But he becomes attracted to a white female co-worker at the shipyard who will eventually accuse him of rape.

Although not a detective novel, *If He Hollers Let Him Go* has distinctive features associated with African American noir.[17] Jones is the model for the existential protagonist who seeks to determine his place in a racist society. Unwilling to settle for second-class treatment by whites yet unable to share the aspirations of the African American bourgeoisie, criticized and persecuted by both races, preyed upon by women (his co-worker and his girlfriend are both femmes fatales), and alienated by his urban environment, Jones solitarily navigates the mean streets of the city. Critics have suggested that Westerns and noir share certain characteristics. Noir tends to be set in cities such as Los Angeles because they represent modern urban equivalents of the western frontier. In both Westerns and noir, a lone individual (a cowboy or gunslinger, a detective or hard-boiled hero) contends with the forces of "civilization" and "savagery."[18] In Chandler, Hammett, and Himes, California symbolizes this dangerous frontier. It is an apocalyptic promised land at the edge of the continent, a postlapsarian paradise, populated by grifters and con artists, wannabe starlets, cultists and racists, diseased individuals seeking a healthier climate, and immigrants attracted by an oasis mirage—all misguided pilgrims, as Nathanael West writes in *The Day of the Locust*, who had "come to California to die."[19]

If He Hollers Let Him Go is a semiautobiographical novel that reflects the disillusionment of African American immigrants who came to the West Coast in search of success, only to watch their dreams die. After serving his sentence, Himes, like his protagonist, moved to Los Angeles. Although he hoped to write screenplays for one of the Hollywood studios, he ended up working twenty-three different jobs during the first three years of the war, only two of which, in the shipbuilding industry, required technical skills.[20] Because southern California during the mid-1940s was experiencing a booming wartime economy, and racism was thought to be less pervasive there than in the North and the South, African Americans came searching for job opportunities and social equality. Jones, for example, believes that he has improved his situation when he gets a job in the shipbuilding industry. He looks manly, self-confident, and upwardly mobile when he puts on his uniform. "Something about my working clothes made me feel rugged, bigger than the average citizen, stronger than a white-collar worker."[21] But negative stereotypes of racial minorities undermine his new self-esteem. Jones becomes ashamed for his race when he watches a film that portrays African Americans as comical and subservient characters (79). Just as the hero in noir becomes morally tainted by the corruption surrounding him—or as Marlowe says at the end of *The Big Sleep*, "part of the nastiness"[22]—so Jones admits that he is unable to maintain a positive self-image in a racist society. "You simply had to accept being black as a condition over which you had no control" (151).

Jones becomes pessimistic about his fate as the novel progresses. He feels "conspicuous, ill at ease, out of place" (79) in a white world where African American men are viewed with suspicion. Accused of assaulting a white woman and pursued by police, Jones goes on the run. After being chased, trapped, and imprisoned, he experiences existential alienation (191). Himes dramatizes an African American man's struggle to realize his dreams in a racist world where his inability to succeed seems predetermined. He contrasts scenes in which Jones is subjected to restricted conditions with scenes in which the protagonist seeks personal freedom and spatial mobility. As a minority, Jones is forced to endure segregation and feelings of intense claustrophobia. Police follow him when he leaves his minority neighborhood and enters white parts of Los Angeles. At work, African American employees are separated from the rest of the building crew, assigned to positions in the ship's deep interior. Jones navigates "a labyrinth of narrow, hard-angled companionways," where he and his fellow "contortionists" toil in poorly lit places that lack ventilation (20). Like the ship, which is dry-docked while under construction, Jones has few opportunities and little mobility. As the novel progresses, he becomes restricted to increasingly smaller and more depressed spaces, including a cabin room where a co-worker frames him for rape, and finally a jail cell "stinking with urine" and "crawling with lice" (196).

Jones only feels in control when he drives his new car. The aptly named Roadmaster restores his virility and gives him a sense of empowerment. He gets an erotic lift as he sits in "the soft springy seat," guides the car into traffic, and smells the "pungent, tantalizing" fumes of "the big Diesel trailers" (162). After a tense day at work, the Buick relaxes him. With his fingers "resting lightly on the steering wheel, just idling along," Jones feels friendly toward whites again (37–38). When he becomes angry, he takes out his frustrations by racing white motorists. One day, on his way to the shipyard, he challenges a

"V-8 full of white guys," nearly sideswipes a Packard, and almost collides with a man driving a coupe. According to Jones, the contest is racial: "I wanted . . . to push my Buick Roadmaster over some peckerwood's face" (12–14). The car fuels such fantasies and makes reality bearable. In his nightmares, which Himes describes in graphic detail, Jones lacks his own transportation (1, 69, 100, 149). And in real life, without his own vehicle, Jones feels defeated and powerless, "as if a car had run over me" (99).

Although the freeway provides physical escape and emotional release from the pressures of life in Los Angeles, ordinary city streets are confining and more problematic. In one scene, after leaving a restaurant, Jones and his girlfriend drive to the exclusive Westside. Dramatic tension increases as the couple ventures into territory where racial minorities are unwelcome. With Jones in the passenger seat, unable to seize control of the vehicle, Alice takes Hill to Washington, turns right on Western, and proceeds north to Sunset, becoming more and more reckless, "jerking" the car as she shifts into high. Weaving through traffic, she rides the dividing line, tailgates other cars, and continues to speed "as if something was after her." Racing west across Vine, she passes the Garden of Allah apartments and tears down the Strip, going "seventy, eighty, back to seventy for a bend, up to ninety again." At the intersection of Sunset and Sepulveda, she speeds south, then west onto Santa Monica Boulevard, running on borrowed time, and heads toward the ocean. The police finally stop her, tell her to leave Santa Monica, and threaten to give her a ticket for venturing into a restricted white neighborhood (61–63).[23]

Himes contrasts the density of a slum such as Harlem, and the hopelessness of an African American population that believes it has nowhere to go, with the openness of a western city such as Los Angeles, and the apparent freedom of movement that it offers its residents. Harlem is suffocatingly crowded, filled with tenement high-rises. It can only be viewed, in its sad inhumanity, from the top looking down. In *The Real Cool Killers*, Himes describes one of these vertically built, densely populated, crime-ridden slums: "It looked indescribably ugly in the glare of a dozen powerful spotlights. Uniformed police stood on the roof [of a building], others were coming and going through the entrance; still others stuck their heads out of front windows to shout to other cops in the street. The other front windows were jammed with colored faces, looking like clusters of strange purple fruit in the stark white light" of a nighttime raid on the neighborhood.[24]

Los Angeles, however, is a sprawling metropolis; a city designed to accommodate the automobile; a space that one can traverse horizontally. Noir exploits this phenomenon by narrating the actions of characters who are always on the make, on the move. Philip Marlowe, for instance, tails suspects and chases crooks in his car, free to travel from one part of town to another, able to chart a course through the asphalt maze of Los Angeles.[25] But Jones has less freedom than Marlowe. He is treated as a criminal suspect because of his race, not as a free agent like the white private eye. He is shadowed by police when he enters white neighborhoods, unable to move independently in segregated society. Harlem "was never meant to be real," as Himes acknowledged in his autobiography.[26] He exaggerated its sordidness in order to emphasize the nightmarish plight of racial minorities in urban America. But Himes gave Los Angeles a maplike reality, naming the streets and boulevards, tracing the actual routes his fictional characters took as they charted a concrete topography. Similarly, he dispelled Jones's romantic illusions, revealing a city that denies minorities equal access and social mobility. Illustrating how racism affects one's experience of urban reality, he plotted the course that Jones follows each day, careful to avoid fearful white drivers, angry pedestrians, and intimidating police.

Himes not only invented African American noir. He inspired Walter Mosley and other African American mystery novelists.[27] The protagonist in Mosley's first novel, *Devil in a Blue Dress* (1990), resembles Bob Jones. During World War II, Easy Rawlins comes to Los Angeles, takes a job in the aircraft instead of the shipbuilding industry, suffers workplace discrimination, and loses his job. Like Jones, Rawlins originally imagined California as paradise. He becomes disillusioned, though to a lesser degree. "People told stories of how you could eat fruit right off the trees and get enough work to retire one day. The stories were true for the most part but . . . [l]ife was still hard in L.A."[28] Rawlins becomes a detective when he accepts an assignment to locate a missing young woman. But police keep him under surveillance, as they do Himes's protagonist, and whites eye him suspiciously as he wanders the city during the course of his search. Rawlins is more optimistic than Jones about the future of racial minorities. As a self-employed private eye, he enjoys a certain independence and financial security. He even exudes some of Marlowe's existential romantic appeal.[29] But unlike Marlowe, a white man who sometimes collaborates with law enforcement, Rawlins is a minority who has been harassed, arrested, and physically abused by police. Like Jones, as well as some of Hammett's pragmatic heroes, he sometimes treats the law with contempt.[30]

Noir examines evils in modern urban society, including destructive capitalist practices, class conflict, street violence, gambling, drug abuse, sexual perversity, and other forms of depravity. Mosley practices noir with a distinctive "black difference," examining racism as yet another symptom of social disease.[31] In each novel, a mystery pertaining to race, involving complex interracial relationships, symbolizes the moral darkness that lies at the heart of society. *Devil in a Blue Dress* exposes the racial background of the titular character. *A Red Death* (1991) examines affinities between African Americans and socialist Jews. *White Butterfly* (1992) investigates prostitution, illegitimacy, and miscegenation. *Black Betty* (1994) implicates a wealthy white family and their colored servants in a case of intrigue. *A Little Yellow Dog* (1996), a story of drug-running, features a large cast of multicultural characters. *Bad Boy Brawly Brown* (2002) traces the converging paths of an African American youth and 1960s militant radicals.

Race plays a role in the hero's relationships. Because he is African American, Rawlins never enjoys as much independence as the traditional lone private eye. He cooperates when police, the Internal Revenue Service, or white citizens in positions of power solicit his services because he needs their legal protection and financial support to survive. In addition, he has contacts in the African American community who provide information and assistance in solving his cases. The typical existential protagonist has few ties to society, like Marlowe, who rents a lonely apartment, despises possessions, and has no long-term relationships; and the Continental Op, an anonymous agent with no family or friends. Rawlins, however, cannot afford to live existentially. As an African American struggling to rise above poverty, and as a single father raising two children, he relies on connections—both white and African American—to help him succeed.[32]

Rawlins interacts with the city's racially diverse population by assuming a series of different personae. In *Devil in a Blue Dress* he says that he learned "proper English" in school (10). Although he speaks "correctly" when talking to whites, he reverts to his natural "uneducated" language when conversing with members of his own race.[33] Marlowe "went to college once and can still speak English if there's any demand for it. There isn't much in my trade," he confesses.[34] He uses hard-boiled slang when speaking with everyone—cops, politicians, rich men, and street people. Rawlins, however, alternates between standardized English and racial vernacular.[35] He adopts different vocal personae, like a trickster in African American folklore and literature. In *White Butterfly* he impresses a snobbish character with his "best white man's English" in order to gain admission to a place that restricts racial minorities.[36] But at home he prefers his native southern racial dialect. For if "you were to talk like a white man" all the time, he says in *A Red Death*, "you might forget who you were."[37]

The traditional private eye works independently. Rawlins, however, needs Raymond "Mouse" Alexander, his best friend, to help him succeed. He acquires bilingual skills in order to work in a racially polarized city where racial minorities and whites not only speak different languages but live separate existences. Similarly, he requires a partner who has different techniques than he has for coping with crime. [38] Rawlins solves cases by cooperating with police, informants, and witnesses. He plays by the rules to a greater extent than his friend. Mouse uses violence to intimidate suspects and eliminate enemies. Unlike Rawlins, who sometimes accommodates authorities, Mouse "had never been chained, in his mind, by the white man. [He] was brash and wild and free." [39] Rawlins and Mouse resemble Himes's protagonists, Coffin Ed Johnson and Grave Digger Jones. One man works within the system, the other outside it. This pairing of opposites reflects a double consciousness. As writers who imitate the traditions of noir, Mosley and Himes present men who resemble white detectives such as Marlowe and Spade—heroes who honor the conventions of the genre and the codes of authority. As innovators within the tradition, who repeat noir with a difference, they self-consciously explore the way that racism affects their subjects, unlike Chandler's and Hammett's fictional characters.

Since Walter Mosley, more writers have entered the field of "black noir," producing an increasing number and an expanding variety of African American heroes and heroines, including cops, private eyes, bail bondsmen, bounty hunters, hired guns, and lone vigilantes. Although whites are still frequently cast as antagonists, other racial and ethnic groups are just as apt to be vilified. Sometimes the multiplicity of races and the complexity of racial relations lead to conflict on the urban frontier. At other times, however, assimilation or coexistence is possible. In such cases, where crimes do occur, racism is seldom the cause.

Violent Spring (1994), by Gary Phillips, illustrates the first case. Here the problems go deeper than the tensions between racial minorities and whites would suggest. Shortly after the 1992 riots, the rebuilding process begins in South Central Los Angeles. When a corpse is discovered during the groundbreaking ceremony for a shopping mall at the corner of Florence and Normandie, an investigation is begun that reveals equally serious conflicts between African Americans and Korean Americans, consumers and merchants, gang members and community residents, city politicians and neighborhood activists, wealthy white developers and impoverished minorities. The private eye, who unites the members of the riot-torn city in the process of solving the puzzle, is likewise an amalgamation of racial, historical, and cultural types. The author alternately describes Ivan Monk as a Mike Hammer clone, as a fan of 1940s film noir, as a character "right out of a Chester Himes novel," and as a blaxploitation hero like Shaft.[40] Although his girlfriend, a successful Asian American judge, shares his passion for justice, she and Monk belong to different races, genders, and classes, which complicates their romantic relationship.

In other novels it is the price of success, not victimization—black self-determination rather than racism—that Phillips explores. In *The Jook* (1999), after losing his job as a wide receiver for the Los Angeles Barons, Zelmont Raines can no longer afford his drug habit, child support payments, or the mortgage on his mansion in the Hollywood Hills. Desperate for money, he takes part in a heist. Phillips criticizes his character's choice, which is motivated by greed. In the process of rising to stardom, Raines, the son of a garbage man, has forgotten his origins. He has become a celebrity who lives in a wealthy white neighborhood, a drug addict, a poor racial role model, and finally a criminal. According to his girlfriend, he has a responsibility to children "in the ghettos and barrios" who buy "the obscenely overpriced shoes" that he endorses for sporting-goods companies. However, Raines dismisses her concern for consumers as well as for workers who get paid "peanuts" to make shoes that sell for hundreds of dollars.[41] *Shooter's Point* (2001), like *The Jook*, contemplates the ethical price of success. This heist novel features an attractive but dangerous vigilante African American heroine, a former Las Vegas showgirl who recovers unreported income stolen from hotel casinos. Las Vegas, like Los Angeles, is portrayed as a metropolitan frontier in the desert with a booming economy, as a hedonistic gambling resort (as opposed to a place that manufactures celebrities) where racial minorities as well as whites ruthlessly pursue the American dream. Unlike the hero in Mosley's and Chandler's novels, the heroine in *Shooter's Point* has no moral code. She works for casinos engaged in illegal activities, taking as her commission a percentage of their ill-gotten gains.

In John Ridley's novels, the show-business capitals of Las Vegas and Hollywood are also represented as lands of illusion where African Americans mistakenly pursue riches and fame. In *Love Is a Racket* (1998), Jeffty Kittridge comes to Los Angeles with the dream of becoming a screenwriter. Although a producer options his script, Jeffty goes to Las Vegas and gambles his paycheck away. The producer then puts his project on hold. Broke and embittered, Jeffty schemes to get revenge by scamming another producer in a con that results in his own death. In *Everybody Smokes in Hell* (1999),

Paris Scott, another failed Los Angeles scriptwriter-grifter, meets his fate in Las Vegas, "the city of slot-machine hopes and jackpot dreams [with] the highest suicide rate" in America. [42] Ridley's protagonist is an assimilated member of the African American middle class and a potentially talented writer with a good education. Instead of seeing himself as a minority who has been denied opportunities, he describes himself as a victim of Hollywood, which has destroyed the dreams of others before him, regardless of race. Ridley reserves his contempt for the entertainment industry capital, quoting Raymond Chandler, who refers to Hollywood as a "degraded community" (2).

Ridley has more in common with Chandler, who associates evil with place, and with Nathanael West, who savages Hollywood in *The Day of the Locust*, than he does with writers in African American noir who examine the role racism plays in the lives of their characters. Gar Anthony Haywood more closely resembles Mosley and Himes because his novels take place during historical moments, in relation to political movements, or in the context of cultural practices that have racial significance. *When Last Seen Alive* (1997) begins in Washington DC during the Million Man March and follows a trail that leads to Los Angeles, where private eye Aaron Gunner, who works out of a neighborhood barbershop, becomes involved in the case. It concerns an African American journalist who has cast shame on his race by inventing a supposedly true story that won a Pulitzer Prize. *All the Lucky Ones Are Dead* (1999) investigates the murder of a young gangsta rapper; the relationships among rap, violence, drugs, and misogyny; and the exploitation of African American culture by music conglomerates.

Although Haywood's novels have a distinct racial flavor, they also bear a certain resemblance to traditional noir, suggesting, as one critic has noted, that formula crime fiction has "an essentially conservative form." [43] Like the archetypal hero, detective Aaron Gunner is an agent of civilization who safeguards society by vanquishing crime. The minority private eye frequently feels alienated from mainstream America, yet he believes in the system and works within it to bring about change. Throughout the series, Gunner is terrorized by a group of African American political militants who accuse him of conspiring with police to imprison minorities. Although the accusation is unfounded, Gunner is not as hip or radical as some African Americans would like him to be. He hates rap music because it glorifies violence, features obscenity, and celebrates disrespect for authority. Gunner is an African American variation on the classic detective who has conventional values and traditional tastes. He listens to old-fashioned rhythm and blues, watches *The Maltese Falcon*, and drives a vintage automobile. [44]

Robert Greer's sleuth is a hybrid as well. C. J. Floyd, a bail bondsman, lives in a minority Denver neighborhood and solves cases that involve African American characters. In *The Devil's Red Nickel* (1997) he complains about the presence of whites in his neighborhood and their purchasing of historic properties owned by minorities. But he also resents the infiltration of African American criminals ("baby cockroaches"), street bums, and gangs.[45] Floyd is a political radical and a social conservative, fighting for the preservation of the African American middle class by fending off the white upper class and low-life racial minorities. He is a contemporary yet nostalgic African American variation on the archetypal detective protagonist, defending his community while preserving his racial identity. He moves in a world that resembles "some grainy 1940s film noir" (171), drives a 1957 Chevy Bel Air, and prefers the music of John Lee Hooker, as he says in *The Devil's Backbone* (1998), to "the hip-hop gangsta rap sounds of Tupac Shakur."[46]

Floyd has a regional as well as a racial identity. Denver, like Los Angeles, is an urban frontier, populated by modern-day Native American criminals and by ecoterrorists who infect herds of cattle with deadly medical viruses. In *The Devil's Hatband* (1996), the first book in the series, the reader learns that Floyd wears a cowboy hat and collects western antiques. His girlfriend's father was born in an experimental African American colony founded in Colorado at the turn of the century, and his two best friends once performed in African American rodeos.[47] Greer's novels take place in a West that is part rural, part cosmopolitan; where minorities have assimilated to some extent, yet remain proud of their heritage; where the bicultural hero combines traits of the nineteenth-century African American pioneer and the twentieth-century white urban detective.

Male protagonists such as Gunner and Floyd handle racial discrimination and professional challenges in modern western society. Female characters face additional obstacles, including sexist treatment at work and problems with families at home. The heroine in *Inner City Blues* (1999), by Paula L. Woods, is a policewoman who lives in Los Angeles. Charlotte Justice is harassed by white male members of the Los Angeles Police Department (LAPD), who make racist and sexist remarks. She is viewed with suspicion by members of her race who distrust the police. She also copes with class prejudice. Her mother, proud of the family's African American upper-class status, and her brother, a lawyer, pressure Justice to quit her blue-collar job. Class differences also come to the surface when she starts dating a successful physician. The title of the novel, *Inner City Blues*, not only alludes to the misery of African American urban experience; it refers to what it feels like to wear a blue uniform. In a scene at a funeral, when the congregation sings the Marvin Gaye song that inspires the title, the heroine experiences a connection with other "young men and women. Eastside or Westside, South Central or South Bay, there were things that bound black folks together beyond the superficialities of skin color or hair texture. It was memory and culture resonating from within, from the way we grieve to the music that had everyone bobbing their heads in the chapel's late afternoon gloom."[48] It is a rare harmonious interlude in a novel that chronicles racial strife, class tension, and social despair.

Although the white detective in traditional noir is a loner with existentialist philosophical leanings, the African American hero is sometimes bound to his racial community by feelings of group solidarity. To an even greater degree, the African American heroine is defined by relationships with family, co-workers, and friends. In *Somebody Else's Child* (1996), by Terris McMahan Grimes, Theresa Galloway is torn by conflicting allegiances.[49] As a Sacramento city employee with a position in the Department of Environmental Equity, Galloway is "responsible for making sure that minority communities don't get more than their fair share of toxic disposal facilities."[50] As an amateur sleuth, she is similarly committed to cleaning up crimes in minority neighborhoods. Here and in subsequent works in the series, Galloway decides to investigate when her mother becomes involved in a mystery. Galloway, a good daughter, wants to help her elderly parent. As a wife and mother, however, she feels guilty neglecting her family; as a career woman, she worries about leaving her job to fight crime on the sly. Grimes raises questions that her male counterparts do not address as explicitly. For example, can a member of the African American middle class still maintain "street" credibility? Easy Rawlins, Aaron Gunner, and C. J. Floyd are respected as tough guys even though they live in comparative comfort among middle-class racial minorities. Galloway, however, is not allowed to have it both ways. Old friends accuse her of acting "better than [black] people" since becoming a suburbanite and a successful professional (77). Galloway returns to her mother's crime-ridden neighborhood in each of the novels in order to demonstrate her commitment to the inner-city community. But the straight-laced civil servant and the middle-aged mother of two admits that the streets are "too mean for me." Unlike Rawlins, Gunner, and Floyd—self-employed single men who are typically childless—Galloway must consider the needs of others before taking personal risks.

In addition to being cautious, heroines such as Galloway, like their male counterparts, have somewhat conservative politics. In *Where to Choose*

(1999), Penny Mickelbury's reluctant detective is a dutiful daughter. Carol Ann Gibson becomes involved in a mystery when she takes a break from her law practice and visits her mother, who lives in a Los Angeles residential community. Founded by African Americans and Mexican Americans as an experimental neighborhood—as a place where different minorities could coexist peacefully—Jacaranda Estates has recently experienced an upsurge in crime. Gibson discovers that various unlawful acts have been committed by Mexican immigrants, who have been secretly housed on the grounds by one of the community's residents as part of a smuggling scheme to import illegal aliens. Mickelbury describes Jacaranda Estates as an urban western utopia—as "an island, an oasis" for low-income minorities.[51] Although it differs in character from the rest of Westside Los Angeles, which has a relatively wealthy and predominantly white population, it resembles the Westside in its exclusivity and homogeneity. The villains in the novel are illegal minority immigrants who breach the security of a gated community, destroy private property, terrorize homeowners, and make life undesirable.

There are significant variations within African American noir. Indeed, one critic has argued that no such tradition exists, given the fact that African American mysteries share few similarities.[52] For example, the domestic heroines in novels by Mickelbury and Grimes have little in common with Himes's existential protagonists. All of these writers, beginning with Himes, consider the effects of violence and crime on African Americans in urban communities. But that hardly makes them unique. Himes once said in an interview that "all Americans" live in a violent society. "There's no reason why [African Americans, like whites] shouldn't write [noir]: It's just plain and simple violence in narrative form."[53] In "The Simple Art of Murder," Chandler echoed these sentiments. Murder, he claimed, was an expression of the universal condition: a result of the "frustration of the individual," regardless of color; a characteristic of "the race," by which he meant the whole human race.[54]

Yet the same critic who maintains that there is no coherent tradition also maintains that African American writers inflect the mystery genre with a "black" sensibility. Certain artists simultaneously resist and accommodate "the dominant culture" by imitating and subverting popular mystery formulas.[55] Traditional noir presents a pessimistic view of Western civilization. African American noir also focuses on depravity, corruption, and crime in society. In African American noir, however, minorities are not only criminals. They are defenders of the law and social avengers, heroes and heroines, ordinary middle-class citizens, business people, conservative homeowners, detectives, and members of the local police. African American noir, according to Paula L. Woods, "lets readers know that African Americans are not just the victims or perpetrators of crimes."[56] They are sometimes the ones who provide hope and solutions as well.

CHAPTER SEVEN

Everybody Comes to California to Die

In the twenty-first century, most African Americans in the West reside in metropolitan areas with large populations. More African Americans live in California than anywhere else in the region, with the greatest percentage of those making their homes in Los Angeles.[1] While the city continues to attract African Americans and other minorities, it also suffers from a reputation as a racial dystopia. The two largest social disturbances that have occurred in the West have taken place in Los Angeles, where overcrowding, segregation, unemployment, and poverty have become increasingly prevalent.

The first major disturbance, known as the Watts Riot, began on August 11, 1965, when a police officer stopped Marquette Frye for reckless driving in South Central Los Angeles. After the young African American man failed a sobriety test, his mother arrived at the scene, started berating her son, and attracted a crowd. When the suspect resisted arrest, the officer radioed for backup support, enraging onlookers who believed that the police were overreacting to a minor street altercation. A riot ensued, resulting over the course of the next several days in thirty-four deaths, more than three thousand arrests, the looting and burning of hundreds of buildings in the neighborhood, and millions of dollars in damages.

The second disturbance, commonly referred to as the Los Angeles Uprising, was inspired by the beating and arrest of Rodney G. King. On March 3, 1991, after a freeway chase, members of the Los Angeles Police Department and the California Highway Patrol apprehended the suspect for speeding. The officers, claiming that King had resisted arrest, subdued him by applying physical force. An amateur video, taken at the time of the incident and later played in the media, revealed that four officers had struck

Headlines on the front page of the *Los Angeles Times*, August 14, 1965, refer to a "Riot," "Anarchy," and "Blood-Hungry Mobs," blaming the events in Watts on "Negro Family Failure" and lack of "Community Leadership." (Copyright 1965, *Los Angeles Times*. Reprinted with permission)

King a total of fifty-six times, shattering one of his eye sockets, breaking a leg, causing nine skull fractures, and producing concussion. When the officers were acquitted on charges related to the beating on April 29, 1992, a protest erupted outside the courthouse. It reverberated dramatically in downtown Los Angeles as people began to riot, burn buildings, and overturn cars. Early the next day, with eight people already dead, Mayor Tom Bradley ordered a curfew and Governor Pete Wilson dispatched the National Guard. By May 4, however, social unrest had infiltrated many parts of the city, accounting for at least fifty-eight deaths, more than two thousand injuries, seven thousand fires, and almost one billion dollars in damages.

African Americans, in particular, were affected by the 1965 riot and the 1992 uprising. Both events began with the arrest of an African American male, led to allegations of racial harassment and police brutality, and ended in warfare that devastated primarily minority areas. Yet most of the news was reported by journalists who were disinterested observers and community outsiders, working for predominantly white media organizations. (In 1965, for example, the *Los Angeles Times* had no African American reporters on staff. It assigned an African American advertising salesman to cover the riot.)[2] The stories of participants, victims, and residents seldom found their way into print.

For many participants, the riot itself was a form of expression. The disenfranchised poor, without political representation and access to media, "performed" their dissatisfaction by staging an urban rebellion. They converted "the one thing the poor can claim as their own, their bodies, into a strength that [could] counteract the might of those at the top of society."[3] While some participants may have exhausted their rage in the act of expressing it, others who were affected by the disturbance channeled their feelings through the performative arts. The Watts Happening Café opened in October 1965, providing an outlet for those hardest hit by the riot. It sponsored painting exhibitions, music and dance classes, and community theater.[4] Similarly, after the uprising, the Los Angeles Contemporary Dance Theatre, inspired by "the energy of street dance and the powerful emotions of personal histories," presented a piece in which it interpreted "the heated emotions which caused the eruption of the Los Angeles riots."[5]

Many of these offerings were construed as forms of practical therapy, as socially useful activities intended to give inner-city African American residents a stake in their war-torn community. However, critics contended that government-funded projects were public-relations campaigns designed to portray civic leaders as interested in addressing racial and economic concerns, when in fact they were merely cosmetic efforts to keep the city's malcontents occupied. One writer described the painting of murals on burned-out buildings as "busywork" in the aftermath of the 1992 episode.[6] Another

May 2, 1992. National Guardsman stands at alert near graffiti that expresses support for Rodney King. (Photographed by Randy Leffingwell. Copyright 1992, *Los Angeles Times*. Reprinted with permission)

argued that the Arts Recovery Program sponsored such murals in order to project an image of Los Angeles as a city "quietly and festively 'healing' its wounds."[7]

Not all responses to the city's two major disturbances were socially acceptable, nor were they pretty. Although civic leaders and local community activists searched for constructive solutions, people with no investment in society reacted quite differently. Eldridge Cleaver recalled how delighted inmates in Folsom Prison were when they heard about Watts. "Sensing a creative moment in the offing, we all got very quiet." Then an African American prisoner extemporized a poem honoring those who had rioted. "'Baby,' he said. 'They walking in fours and kicking in doors; dropping Reds and busting heads; drinking wine and committing crime, shooting and looting; high-siding and low-riding, setting fires and slashing tires; turning over cars and burning down bars; making [LAPD chief William H.] Parker mad and making me glad; putting an end to that "go slow" crap and putting sweet Watts on the map— my black ass is in Folsom this morning but my black heart is in Watts.'"[8] Twenty-seven years later, disaffected minorities once again challenged popular sentiment. An art critic noted that the 1992 uprising inspired not only conservative murals but politically incendiary hip-hop graffiti, much to the consternation of business owners and residents.[9]

Responses to the demonstrations in Watts and Los Angeles most appropriately found expression in the performative arts. People could re-create the riot and uprising, the physical movements of people, in dance; react spontaneously to current events by improvising rhymes or composing graffiti; and attempt to heal communities by bringing audiences together to witness live theater. These events also inspired "demonstrative" literature: protest pieces produced by the Watts Writers' Workshop; song lyrics dealing with racial rebellion; "street" journalism; and Anna Deavere Smith's play *Twilight: Los Angeles*, featuring interviews with people involved in the 1992 uprising. Like other forms of representation, literature also prompted debates about the purpose of art. Should African American artists seek nonviolent solutions to urban unrest, or should they advocate open rebellion against white society?

During the twentieth century the African American population in Los Angeles increased dramatically. Between 1900 and 1960 the number of African American residents swelled from 2,131 to 334,916.[10] African Americans believed there were fewer racial restrictions and more job opportunities on the urban frontier. By the beginning of the civil rights decade, however, that perception had changed. Watts, a neighborhood in South Central Los Angeles where many African Americans lived, had transformed from a paradise into a slum. Though it had its share of sunshine and palm trees, by midcentury Watts also had higher unemployment and poverty rates than the rest of city; an oppressive police force; businesses that exploited African American customers; little affordable housing in its overcrowded community; substandard social service agencies and educational facilities; and a lack of cheap public transport, which prevented the poor from commuting from Watts to other parts of Los Angeles in search of better alternatives.[11]

In the aftermath of the Watts Riot, Governor Edmund G. Brown appointed a committee, headed by John A. McCone, a former director of the Central Intelligence Agency, to determine what had caused the recent racial unrest. On December 2, 1965, the predominantly white, eight-man committee issued a report entitled "Violence in the City." It blamed the riot on African American immigrants who had come to Los Angeles with unrealistically "high hopes and great expectations." Although "the Negro districts of Los Angeles are not urban gems, neither are they slums," the committee reported. Watts, for example, had one- and two-story houses, parks, playgrounds, and trees. "Compared with the conditions under which Negroes live in most other large cities," the panel concluded, the quality of life here was "superior."[12]

Critics claimed that the report whitewashed reality. They cited Marquette Frye, whose arrest had started the riot, as an example of those who had come to Los Angeles, seduced by the myth of the urban frontier. Frye had been born in a small Oklahoma farming community. His family had later relocated to Hannah, Wyoming, believing that the mining boomtown offered greater prospects for economic success. For the next thirteen years, according to one biographer, the family had lived like the first pioneers in a picturesque settlement, nestled on top of "the Continental Divide just south of what had been the great Overland Trail."[13] With the collapse of the mining boom, the family had moved to Los Angeles, like thousands of other racial minorities. After living in Watts, Frye decided that he had been happier in rural Wyoming, where there had been fewer African Americans but also less racism.[14] His dissatisfaction with life in Los Angeles was echoed on August 11, 1965, by thousands of others who rioted.

Some African Americans rejected the official myth of Los Angeles, supported by civic boosters and state politicians. They complained about the reality of African American urban experience. Los Angeles was not only the land where dreams could come true but also the site of nightmarish social unrest. African American writer Otis O'Solomon claimed that "the make-believe capital of the world" had produced "a violent new spectacle" featuring "a large, mostly black cast."[15] In addition to Hollywood, Disneyland, and other magical places, there were inner-city slums populated by rebellious racial minorities.

According to the official myth, Los Angeles had many amenities: a good climate, wide-open spaces, and a high standard of living. Racism was rare, social discontent was uncommon, and violent dissent was unheard of. According to the countermyth, racial discrimination, separate and unequal living conditions, unemployment, and poverty were characteristics of life in Los Angeles. Over time, anger had increased in the inner-city community and talk of rebellion had grown. The *Los Angeles Times*, reflecting the views of its largely white audience, referred to the events in Watts as a riot. Words like "terrorism," "anarchy," "out-of-control," "mob violence," and "mass murder" were used to characterize the actions of the participants in front-page reports and news editorials.[16] The consensus seemed to be that people were overreacting to circumstances, behaving irrationally, or in the words of the McCone Commission Report, published later that year, allowing themselves to be "caught up in an insensate rage of destruction."[17] Some compared the National Guard and local police that were fighting in Watts with American military troops that were participating at the same time in the Vietnam War. "Modern Negro violence is not simply rioting but an urban form of guerilla warfare. . . . This situation is very much like fighting the Viet Cong," Chief Parker explained.[18]

However, subsequent surveys and sociological studies have suggested that Parker's analogy was not entirely accurate. Although mobs may be violent, as studies have shown, they tend to be rational. And in Watts the people were not rioting for a communist cause. According to one survey, the rioters in 1965 "were not primarily the unemployed, ill-educated, uprooted, and criminal."[19] They were "better-educated and economically advantaged" residents of the inner-city community, one-third to one-half of whom described themselves as "active spectators," or more than passive observers.[20] Unlike communist insurgents, with whom they were compared, the majority of rioters, according to statistical surveys, believed in capitalism and democracy. They protested because they felt that they had been denied equal access to the American dream, not because they advocated a new ideology.[21]

In order to give African Americans a stake in the dream, Budd Schulberg founded the Watts Writers' Workshop. Schulberg was an affluent white man, a political liberal, and a well-known screenwriter and novelist. He believed that the disturbance in Watts was "a rebellion that had been years in the making," a response by the disenfranchised to "a society that was selling swimming pools and golf courses and at the same time warning [racial minorities] to keep off the grass."[22] He established the workshop, which gave African Americans a chance to express their frustration while honing writing skills that could later be marketed, thus affording them economic opportunities that they had long been denied. With connections in the publishing world as well as in Hollywood, Schulberg attracted the support of an eclectic group of celebrities, including John Steinbeck, Norman Mailer, Sam Goldwyn, Groucho Marx, and Shirley MacLaine. In 1966, NBC television broadcast *The Angry Voices of Watts*, featuring poems, essays, and stories written by workshop participants. Schulberg edited these pieces for publication the following year. *From the Ashes* was inspired by his faith in the future. As Schulberg claimed in the book's introduction: "From the ashes, out of the rubble, out of apathy, despair, neglect, and hopelessness might rise a black phoenix" (18).

Although Schulberg was optimistic, the writers themselves were ambivalent. Some, like Blossom Powe, believed that social upheaval might lead to the integration of racial minorities in mainstream society. "Time . . . crawling slowly, / Starts to sift through the ashes / Of this black kind of Phoenix / With trembling hands— / Crying! Brooding! Trying somehow / To create . . . a new mosaic" (203–4). Others, like Johnie Scott, prophesied: "We were never children of the sun / who might bask beneath golden rays and burn red. . . . / We are yesterday people / who cannot live in tomorrow" (127–28). Harry Dolan claimed that it would take more than a riot—"a spontaneous, explosive reaction"—to end white oppression. Next time there would be an organized underground movement prepared to wage "Armageddon" (34–35). Most poets, however, expressed doubts about whether African Americans should use violence to resolve racial grievances. Johnie Scott applauded "angry black braves" who went on the warpath in Watts while mourning those who were slain (132). Vallejo Ryan Kennedy also had mixed reactions to the 1965 riot. "What I felt was heaven to feel / What I saw was hell to see" (141).

Some praised Schulberg for subsidizing the Watts Writers' Workshop, while others accused him of exploiting African American poets. Maya Angelou lauded his efforts.[23] But Quincy Troupe condemned his harvesting and editing of minority literature, calling Schulberg a sharecropper who had exercised "censorship," rendering the contributors' poetry "sterile."[24] One year after the appearance of Schulberg's anthology, Troupe published his own edited collection of writings, entitled *Watts Poets: A Book of New Poetry.* Unlike Schulberg, who had allegedly sanitized and commercialized the work of African American artists, Troupe theoretically preserved African American artistic integrity by rejecting white sponsorship and independently publishing his collection of alternative poetry. In a prose manifesto that prefaced the book, one of the contributors defined the mainstream publishing industry as a capitalist enterprise, as an exploitive white practice motivated by ruthless competition, self-interest, and greed. "Traditional African communalism never lent itself to indiscriminate rivalries or to wanton destruction of people and goods," argued Milton McFarlane. He urged African Americans to resurrect African tribal traditions. By rejecting the mainstream press they could avoid exploitation, and by forming racial cooperatives, which would publish their work, they could they ensure their successful survival.[25]

A number of poems expressed anti-capitalist and anti-imperialist views. According to the writer Fanita, the pursuit of commerce in the African American community had resulted in self-exploitation, in a pimp culture dependent on the prostitution of women. "Daddy, I know you're still pretty / drugged because I didn't make / my quota last night. . . . / A bitch knows her man needs money, / and she must be crazy / if she can't stay on her job. . . . / Jest watch me, Daddy. I'm a bad whore. / I'm jest goin' to TAKE THIS FOOLS MONEY" (13–14). K. Curtis Lyle wrote about African Americans who preyed on their people by selling drugs to make money: "[B]rothers in search of cosmic states / in quest of no-returns, / I mean . . . lookin for some LBS. / of stomp-down righteous smack / call me Hezekiah, / Ezekial or some other o weird / biblical name / but, / I can get it for you wholesale" (44). Charles K. Moreland Jr. complained that some African American men were unable to work because they had fought in imperialist wars overseas: "[S]horty blue caint steal / shorty blue caint git a job neither. / all he can do is sell them bottles. / he aint got sense to do nothing else. / shorty blue crazy. / he a stupid black niggah. / he got shell shocked in korea" (29). Others were haunted by the memory of wartime atrocities, which K. Curtis Lyle compared to the horrors of life in South Central Los Angeles: "[Y]ou suffer for all the yellow children / sitting paralyzed in napalmed rice paddies / you suffer for Black women, / eyes bugged-out behind 9 illegitimate / children & food enough for only 4 / you suffer for being stigmatized as / an american; convenient platitudes / for an Olympic yr. or a Vietnam War" (47).

If African Americans in the Watts Riot were like Viet Cong warriors, as Chief Parker suggested, then so were some militant poets, at least in terms of their politics. They opposed America's presence in the Vietnam War and believed in racial "communalism" instead of white-run democracy. While some of these poets examined the destructive effects of racism, war, drugs, prostitution, and poverty, others sought constructive solutions to the problems that beset inner cities. These artists advocated self-pride, family unity, African nationalism, and solidarity with other racial minorities. Elaine Brown claimed that African American men had been separated from their families by slavery. Now they were returning home and reclaiming their place in society: "Poppa was made to go / Four-hundred years / To be exact / Lashed on his back / Just because he was black / But oh / Yes, child, Poppa's Come Home" (52). Herbert A. Simmons observed that family unity was "the key to survival . . . / over nebulous cultures / Bent on aggrandizement and genocide" (39). The "family" symbolized a strong African American community and a racial group consciousness. K. Curtis Lyle heralded "the coming of the Black Nation"

(47). Lance Jeffers, appropriating Walt Whitman's voice as well as his vision, celebrated the masses when he said: "I sing my people" (32). His "people" included tribes of all nationalities: African Americans who had marched for civil rights in the South; Comanches who had fought whites on the western frontier; and Aztecs in Mexico who had battled the European invader Cortés (35).

In 1971, another group of artists commemorated the riot by recording an album of poetry. The Watts Prophets—including Dee Dee MaNail, Anthony Hamilton, Richard Dedeaux, and Otis O'Solomon—released *Rappin' Black in a White World*. [26] Their work was influenced by 1960s beat poetry and served as an inspiration for later African American rap. [27] Unlike some of Quincy Troupe's poets, who advocated nonviolence, the Watts Prophets believed that rebellion was necessary to achieve racial equality. In "Take It" they urged African Americans to overthrow the establishment. Why preserve a system that treated them like second-class citizens? "Ask not what you can do for your country," they said in "Amerikkka." "What in the fuck has it done for you?" In "Watch Out Black Folks" they warned that "revolution is coming." The Watts Prophets were poets of the racial apocalypse. In "Dem N°gg°rs Ain't Playing" they envisioned fires that would "light up the nights."

The riot produced disarray in the African American artistic community. Some poets were committed to rebuilding society; others vowed to destroy it. But most were divided. Certain members of the Watts Writers' Workshop accepted white guidance and sponsorship while sympathizing in their poetry with minority underground movements and terroristic activities. Troupe claimed that Budd Schulberg had censored these writings. But Troupe's own group of poets produced works that were far from ideologically pure. One writer rhymed: "believe it, my friend / That this silence can end / We'll just have to get guns / And be men" (50). However, another one condemned "this age of violence" when "Non-violence fell, / And Christianity died" (42). As for the Watts Prophets, much of their rap was rhetorical. Although they preached revolution, they used words rather than bullets to express their political views. Perhaps they believed that by warning people that racial Armageddon was possible they could prevent it from happening.

Twenty-seven years later, however, the doomsday predictions came true. Since 1965 the situation had continued to deteriorate in South Central Los Angeles. By the time of the uprising, almost one-third of residents lived below the poverty level, more than half of the adult population had dropped out of the workforce, and a greater percentage of households were on welfare than ever before. [28] An independent commission appointed after the beating of

King concluded that a disproportionate number of African Americans were segregated in low-income "ghettos" where they were subject to surveillance and physical harassment by the LAPD.[29] It had been possible to dismiss the earlier instance of social unrest as a riot by viewing it as an isolated and irrational outbreak in an otherwise peaceful metropolis. The second event was more commonly viewed as an uprising—as an organized rebellion against long-standing social, political, and economic injustices. "It's Watts all over again," said the city district attorney.[30]

However, the causes of the uprising were more complex and the effects more damaging. Other minorities had immigrated to Los Angeles and become disenchanted in the years since the Watts Riot. Approximately half of those arrested for looting and rioting during the Los Angeles Uprising were male Latinos.[31] Anger was directed not only at whites but also at Korean American merchants who had uneasy relations with African American customers. More groups were involved, as were more parts of the city. Once again the violence began in South Central Los Angeles, but this time it spread to Hollywood and to affluent Westside communities, causing greater financial damage and resulting in more deaths and injuries.[32]

The media also played a more prominent role, complicating perceptions of urban reality. Some journalists dubbed the disturbance a "riot," while others called it an "uprising," comparing it to the "revolt" that had occurred in Los Angeles twenty-seven years earlier.[33] Television series such as *Knots Landing* and *Fresh Prince of Bel-Air* subsequently incorporated the uprising into their story lines, treating it seriously or superficially, depending on one's point of view.[34] George Halliday's amateur video, which captured King's beating, was a perfect example of the way media could be used to interpret occurrences. In the 1992 trial the prosecution used the videotape to illustrate that the four accused members of the LAPD had treated King with unnecessary brutality. The defense argued, however, that the tape told only part of the story. Not recorded on video was the fact that King had resisted arrest by refusing to get out of his car and that he had not complied with repeated requests to submit to authorities. The defense attorneys also interpreted the video differently. Analyzing it frame by frame, they concluded that not all of the alleged blows had made contact with King and that the police were therefore not guilty of abusive behavior. Later, observers agreed that by playing the video over and over the defense had managed to desensitize the jury to the violence onscreen. By interrupting the continuous visual narrative and focusing on a series of discrete frozen images, they had deprived the video of its dramatic momentum.[35] "Many people were shocked by the jury's verdict because it seemed to be clearly at odds with 'reality,'" noted one journalist.[36] But in this instance, reality consisted of a piece of visual evidence that could be read in various ways.

As a result of three incidents—the courtroom dispute and the public debate over the 1991 video; the predominantly white jury's acquittal of the officers in the 1992 case; and an ethnically mixed jury's conviction of two of those officers in the 1993 federal trial—there developed a greater awareness that people perceived reality differently, depending on their race, where they lived, and whether they trusted or distrusted the LAPD. At the same time, people continued to search for the "truth" by sifting through conflicting accounts of urban experience. In 1992, Lynell George, an African American journalist, published *No Crystal Stair*, a collection of essays reporting on life in South Central Los Angeles. The work intentionally lacked structure and thematic coherence, reflecting the fractured existence of alienated inner-city minorities. In personal musings, pieces of cultural reportage, and biographical portraits of local residents, George commented on the fragmentation of the ethnic community. In the first chapter, she recorded what it was like to be at the scene of the uprising: "I'm already speedily taking notes, as if the act of writing down what I see and hear will bring about some sense of order."[37] But later her scribblings are hard to decipher, and her incomplete sentences remind her of hopes for a better future that have not been fulfilled. In another chapter, one of her subjects confirms this impression by referring to South Central as one of the city's "most fragmented areas," lacking government funding and civic support (68). But another resident says that this claim is distorted. The mainstream media "have done an expert job of obliterating [the community's] cohesive past" by emphasizing the divisive and destructive aspects of the recent social unrest (167).

George distinguishes herself from the rest of the media by offering "an alternative vision" of life in South Central Los Angeles. Other reporters, presumably white, view African Americans as "thems," "theys," and "thugs." Unacquainted with members of the inner-city community, these "outsiders" in their "ignorance" portray racial minorities in stereotypical terms (5). As an African American woman capable of navigating the urban terrain, George claims to have greater credibility and more expertise. Rather than merely offering an alternative vision, she provides a perspective that is allegedly keener, more accurate. She asks the reader to dismiss previous inauthentic, ill-informed, and unreliable narratives and to trust her own work instead.

Writers who searched for the truth after the 1992 uprising defended the value of their work by emphasizing its journalistic integrity. Anna Deavere

Smith interviewed more than two hundred people for her play *Twilight: Los Angeles*. Like George, she portrayed a fragmented city made up of gang-bangers, neighborhood activists, career politicians, undocumented workers, affluent residents, artists, homeless people, and members of the entertainment community. By juxtaposing their various responses to the recent unrest, Smith underscored the potential for conflict that existed in contemporary urban society.

There was no consensus in *Twilight: Los Angeles*, for the uprising meant different things to each individual. The "truth" resided in the honest opinions of people who were represented in the play by their actual words. Smith described the play as one in a series of works based on real-life events. The series, entitled *On the Road: A Search for American Character*, explored the notion that "you could be found in your language," that meaningful ideas and emotions were revealed in a person's unrehearsed and uncensored speech—in voice rhythms, verbal tics, and idiosyncratic expressions.[38]

Smith impersonated these people and repeated their words in her dramatic performances. Although the wide range of views expressed by the interviewees was bewildering, the arranging of the order in which the speakers appeared and the juxtaposition of their thoughts for dramatic effect imposed patterns of meaning on the otherwise unwieldy material. Forced to select from more than two hundred interviews, Smith included some and not others. Because she made changes in the cast periodically, there was no single "text." (The 1993 stage version, the 1994 published edition, and the 1999 PBS production are three of the best-known textual variants.) In the published edition she arranged the words on the page in free verse, investing colloquial speech with the power of lyrical poetry.[39]

Different versions of *Twilight: Los Angeles* offer contradictory accounts and shifting impressions of the same individual. For example, in the published edition, Smith's interview with Rodney King's aunt takes place in the back room of the aunt's Pasadena boutique. Angela King is described as a "powerful" woman who discusses the beating of her nephew while focusing her "direct gaze" on Smith.[40] During King's speech, Smith hears the pounding of "two hammers," which sounds "like a dialogue." In the broadcast production, however, the setting is homier, there are no background acoustics, and the speaker appears more relaxed and less confrontational. Smith achieves a subtler dramatic effect by having her character narrate her story in a seemingly casual style. Now King sits on a couch, flips through a magazine, and makes only occasional eye contact with the camera during the course of her monologue.[41]

Other characters undergo more extreme transformations. In the published version of *Twilight: Los Angeles*, Professor Cornel West sits behind a fortress-like desk. Surrounded by papers, he pontificates on the meaning of the recent unrest: "On the one hand / there's / like duh frontier myth in America / right?" He defines the frontier myth as a version of Manifest Destiny, which justifies the "conquest and dispossession of / duh / people's land." Thus, he reasons, the 1992 uprising can be viewed as a contemporary example of westward expansion, in which African Americans acted like "*cow*boys," like "Rambo," like gangsters, getting theirs while they could (41–43). West "performs" for his audience, lecturing like an academic and at the same time sounding like a clown ("duh"). In the film, there is no pose or pretension. West sits in an armchair, directly facing the camera, and delivers a briefer address in which he speaks from the heart. Telling viewers that the uprising was a sign of "black sadness," he seems emotionally moved, less remote, and consequently more sympathetic.

The various opinions expressed in the play, and Smith's changing interpretations of the people who express those opinions, are appropriate given the confusion that is typically caused by urban unrest. It is difficult to analyze the two major outbreaks of violence that have occurred in Los Angeles during the last forty years; to agree on what happened and why; to understand the significance of these momentous events; and to gauge the effect that they had on society. People entertain wide-ranging, sometimes contradictory views. They express disagreement, doubt, and confusion. Were these anarchic riots or organized uprisings? Were the participants poor people who felt they had nothing to lose, or educated middle-class citizens? To what extent were they motivated by political, economic, and racial concerns? Were they bent on destruction, or did they merely seek to improve existing conditions?

In a poll that was taken immediately after the uprising, Los Angeles residents appeared personally divided as well as racially polarized. Seventy-one percent condemned the verdicts in the King beating case. However, almost exactly the same percentage of people believed that the violent response to the verdicts was wrong. Whites, who were less likely to have been touched by the violence, were more likely to feel pessimistic about the state of society. African Americans were more optimistic than whites and Latinos that "something good" would transpire.[42]

Like the uprising, Anna Deavere Smith's play was a disturbing as well as a healing experience. It provoked controversy among theatergoers when it premiered in Los Angeles. Yet it brought people together to relive the spectacle that had disrupted the city. Smith voiced contradictions, explored oppositions, and celebrated diversity while at the same searching for meaning and unity. In the process of "acting" she attempted to locate the "truth." She represented dozens of characters, some of whom doubted whether their fair representation in a racist society was possible. She let them speak for themselves, but she imposed interpretations on the material by arranging, editing, and substituting parts of the text.[43]

Accounts of the uprising were personal, sometimes confusing, but intent on capturing the chaos of the event and characterized by a feeling of urgency. Lynell George, with access to members of the inner-city community, documented the devastation in a series of personal essays and first-person interviews. Anna Deavere Smith performed the results of her research, making the audience reexperience the historical moment by witnessing the testimony of the uprising's participants. In 1992, *High Performance* magazine published a special edition, entitled "The Verdict and the Violence," in which several contributors, like Smith, interpreted rebellion as a form of dramatic expression. "Art and mobs require critical mass," argued Sam Eisenstein. In both cases, "[s]omething lines up the ions and a picture begins to take shape."[44] Adam Leipzig believed that theater needed to reflect the new shape of society by becoming more politically activist. He called for a "theater of insurrection," claiming that people were "tired of lots of talk and no action" (7).

As a result of the Watts Riot, a schism developed between the mainstream media and minority artists. Members of the Watts Writers' Workshop were perceived as sellouts because they accepted support from white Hollywood liberals, while contributors to Quincy Troupe's collection of poetry and groups such as the Watts Prophets were allegedly more committed to the overthrow of capitalism and white-run society. After the uprising, similar tensions appeared. When Anna Deavere Smith, a member of the East Coast theatrical world, was commissioned by the producer and director of the Mark Taper Forum to write a play about the recent events in Los Angeles, regional artists complained that the Taper had not given them the same opportunity.[45] Other writers, such as Lynell George, offered an insider's perspective on the local community and took pride in a lack of corporate funding or commercial support. Wanda Coleman, the guest editor of *High Performance* magazine, stated that the goal of the special issue was to include as many unheard "voices" as possible (1). The contributors volunteered their time and received no compensation (2–3).

The uprising was more complex than the riot, involving more participants from more walks of life, as well as more media. Responses to the uprising were correspondingly wide-ranging. A greater cross-section of society received representation in *Twilight: Los Angeles*. A more diverse sampling of artists appeared in print, too. Wanda Coleman wrote that the contributors to "The Violence and the Verdict" crossed the "boundaries of aesthetics, age, economics, ethnicity, gender, and sex-orientation" (1). African American artists, however, remained at the forefront of change, perhaps because the uprising, as well as the riot, had a greater impact on African Americans than on other minorities. A significant number of those who contributed to the Watts Writers' Workshop, Troupe's poetry anthology, and the Watts Prophets were men. But after the uprising, African American women such as Smith, George, and Coleman played greater roles. They represented more voices and presented more eclectic materials. The uprising, like the riot, not only created a dramatic disturbance in the urban environment; it caused a reconfiguration of the artistic landscape as well.

CHAPTER EIGHT

Women Rewriting History

In 1963, a young woman named Billy, living in a small Texas town, becomes pregnant with a married man's child. Desperate, she tries to raise money to pay for an illegal abortion. Then she learns that her mother's grave site has been sold to developers who plan to bulldoze the property. Remembering that her mother had been buried along with her jewelry, Billy goes to the cemetery before the grave is destroyed in order to retrieve what she considers her rightful inheritance. Her mother's friends, relatives, and former lesbian lover have similar plans. They race Billy to Arizona in a contest to recover the cache.

Getting Mother's Body (2003), by Suzan-Lori Parks, was published on the fortieth anniversary of Martin Luther King Jr.'s civil rights march on Washington. The African American characters travel across the West on the eve of this historic event. [1] They participate in a movement that has equally dramatic significance. What begins as a treasure hunt becomes an emotional, psychological, and spiritual pilgrimage. During the course of the novel, Billy falls in love, decides not to have an abortion, makes peace with the ghost of her mother, and comes to terms with her past. Other members of the expedition learn valuable lessons, undergo personal changes, or experience religious epiphanies. The journey, like the march, represents an important rite of passage for the novel's African American characters.

Parks not only situates her story in the tumultuous past but locates her characters in a region that is particularly volatile. In the East, hundreds of thousands of protesters prepare to march peacefully. Meanwhile, in a sparsely populated, remote part of the West, a small group of African Americans embarks on a more violent and hazardous quest. Some hope to get rich when they reach Arizona. Others want to abandon the search for treasure, head further west, and look for someplace to begin life anew. But the African American sojourners discover that they are unwelcome wherever they go. They are arrested for speeding, imprisoned, and harassed by white police (166–68). They pass a gas station with a sign that reads: "We don't serve NO niggers" (187). "This is 1963," says one of the characters. But it still "ain't safe you going [to Arizona] all by yrself" (121).

In addition to Parks, other African American writers have recently documented the regional historical struggles of racial minorities. In *Flyin' West* (1992), Pearl Cleage celebrates the Exodusters, former slaves who came to Kansas after the Civil War, hoping to farm. In *Paradise* (1997), Toni Morrison models her characters on African American pioneers in Oklahoma who founded segregated communities. In *Magic City* (1997), Jewell Parker Rhodes reexamines a Tulsa race riot in the early twentieth century. In *Parable of the Sower* (1993) and *Parable of the Talents* (1998), Octavia Butler writes about more recent civil disturbances. These authors find inspiration in actual events that have occurred in the West, both on rural frontiers and in modern urban environments.

Some recent fictional histories have been written by men. David Anthony Durham, in *Gabriel's Story* (2001), chronicles an African American cowboy's coming-of-age during a cross-country cattle drive. In *Oscar Wilde Discovers America* (2003), Louis Edwards describes the Englishman's tour, including his stopovers in several western locations, from the point of view of his Negro valet. Most recent fictional histories, however, have been written by women who present western history from the equally neglected perspectives of women and racial minorities.[2] Instead of exploring how the viewpoints of these two groups are essentially similar, the writers illustrate how these perspectives are frequently different, sometimes antagonistic, and often irreconcilable. In *Flyin' West*, the members of a racial matriarchy conspire to kill an African American man who threatens their farm. In *Paradise*, the African American elders in a small town wield their patriarchal authority over women in a nearby community. In *Magic City*, a misunderstanding between an African American man and a white woman causes a riot. However, in *Parable of the Sower* and *Parable of the Talents*, an African American woman attempts to overcome racial and gender differences by creating a multicultural western utopia.

In each work, characters journey across the American West in pursuit of a dream: to establish an ideal civilization where racism and sexism no longer exist. Each writer considers the same set of questions: What constitutes a perfect society? Is it possible for men and women, and members of different races, to coexist peacefully? Or must some people be sacrificed so that others may thrive? The West has often been imagined as a mythical promised land. But is it a free and accessible space, or an exclusive paradise, open to few? Is it a segregated or integrated community, or a rural or urban frontier?

In *Flyin' West*, Pearl Cleage pays tribute to the Exoduster movement, one of the most significant episodes in western American history. Beginning in the late 1870s, thousands of African Americans left the South in a mass migration or exodus, seeking freedom, cheap land, and economic opportunities on the western frontier. Cleage's characters settle in Nicodemus, Kansas, in actuality the largest and most successful of these experimental communities. Sophie Washington, a homesteader, lives with her friend, Fannie Dove. An elderly neighbor, Miss Leah, stays with the women while she recovers from a bout of ill health. Complications occur when Fannie's sister and brother-in-law, Minnie and Frank, come from England to visit. As a gift, Sophie and Fannie add Minnie's name to their deed. But after Frank loses at cards, he beats his wife and makes her sign over her share of the property to pay off his debt. To punish Frank for beating his wife and to prevent him from stealing their farm, the women kill Frank and bury his body, thereby securing their personal safety as well as saving their property.

Cleage has two ideological purposes, the first of which she acknowledges. In a note preceding the text of the play, she states that the Homestead Act of 1860 permitted Americans to settle parts of the western frontier. She adds that minority homesteaders pursued similar goals by participating in the "Exodus of 1879."[3] Cleage maintains that the African American exodus was not just an isolated racial phenomenon; it was part of a national pioneering trend in the late nineteenth century. In addition to suggesting that African Americans as well as whites participated in this widespread migration, she reminds her audience that women joined men in this enterprise. Benjamin "Pap" Singleton is the patriarchal figure usually credited with leading the African American exodus. Although women participated, they were not listed as "actors or speakers" in most historical sources.[4] Cleage redresses this imbalance by writing a play in which African American women take center stage. Although Nicodemus was named after a male African slave, it is represented here as a matriarchal society. Women warriors protect their "sisters" from a man who threatens their existence on the western frontier (9).

Cleage writes about a town that existed in the late nineteenth century. However, as a self-confessed "third-generation black nationalist and radical feminist" she imagines the town in such a way as to reflect her contemporary political views.[5] In the play, Nicodemus is a progressive society where ex-slaves govern themselves and women are equal to men. "I [didn't] want no white folks tellin' me what to do all day, and no man tellin' me what to do all night," says Sophie, explaining why she left Tennessee (21). By contrast, most of the leaders in the real Nicodemus were men, and one of the original founders was white.[6] Furthermore, most founders of African American western townships were "speculators aiming to profit by fostering a migrant population's quest for social equality and financial security."[7] Yet the characters suggest that the community has been hurt by commercial entrepreneurs. According to Sophie, women must "protect their land from speculators and save Nicodemus!" (52). In particular, they must guard against Frank, a gambler with a speculator's mentality. After losing at cards, he tries to sell the women's property out from under their feet. However, the women believe in preserving and sharing the land, not exploiting or selling it. Sophie and Fannie add Minnie's name to their deed. They help their elderly neighbor, Miss Leah, manage her farm. Although the real Nicodemus went bust eventually, at the end of the play the town seems secure. The women save the community by murdering Frank—a greedy, self-hating mulatto who tries to improve his economic and social position by selling to whites. In the last scene, Cleage presents an imaginary Nicodemus that is a proud, self-sustaining, proto-feminist, African American agricultural cooperative. "It's not paradise yet, but it can be," says Sophie (53).

One critic suggests that Cleage brings "us to grips with our American past and [helps] us understand and acknowledge its impact on our present conditions."[8] She stages a "historical community for another community," writing for an audience of contemporary African American women who share her political views.[9] Because her purpose is not to represent the real Nicodemus, Cleage makes no effort to be historically accurate. She creates an imaginary yet supposedly possible paradise in order to suggest that African American women can be economically independent and politically powerful. Yet troubling questions remain. How can a better society be achieved or maintained? In the play, the women escape oppression by leaving the South, going west, and purchasing land on the open frontier. Today, where in the United States can one find the same opportunities? The women kill Frank when he threatens to destroy their future. Is this the price they must pay in order to realize their dreams? Is it permissible to use violence if the cause is deemed just?

Nicodemus, Kansas, ca. 1885. (Kansas State Historical Society).

How long can a community without men, where there is no reproduction, continue to thrive? The women shut themselves off from the rest of the world. Is that healthy or feasible?

Toni Morrison addresses these questions in *Paradise*. Like Cleage, who writes about the Exoduster migration, Morrison was inspired by the story of pioneers in Oklahoma who founded African American townships at the turn of the century. [10] At least thirty such sites were established between 1889 and 1916. They were settled by African Americans who came west for one of three reasons: to escape racial oppression, to enhance their social status, or to improve their economic condition. Although they believed in voluntary segregation and self-help, according to scholars, "integration into the mainstream of American life constituted their ultimate goal." [11] Many early African American settlers hoped to earn white respect and acceptance by succeeding on the western frontier.

Like the fictional Nicodemus, which to some extent resembles its original namesake in Cleage's historical play, the towns in Morrison's novel share some of the characteristics of actual African American Oklahoma communities. Founded in 1890, the fictional town of Haven is a refuge for ex-slaves who were rejected by whites, Choctaw Indians, and other African Americans after leaving the South. Although the town initially thrives, during the course of the twentieth century its population gradually dwindles. Hoping to revitalize their dying community, the remaining members relocate and rename the town Ruby. Like Haven, Ruby is a segregated frontier oasis. Here, "if they stayed together, worked, prayed and defended together, they would never be . . . run out of town." [12] The people in Ruby are safe from persecution and free from the pangs of mortality. The town is an immortal paradise where no one has died (199). (In fact, several real African American Oklahoma communities claimed that their residents enjoyed greater longevity.) [13] In addition, the citizens of Ruby are sexually pure (217), like actual African American settlers who once advertised that they lived in a town where prostitution, adultery, and interracial and premarital sex were prohibited. [14]

Ruby is an exaggerated version of a racial utopia. The African Americans who live there resist integration, unlike some of their historical counterparts who considered mainstream social acceptance a desirable end. Ruby's residents also stay separate from the rest of their race because lighter-skinned African Americans originally rejected them and forced them to live by themselves. The elders go to violent extremes to make sure that Ruby remains racially and sexually pure. They murder the women who live in a former convent nearby, blaming them for a plague of disasters that afflict the com-

Western black townships were usually governed by men. Here, the Boley, Oklahoma, town council, ca. 1907–10. (Oklahoma Historical Society)

munity, including adultery, unwanted pregnancies, abortions, stillbirths, and miscarriages (11).

The women are executed in a fanatical effort to restore what was once a utopia. Morrison criticizes the decision, suggesting that the Convent, in spite of its flaws, is a relatively benign, racially integrated, matriarchal community, unlike Ruby, a racially segregated town where "the stallions" control "the mares and their foals" (150). Like Cleage, Morrison shows compassion for a group of women who are persecuted or ostracized by the rest of society. But Cleage believes that women are justified in using violence if necessary to safeguard their persons and property. Morrison scorns violence, which she associates with her male instead of her female characters. The elders in Ruby are farmers, ranchers, land speculators, and real estate entrepreneurs (82). One of them decides to attack the women at the Convent because he covets their property (277). Morrison attributes predatory, acquisitive, and territorial tendencies to a ruthlessly aggressive patriarchal society.[15]

The characters in Nicodemus and Ruby offer historical justifications for the way they behave. In *Flyin' West* the women perform a regular "ritual." They stand in a circle, hold hands, and remember why they "left Memphis and came West to be free." First, "crazy white men" made them feel unsafe in their homes. Then Pap Singleton came to their church and offered to lead them to a promised land on the Kansas frontier (41–42). The women renew their sense of purpose by recounting their journey. Holding hands in a circle, they demonstrate their group solidarity. Repeating the story at regular intervals gives them the strength to persevere until they can realize their dreams.

Like the women of Nicodemus, the citizens of Ruby participate in ceremonial rituals. They remember how the original founders were rejected by other Oklahoma residents in a story referred to as the Turning Away (13–14). In the Disallowing Pageant, in which they reenact this traumatic event, the residents yell at the immigrants: "Get on way from here! Get! There's no room for you!" (210). Cleage imagines that history can be inspirational. However, Morrison suggests that it can negatively affect those who live in the present. It causes the townspeople to turn inward, to remember the past, and to nurse former grievances. In the process of doing so, they become bitter and afraid of "Out There": "a void where random and organized evil erupted. . . . Out There where your children were sport, your women quarry. . . . Out There where every cluster of white men looked like a posse" (16). Because the townspeople see themselves as the chosen people and the rest of the world as their enemy, they feel justified in going to any extremes to ensure their survival.

The town, which has a sense of purpose and a specific identity, differs from the Convent, which changes missions throughout the nineteenth and twentieth centuries. Once a refuge for Catholics in a predominantly Protestant state, then the home of a local embezzler and a boarding school for Native American girls, the building, still known as the Convent, now houses a racially mixed assortment of women with different personalities, interests, and aims. Before they die, however, they unite as a group.[16] Connie, inspired by a mysterious god (283), tells the other women: "If you want to be here you do what I say" (262). She presides over cleansing rituals, and under her influence the women start having mystical dreams (285).

By the end of the novel, the Convent has begun to resemble the town. The women become inspired by a spiritual purpose, they exhibit clannish behavior, and they stage ceremonies that seem strange and hysterical. It is unclear to what extent Morrison means to compare and contrast the Convent with Ruby. When the novel was published, one reviewer called Paradise "heavy-handed, schematic," complaining that the contrasts between the town and the Convent were obvious.[17] Another described the men as one-dimensional macho oppressors, the women as victims, scapegoats, and martyrs.[18] But a third wondered if there was any real difference between the communities. Both the people in Ruby and the members of the Convent practiced rituals. Although Morrison seemed to prefer the rituals in the feminist Convent over those in the patriarchal community, the reviewer thought that rituals in general deluded participants by removing them from contact with reality. "Why cure a myth that you don't like by trying to substitute a myth that you do like? Why not eschew myth altogether?" asked the reviewer.[19] Such a solution, however, may not be possible. Unlike Cleage, Morrison questions whether paradise can exist in a nonmythic realm. Her earthbound communities are, like Ruby, exclusive, oppressive, and static, or, like the Convent, mortally doomed. At the end of the novel, the women, who may or may not have been killed by the people of Ruby, seem to exist in a nebulous state that is neither earthly nor heavenly.

While some writers examine communities on the rural frontier, others chronicle movements and gatherings in urban locales. Jewell Parker Rhodes sets her novel in Tulsa, Oklahoma, which was known as "Magic City" at the turn of the century because many companies associated with the oil industry had their headquarters there. Although Tulsa was a boomtown, it was also a site where race relations were tense. In 1921 a riot erupted when an African American man who shined shoes was accused of attacking a white woman who worked as an elevator operator in a local hotel. White vigilantes invaded Greenwood, the part of Tulsa where most African Americans lived, and over the course of several days they destroyed more than a thousand businesses, churches, and homes. They killed, and in some cases lynched, dozens of residents. Some African Americans fled the city. Others were imprisoned or sent to internment camps.[20]

In *Magic City*, a dramatic re-creation of one of the most deadly disturbances in the twentieth-century American West, Rhodes imagines the riot from the perspectives of two fictional characters: Mary Keane, the alleged victim, and Joe Samuels, the man who was falsely accused of assault (loosely based on the real Sarah Page and Rick Rowland). As their stories unfold, it becomes clear that Tulsa's reputation as a modern western paradise belies the social reality. Joe lives in Greenwood, a segregated, low-income minority neighborhood. After being arrested for rape, he spends time in prison. Throughout the novel he dreams of escaping to California, where he believes life will be better. Mary, like Joe, has few opportunities. "Oil men said Tulsa was a 'magic city.' A boom town. But her family had always been poor."[21] Her father has wasted his money fruitlessly scouting for oil. Now he owns a farm where she does most of the chores in addition to working full-time at the local hotel. She fantasizes about running away with a farmhand who subsequently rapes her, thus dashing her hopes for romance. She then makes matters worse by blaming Joe for the crime.

Greenwood, the black section of Tulsa, Oklahoma, after the riot in 1921. (Tulsa Historical Society)

Rhodes shows compassion for Mary, even though the white woman is responsible for inciting a riot. The author suggests that Mary is a victim, like Joe. Having been physically overworked by her father for years, then raped by a man in a moment of fear, Mary, on the day of the incident, is exhausted, confused, and hysterical. In the West, as Rhodes envisions it, women and racial minorities, along with natural resources, are exploited by whites. Just as white settlers once dispossessed Native Americans during the land rush in the late nineteenth century, so present-day whites have dispossessed Tulsa's African American residents. Joe's grandfather was one of the "sooners" who came to Oklahoma to farm, but a white investor purchased the grandfather's homestead for a small sum of money, then became rich drilling for oil (110). Like the Native Americans who were forced onto reservations, African American families such as the Samuels later moved into Greenwood, while whites on the other side of town continued to thrive. Now, in the early 1920s, the population is no longer divided between settlers and Native Americans but rather between urban Ku Klux Klan "cowboys" and "niggers" (223).

Rhodes seems more pessimistic than Cleage yet more optimistic than Morrison. Cleage situates her characters on the open frontier and imagines the West as a New World where African Americans can sow the seeds of a better society. Rhodes places her characters in a dystopic urban environment. She describes "Magic City" as a myth for minorities; the real Tulsa is a "Wild West" ruled by a lynch-mob mentality (138). Cleage demonstrates that African Americans can live separately and succeed on their own, whereas Rhodes shows that racial minorities are forced into segregated neighborhoods and denied economic and social equality. Morrison suggests that the citizens of Ruby are at fault for not welcoming others into their town. But the people of Greenwood accept Mary when she comes to apologize for having incited the riot (232). It is whites, not African Americans, who are quick to judge and condemn.

Like her counterparts, Rhodes writes about the persecution and marginalization of women and racial minorities in western communities. In addition, she sympathizes with all individuals who differ from the norm or who challenge the oppressive majority. One of the few people who befriend Mary and Joe is a lonely albino, a resident of Tulsa who is socially ostracized, repulsive to women, and "nearly invisible" (51). Another man, considered a hero in Greenwood, is a socialist Jew—a labor-union organizer—who is lynched, burned, and essentially crucified for attempting to "make things better" for racial minorities (54–55). Sometimes characters succeed in overcoming their differences. In doing so, they reaffirm the universality of the human condition. In one instance, Mary crosses the color line, goes to Greenwood, and visits Joe's home. Standing in the kitchen with Joe's sister, Hildy, she has a quiet epiphany. She realizes that she has done "the same living as Hildy— wiped a sink dry, washed greens, cooked with fatback boiling in the water. She'd dusted, hung out wash, folded linens, and nights, exhausted, she'd stared at the same moon. Like Joe, the other colored—Negro—men. Now she knew Greenwood was flowers, pastel homes with sweeping porches, and Hildy" (215).

Rhodes once said in an interview that "migration in and of itself doesn't solve problems. The literal moving across landscapes does not make you whole." [22] Joe shares this philosophy. After escaping from prison, returning to Greenwood, and surviving the riot, he has the chance to leave town. But he decides to stay, vowing to rebuild the community, to transform the burned slum into a real "Magic City" (265–68). According to Rhodes, what matters is a character's spiritual journey: Joe's realizing that instead of going to California he can find fulfillment at home, or Mary's discovering that she and Hildy share a common humanity. Rhodes, like Morrison, seems to believe in the possibility of symbolic rebirth. Like the women in *Paradise* who survive the massacre at the Convent by some miraculous means, reappearing as heavenly spirits in physical form, the people of Greenwood rise phoenix-like, out of the ashes, in order to resurrect their dream of a "glorious kingdom" on earth (266).

Octavia Butler, another contemporary female African American novelist, writes about the necessity of rebuilding communities. Unlike Rhodes, she considers geographic migration just as important as spiritual conversion or ideological change. In *Parable of the Sower*, the heroine, Lauren Olamina, lives in southern California at the beginning of the twenty-first century, at a time when crime is overwhelming the region. After a gang destroys the "unwalled little city" of Robledo, she leads a group of survivors to safety in the Pacific Northwest. [23] Lauren, a preacher's daughter, becomes a prophet of the postmodern age. During the journey she converts her followers to the Earthseed religion. According to Lauren, in a collection of verses called *Earthseed: The Books of the Living*, the one constant factor in human existence is change. People must adapt in order to survive in an unstable world. With civilization on the verge of extinction, it therefore becomes necessary to create a new social order. Earthseed, an agricultural settlement founded by Lauren and her group of disciples, becomes the first post-apocalyptic frontier development.

In the novel, the future resembles the present as well as the past. Writing in the mid-1990s, Butler portrays a twenty-first century that mirrors 1990s urban America. In Robledo, home invasions, street crimes, and riots are common occurrences. So are practices that existed in earlier centuries. Some people have barricaded themselves in their homes because they feel unsafe in society, while others have become "debt slaves," or poorly paid employees, of powerful business conglomerates (259). One character says: "This country has slipped back 200 years" (274). In response, Lauren organizes an exodus, a "modern underground railroad" (262), that offers the hostages a means of escape.

Like her counterparts, Butler has a historical consciousness. She compares events in the future to those in the past, such as slavery. Even the present (the mid-1990s) becomes part of the past when viewed from the perspective of the twenty-first century.[24] Butler's futuristic-historical novel has similarities with contemporary-historical works in western African American literature. Each work charts a physical and spiritual journey, from bondage to freedom. The journey culminates in the building or rebuilding of a special community, which is patriarchal or matriarchal in origin. The population is African American, or racially diverse (like Earthseed), but not exclusively white. At some point it becomes necessary to use violence to save this society. The people of Nicodemus and Ruby murder their enemies. The residents of Greenwood defend their neighborhood during the riot (194). Even Lauren kills in order to ensure the survival of the Earthseed experiment (164).

These works share certain characteristics, but they also differ in significant ways. Cleage and Rhodes believe in the perfectibility of human society. Nicodemus would be an ideal Garden of Eden except for the presence of Frank. By removing the snake—by killing the man who threatens their fall—the women restore Nicodemus to its prelapsarian state. In addition, Joe imagines that Greenwood will one day be resurrected as a "kingdom" for racial minorities in the American West (266). But others are less ambitious and more pessimistic than Joe. Morrison, for example, criticizes the concept of paradise. The townspeople of Ruby go to ruthless extremes to create a space that is strictly governed, exclusive, unchanging, and sterile.[25] Like Morrison, Butler suggests that people, despite their best intentions, are inherently flawed. Although the members of Earthseed create a better civilization, it is not a utopia. As Butler once said in an interview, "I don't believe that imperfect human beings can form a perfect society."[26]

Yet people can improve their lives if they are willing to change. The residents of Ruby refuse to interact with outsiders or keep pace with the times. They become isolated, fearful, diminished in number, and spiritually numb.

But Lauren survives by interacting with the surrounding community. In *Parable of the Sower* she recruits among the general population, enlists a diverse group of people, and organizes them successfully in a multicultural colony. In the sequel, *Parable of the Talents*, Earthseed is attacked and destroyed, and Lauren, as she writes philosophically in one of her verses, is once again "cast from paradise— / Into growth and destruction, / Into solitude and new community, / Into vast, ongoing / Change."[27] In this sequel, Butler narrates Lauren's continuing quest to pioneer a stable new world. The heroine gathers another flock of disciples; establishes a network of colonies, workshops, and colleges; receives national recognition as a political leader in the twenty-first century; and sees her first mission launched into space. But Lauren dies before she herself can explore the final frontier. The dream of a perfect society may not be achievable, and Lauren may not live to realize her goal, but she inspires a new generation of followers to achieve "the next stage of growth" (363).

Earthseed is an ideological movement, a continuing exploration of physical space, and a temporal, "ongoing" phenomenon. Butler and her counterparts set their works in the past or the future because they imagine the quest to create a perfect society as a process that occurs over time. The problems that afflict civilization (racism, sexism, violence, and crime) have their roots in the past. They extend into the present as well as the future. Cleage believes that her historical characters resonate with a contemporary audience of female African American radicals. Morrison chronicles a history that begins with the founding of Haven in the late nineteenth century and culminates in a fatal incident at the Convent in 1976. Rhodes and Butler, writing about the past and the future, are inspired by recent events in the American West. Their novels, which address urban riots and apocalyptic upheavals, must be read in relation to the 1992 uprising in Los Angeles and other recent civil disturbances.

History, however, does not always provide a key to understanding these works. Fannie writes a book "about all of us" women who were part of the exodus (17), but Miss Leah complains that "[e]verything can't be wrote down" (48). Histories only acknowledge the men who participated in nineteenth-century African American westward migration, so Cleage writes a play that features women in significant roles, just as Miss Leah whispers a promise into her granddaughter's ear: "I'm going to tell you about your mama and her mama and her gran'mama before that. . . . I'm gonna tell you all about 'em. Yes, I sure am" (86). Cleage respects the written word as well as the oral tradition. Fannie's book, Cleage's play, and the grandmother's stories present equally valid accounts of the African American woman's western experience.

Rhodes also uses her imagination to fill in historical gaps. She joins other artists and scholars in an effort to right (and re-write) the past.[28] One historian, in a recent account of the 1921 riot, "scrutinizes sources that have often been slighted: the observations of black journalists, reminiscences by African American witnesses, briefs written by black lawyers, and impressions penned by black poets."[29] Rhodes creates fictional characters who comment on the action instead. Some figures are ghosts, like the spirit of Harry Houdini. The legendary escape artist encourages Joe to break free from his shackles in prison (152). Many of the people in the novel live in a nightmarish world or believe in dreams that are more real than their concrete reality. Like Cleage, who stresses the importance of the oral tradition, Rhodes considers various ways of documenting human experience. Incorporating necromantic rituals "whereby the living communicate with the dead," African dances, Negro spirituals, and rhythm and blues, Rhodes, in the words of one critic, "deconstruct[s] the conventional format of the historical novel."[30]

Like her counterparts, Morrison experiments with methods of representation. Instead of tracing the history of Haven and Ruby in a chronological fashion, she moves backward and forward in time. Instead of choosing a single narrator to tell a unified story, she allows various characters to interpret events. For Morrison, westward migration is not a simple teleological journey, culminating successfully in the settlement of the U.S. frontier. It is a complicated enterprise, unfolding in nonlinear time, resulting in tragedy. Ruby's unofficial historian offers several "editions" of the truth instead of a reliable account of what happens at the end of the novel.[31] Rumor has it that the men went to the Convent, but the women "took other shapes and disappeared into thin air." According to another source, the men evicted the residents, who "took off" in their car. Or, as the historian suspects, the men murdered their victims and then denied having committed the crime (296–97).

In literature, writers and readers can give their imaginations free rein. Morrison states that one of the women in the Convent is white. But she allows readers to speculate about which one it is. She presents various stories, different interpretations of confusing events, and an unclear conclusion. Unlike the historian, Morrison searches for no explanations, offers few facts, and privileges no single truth. Butler also explores alternative possibilities and imaginary worlds in her literature. She once said in an interview that she chose to write science fiction because it was "the freest genre" she knew.[32] In her novels, she envisions future societies where African American women often play significant roles. She and other contemporary female African American writers participate in a similar quest. They strive to imagine a better world that includes women and racial minorities. The journey by these writers begins on the early frontier and ends with the foundation of a future civilization among the celestial stars.

Notes

Introduction

1. I use the term "African American" throughout most of this study, realizing that the choice may not please everyone. "African American" is a contemporary term that may seem anachronistic when used to describe people who lived in an earlier time. To some, "black" might seem like a more appropriate term. But as I discovered in the course of writing this book, some readers believe that "black" has pejorative connotations, although others do not. Therefore I use "African American" as a neutral term. I use "black" and "white" as oppositional terms, in some cases, and I use "black" when there is no other choice, as in the accepted phrase "the black nationalist movement." In the same spirit of accuracy, I use the term "Negro" as it was used to refer to such movements as "the New Negro Renaissance." Other words and phrases, used by writers, speakers, or fictional characters, some of them acceptable, some of them clearly offensive, occasionally appear in this study and are marked as quotations.

2. Guy Logsdon, "Rodeo," in *The Reader's Encyclopedia of the American West*, ed. Howard R. Lamar (New York: Harper and Row, 1977), 1028.

3. Jim Bob Tinsley, *He Was Singin' This Song: A Collection of Forty-eight Traditional Songs of the American Cowboy, with Words, Music, Pictures, and Stories* (Orlando: University Presses of Florida, 1981), 192.

4. Mark Arax, "The Black Okies: A Lost Tribe's Journey to a Land of Broken Promises," *Los Angeles Times*, August 25, 2002, A1, A24–25.

5. Frederick Jackson Turner, "The Significance of the Frontier in American History," in *Rereading Frederick Jackson Turner*, ed. John Mack Faragher (1893; repr., New York: Henry Holt, 1995), 48. Subsequent references to this edition appear in the text.

6. For information about the number of people of African origin residing in the region from the early sixteenth through the late nineteenth century, see Quintard Taylor, *In Search of the Racial Frontier: African Americans in the American West, 1528–1990* (1998; repr., New York: Norton, 1999), 33, 76, 104, 135.

7. Samira Kawash suggests that "the color line metaphorizes racial distinction as spatial division. Historically, the idea of race has a long-standing relation to the idea of geography" (*Dislocating the Color Line: Identity, Hybridity, and Singularity in*

African-American Literature [Stanford: Stanford University Press, 1997], 8). I suggest that the frontier line works in a similar way.

8. Turner, "Significance of the Frontier," 32–33, 36–38.

9. Pleasant published a brief summary of her life in a small journal in 1901. For further information about this important historical figure, see Lynn M. Hudson, "Mining a Mythic Past: The History of Mary Ellen Pleasant," in *African American Women Confront the West, 1600–2000*, ed. Quintard Taylor and Shirley Ann Wilson Moore (Norman: University of Oklahoma Press, 2003), 56–70.

10. For a penetrating analysis of Turner's use of metaphorical language and imagery, see William R. Handley, *Marriage, Violence, and the Nation in the American Literary West* (Cambridge: University of Cambridge Press, 2002), 43–66.

11. Some of the seminal works that have contributed to a redefinition of western American literature include Kenneth Lincoln, *Native American Renaissance* (Berkeley: University of California Press, 1983); Ramón Saldívar, *Chicano Narrative: The Dialectics of Difference* (Madison: University of Wisconsin Press, 1990); Moses Rischin and Josh Livingston, eds., *Jews of the American West* (Detroit: Wayne State University Press, 1991); Anne Goldman, *Continental Divides: Revisioning American Literature* (New York: Palgrave, 2000); and Krista Comer, *Landscapes of the New West: Gender and Geography in Contemporary Women's Writings* (Chapel Hill: University of North Carolina Press, 1999).

12. Exceptions include John Ford's film *Sergeant Rutledge* (1960) and William Eastlake's novel *The Bronc People* (1958).

1. Beckwourth's Pass

1. The memoirs, however, were not published until 1973. See Martin Cole and Henry Welcome, eds., *Don Pío Pico's Historical Narrative* (Glendale: Arthur H. Clark, 1973).

2. According to Quintard Taylor, *In Search of the Racial Frontier: African Americans in the American West, 1528–1990* (1998; repr., New York: Norton, 1999), 47.

3. James P. Beckwourth, *The Life and Adventures of James P. Beckwourth, Mountaineer, Scout, and Pioneer, and Chief of the Crow Nation of Indians, Written from His Own Dictation by T. D. Bonner* (1856; repr., Lincoln: University of Nebraska Press, 1981), 14. Subsequent references to this edition appear in the text.

4. Gordon B. Dodds, "Beckwourth, Jim [James Pearson]," in *The Reader's Encyclopedia of the American West*, ed. Howard R. Lamar (New York: Harper and Row, 1977), 85.

5. Based on population statistics in these territories and states in the early and mid-nineteenth century. See Taylor, *Racial Frontier*, 54, 76, 81, 94.

6. The first U.S. census conducted in Montana Territory listed 183 "negroes" in 1870. See Taylor, *Racial Frontier*, 104.

7. For information on Rose see Taylor, *Racial Frontier*, 48–50; Dodds, "Rose, Edward," in Lamar, *Reader's Encyclopedia of the American West*, 1046–47; Hiram Martin Chittenden, *The American Fur Trade of the Far West*, 2 vols. (1902; repr., Lincoln: University of Nebraska Press, 1986), 2:675–79; and William Loren Katz, *The Black West* (1987; repr., New York: Touchstone, 1996), 26–28. There is little information on Harris, except on the Internet. See "Black Pioneers" (www.endoftheoregontrail.org /blackbios.html); "Applegate Trail: The Run of the South Road Expedition" (www. webtrail.com/applegate/biography.html); and "Moses Harris" (www.usgennet.org /alhnerns/ahorclak/harris.html).

8. Quoted in Katz, *The Black West*, 24.

9. Lawrence Cortesi, *Jim Beckwourth: Explorer-Patriot of the Rockies* (New York: Criterion, 1971). The book is a novelization of Beckwourth's autobiography, intended for adolescent readers.

10. Emerson Bennett, *The Prairie Flower; or, Adventures in the Far West* (1850; repr., Cincinnati: James, 1853), 27.

11. For a discussion of the ways in which the Crow tribe benefited from trade with American fur companies and with African American representatives of those companies, see Chittenden, *American Fur Trade*, 1:3–17; Frederick E. Hoxie, *The Crow* (New York: Chelsea, 1989), 54; Hoxie, *Parading through History: The Making of the Crow Nation in America, 1805–1935* (Cambridge: Cambridge University Press, 1995), 65–70; and Keith Algers, *The Crow and the Eagle: A Tribal History from Lewis and Clark to Custer* (Caldwell: Caxton, 1993), 49–50, 69–70.

12. Robert H. Louie, *The Crow Indians* (1935; repr., New York: Holt, Rinehart and Winston, 1956), 215.

13. Louie, *The Crow Indians*, 215.

14. Francis Parkman Jr., *The Oregon Trail* (1849; repr., New York: Penguin, 1983), 178.

15. Bernard DeVoto cites this information in the introduction to a later edition of Beckwourth's autobiography. See *The Life and Adventures* (New York: Knopf, 1931), xix.

16. Lewis Garrard, *Wah-to-yah and the Taos Trail, or Prairie Travel and Scalp Dances, with a Look at Los Rancheros from Muleback and the Rocky Mountain Campfire* (1850; repr., Norman: University of Oklahoma Press, 1955), 236–37.

17. Elinor Wilson questions whether Beckwourth's "Negroid" characteristics would have been visible (*Jim Beckwourth: Black Mountain Man and Chief of the Crows* [Norman: University of Oklahoma Press, 1972], 18). Other scholars debate the exact nature of Beckwourth's ancestry. Hubert Howe Bancroft claims that Beckwourth's mother was a full-blooded "negro" (*The Works of Hubert Howe Bancroft*, vol. 25 [San Francisco: History, 1890], 352 n. 15). Charles G. Leland, who edited the 1892 English edition of the autobiography, and DeVoto, who edited the 1931 American edition, speculate that Beckwourth's mother was one-quarter "black" (Leland, "Preface to the New English Edition," in Beckwourth, *The Life and Adventures* [London: Unwin, 1892], 9; DeVoto, "Introduction," xxxi). Harvey L. Carter believes that Beckwourth was part "white," part "black," and part "Indian" (introduction to *Trappers of the Far West: Sixteen Biographical Sketches*, ed. LeRoy R. Hafen [Lincoln: University of Nebraska Press, 1983], xii).

18. For information about Bonner and his collaboration with Beckwourth on the autobiography see Raymond Friday Locke, *James Beckwourth: Mountain Man* (Los Angeles: Melrose Square, 1995), 171–72; and Louise Amelia Knapp Smith Clappe, *The Shirley Letters, Being Letters Written in 1851–52 from the California Mines*, ed. Carl I. Wheat, vol. 1 (1854–55; repr., San Francisco: Grabhorn, 1933), 147.

19. Noreen Groover Lape, *West of the Border: The Multicultural Literature of the Western American Frontiers* (Athens: Ohio University Press, 2000), 25.

20. I am indebted to Katz, who first made this point, most convincingly, by juxtaposing a photograph of Beckwourth with an illustration that makes Beckwourth appear to be white (*The Black West*, 32–33). I have also juxtaposed a photograph and an illustration of Beckwourth, but in addition I analyze other illustrations in the autobiography that show Beckwourth assuming a range of identities.

21. Washington Irving, *The Adventures of Captain Bonneville, U.S.A., in the Rocky*

Mountains and the Far West, ed. Edgeley W. Todd (1837; repr., Norman: University of Oklahoma Press, 1986), 69.

22. George Frederic Ruxton, *Ruxton of the Rockies: Autobiographical Writings by the Author of "Adventures in Mexico and the Rocky Mountains" and "Life in the Far West,"* ed. LeRoy R. Hafen (1950; repr., Norman: University of Oklahoma Press, 1982), 227–28.

23. Captain Mayne Reid, *The Scalp Hunter* (1856; repr., London: Routledge, n.d.), 119–20, 129–30.

24. See George Frederic Ruxton, *Life in the Far West* (New York: Harper, 1849), 16; Garrard, *Wah-to-yah and the Taos Trail*, 191, 217; and Bennett, *The Prairie Flower*, 30, 32–34. In *The Mountain Man Vernacular: Its Historical Roots, Its Linguistic Nature, and Its Literary Uses* (New York: Peter Lang, 1985), Richard C. Poulson fails to mention that the terms "mountain man," "niggur," and "coon" are interrelated.

2. The Pioneering Adventures of Oscar Micheaux

1. Joseph A. Young, *Black Novelist as White Racist: The Myth of Inferiority in the Novels of Oscar Micheaux* (New York: Greenwood, 1989), 65.

2. Donald Bogle, *Toms, Coons, Mulattoes, Mammies, and Bucks: An Interpretive History of Blacks in American Films* (1973; repr., New York: Continuum, 1991), 114–16. For similar critiques of Micheaux's films see John Kisch and Edward Mapp, *A Separate Cinema: Fifty Years of Black-Cast Posters* (New York: Farrar, Strauss and Giroux, 1992), xvii; and Stephen F. Soitos, "Micheaux, Oscar," in *The Oxford Companion to African American Literature*, ed. William Andrews, Frances Smith Foster, and Trudier Harris (New York: Oxford University Press, 1997), 495.

Unlike Bogle, J. Ronald Green argues that Micheaux represented the African American "middle class," not the "bourgeoisie." He discusses the pejorative ideological associations that cling to the latter term, reminding readers that most of Micheaux's contemporary audience would have fallen into the first class of viewers. See *Straight Lick: The Cinema of Oscar Micheaux* (Bloomington: Indiana University Press, 2000), 31–40.

3. Critics who have contributed to the rehabilitation of Micheaux's reputation include bell hooks, "Micheaux: Celebrating Blackness," *Black American Literature and Film* 25 (summer 1991): 351–60; Mark A. Reid, *Redefining Black Film* (Berkeley: University of California Press, 1993), 11–14; Jane Gaines and Charlene Regester, "Micheaux, Oscar," in *Encyclopedia of African-American Culture and History*, ed. Jack Salzman et al., vol. 4 (New York: Macmillan, 1996), 1774; Pearl Bowser and Louise Spence, "Identity and Betrayal: *The Symbol of the Unconquered* and Oscar Micheaux's 'Biographical Legend,'" in *The Birth of Whiteness: Race and the Emergence of U.S. Cinema*, ed. Daniel Bernardi (New Brunswick NJ: Rutgers University Press, 1996), 57, 71–72; Green, *Straight Lick*, xv, 34–35; Susan Gillman, "Micheaux's Chestnutt," PMLA 114 (October 1999): 1080–88; and Soitos, "Micheaux, Oscar," 495.

4. *Midnight Ramble: The Story of the Black Film Industry*, directed by Bestor Cram and Pearl Bowser (WGBH: Boston, 1994).

5. Pearl Bowser and Louise Spence, *Writing Himself into History: Oscar Micheaux, His Silent Films, and His Audience* (New Brunswick NJ: Rutgers University Press, 2000), 212.

6. Young, *Black Novelist as White Racist*, 10, ix.

7. Robert Bone, *The Negro Novel in America*, rev. ed. (1958; New Haven: Yale University Press, 1965), 49.

8. I agree with M. K. Johnson, who argues in "'Stranger in a Strange Land': An African American Response to the Frontier Tradition in Oscar Micheaux's *The Conquest: The Story of a Negro Pioneer*" (*Western American Literature* 33 [fall 1998]: 249) that *The Conquest* critiques "the myth of the West and the myth of racial uplift." However, Johnson fails to consider subsequent works, such as *The Homesteader* and *The Wind from Nowhere*, in which Micheaux seems, at least on the surface, to revise his critique. I would like to acknowledge Johnson's insights while at the same time extending the author's project by considering Micheaux's three novels together and by complicating the thesis that Johnson sets forth.

In "Reclaiming the Frontier: Oscar Micheaux as Black Turnerian" (*African American Review* 36 [fall 2002]: 357–81), Dan Moos claims that Micheaux was inspired by Frederick Jackson Turner, who believed that the West offered homesteaders a chance for success, and by Booker T. Washington, who provided African Americans with the tools for achieving success. Moos maintains that Micheaux never lost faith in the West, whereas I claim that he did. As a result, Moos and I differ in our interpretations of the second and third works in Micheaux's homesteading trilogy.

9. For a fuller account of this conflict as it appears in Garland's work, see Donald Pizer, *Hamlin Garland's Early Work and Career* (Berkeley: University of California Press, 1960), 2, 38–44.

10. Bowser and Spence, *Writing Himself into History*, 38.

11. Frederick Jackson Turner, "The Significance of the Frontier in American History," in *Rereading Frederick Jackson Turner*, ed. John Mack Faragher (1893; repr., New York: Henry Holt, 1995), 47.

12. Houston A. Baker Jr., *Long Black Song: Essays in Black American Literature and Culture* (Charlottesville: University Press of Virginia, 1972), 2.

13. The impression one gets in reading the trilogy, that Micheaux (or his fictional counterpart) was the only African American homesteader in the region, has been contradicted by anecdotal and historical evidence. In the late nineteenth century, Reverend John C. Coleman, an official in the African American Methodist Episcopal Church and the president of the Northwestern Homestead Movement, "championed agriculture because this was the best strategy to help [black] homesteaders obtain a 'permanent footing' and an 'independent existence.'" Whereas in 1870 there were only 94 African Americans out of 13,000 people in South Dakota Territory, ten years later there were almost 400 more. Henry Lewis Suggs, "The Black Press, Black Migration, and the Transplantation of Culture on the Great Plains of South Dakota, 1865–1985," in *The Black Press in the Middle West, 1865–1985*, ed. Suggs (Westport CT: Greenwood, 1996), 297–99.

In *Oscar Micheaux: A Biography* (Rapid City SD: Dakota West Books, 1999), Betti Carol VanEpps-Taylor writes that Micheaux "could hardly have resided in South Dakota during the homestead period without being aware of the large Sully County Colored Colony thriving not far to the northeast. Begun in Fairbanks Township on the banks of the Missouri River northeast of Pierre in 1884 by Norval Blair, an ex-slave from northern Illinois, and his adult children, it had prospered. During the homestead boom of 1905–1910, a number of African American families tried their luck in western Sully County, and by the 1910 census, the immediate area was home to at least 13 black homesteading families." In addition, the "sizeable African American Yankton colony, begun in the 1880s," was still thriving in the southeast corner of the state, and there were smaller African American homesteading communities in nearby northwestern Nebraska (53–54). Ted Blakely, an African American and a historian from Yankton, whose ancestors homesteaded there in the early twentieth century, has continued to challenge "Micheaux's notion of being the only African American in the area" (Bowser and Spence, *Writing Himself into History*, 222).

For a history of African American homesteading in the late nineteenth and early twentieth centuries, focusing on individual farmers as well as on minority rural communities, see Quintard Taylor, *In Search of the Racial Frontier: African Americans in the American West, 1528–1990* (New York: Norton, 1998), 143–56; and William Loren Katz, *The Black West* (1987; repr., New York: Touchstone, 1996), 167–98.

14. No one knows the extent to which Micheaux, in his first work, mixed fiction with fact. While some of the author's descendants believe that there was such a woman "who caught his eye and perhaps broke his heart," investigators caution that Micheaux may have invented this ill-fated love affair (VanEpps-Taylor, *Oscar Micheaux*, 57). Bowser and Spence refer to the semiautobiographical heroes who appear in most of Micheaux's novels and films as "biographical legends" (*Writing Himself into History*, 5). Green, however, contends that *The Conquest*, in particular, is "fundamentally trustworthy as autobiography and as history" (*Straight Lick*, xi).

15. Oscar Micheaux, *The Conquest: The Story of a Negro Pioneer* (1913; repr., Lincoln: University of Nebraska Press, 1994), 199. Subsequent references to this edition appear in the text.

16. For histories of the Rosebud Reservation in South Dakota and for accounts of the Sioux in particular, see Doane Robinson, *A History of the Dakota or Sioux Indians* (1904; repr., Minneapolis: Ross and Haines, 1956), 459–69; Robert M. Utley, *The Last Days of the Sioux Nation* (New Haven: Yale University Press, 1963), 200–230; and Herbert S. Schell, *History of South Dakota* (Lincoln: University of Nebraska Press, 1968), 133–34, 253–55, 320–32.

17. Johnson, "'Stranger in a Strange Land,'" 245.

18. Johnson, "'Stranger in a Strange Land,'" 248.

19. J. Lee Greene, *Blacks in Eden: The African American Novel's First Century* (Charlottesville: University Press of Virginia, 1996), 6.

20. Oscar Micheaux, *The Homesteader: A Novel* (1917; repr., Lincoln: University of Nebraska Press, 1994), 163. Subsequent references to this edition appear in the text.

21. Greene, *Blacks in Eden*, 168.

22. Oscar Micheaux, *The Wind from Nowhere* (New York: Book Supply Co., 1944), 384–85. Subsequent references to this edition appear in the text.

23. In race melodramas in general, and in one of Micheaux's films in particular, Jane Gaines detects the presence of "racial themes which reorganize the world in such a way that black heritage is rewarded over white paternity; [these works] are schematic renunciations of the prevailing order of things in white American society where, historically, the discovery of black blood meant sudden reversal of fortune, social exclusion, or banishment" ("*The Scar of Shame*: Skin Color and Caste in Black Silent Melodrama," in *Imitations of Life: A Reader on Film and Television Melodrama*, ed. Marcia Landy [Detroit: Wayne State University Press, 1991], 331). The same theme appears in the last two novels in Micheaux's western trilogy.

24. David Grimsted, "Vigilante Chronicle: The Politics of Melodrama Brought to Life," in *Melodrama: Stage, Picture, Screen*, ed. Jacky Bratton, Jim Cook, and Christine Gledhill (London: British Film Institute, 1994), 200.

25. Bernard W. Bell, *The Afro-American Novel and Its Traditions* (Amherst: University of Massachusetts Press, 1987), 33–36. Also see Bone, *Negro Novel in America*, 21–25.

26. Bowser and Spence, *Writing Himself into History*, 24.

27. Recently, commentators have begun to address the passage in *The Conquest* in which Micheaux's narrator defends the practice of "knocking down" passengers (VanEpps-Taylor, *Oscar Micheaux*, 25; Bower and Spence, *Writing Himself into History*, 6–7).

28. For an excellent history of the profession, an analysis of the work culture, and interviews with individual porters, see Jack Santino, *Miles of Smiles, Years of Struggle: Stories of Black Pullman Porters* (Urbana: University of Illinois Press, 1989).

29. Schell, *History of South Dakota*, 176.

30. Janis Hebert, "Oscar Micheaux: Black Pioneer," *South Dakota Review* 11 (1973): 63; see also John Milton, *South Dakota: A Bicentennial History* (New York: Norton, 1977), 100.

31. Bowser and Spence, *Writing Himself into History*, 8.

32. In discussing the films of Micheaux, Thomas Cripps writes that in "only a few cases" do "blacks succeed after working hard." Because they lack equal job opportunities, they tend not to believe in "the puritanical work ethic," relying on luck, "the quick score," and "bonanzas" to compensate for economic injustices (" 'Race Movies' as Voices of the Black Bourgeoisie: *The Scar of Shame*," in *Representing Blackness: Issues in Film and Video*, ed. Valerie Smith [New Brunswick NJ: Rutgers University Press, 1997], 50). In his pioneer trilogy, although Micheaux advocates farming or working hard, his heroes triumph by other means (the melodramatic death of a rival, rescue by a woman on horseback, the discovery of valuable ore). In *The Conquest*, the amount of attention devoted to speculative real estate ventures and plans for getting rich quickly foreshadows the reliance on plot and the importance of scheming in Micheaux's later novels.

33. VanEpps-Taylor, *Oscar Micheaux*, 76–77.

34. Young claims that the "structural divisions" in *The Conquest* are signs of Micheaux's flaws as a novelist (*Black Novelist as White Racist*, 75). Arlene A. Elder, however, believes that they signify "Micheaux's self-conscious emotional division between personal ambition, marked by intense frontier individualism, and his hope of being not only a racial representative but a leader of his people and a model for them" (*The "Hindered Hand": Cultural Implications of Early African American Fiction* [Westport CT: Greenwood, 1978], 299). Johnson agrees, describing the first half of the novel as "an account of a determined individual conquering his environment," in the tradition of western American literature, and comparing the second half to earlier works in African American fiction dealing with manhood and race (" 'Stranger in a Strange Land,' " 232).

35. Jane Gaines, "Fire and Desire: Race, Melodrama, and Oscar Micheaux," in *Black American Cinema: Aesthetics and Spectatorship*, ed. Manthia Diawara (New York: Routledge, 1993), 66. See also Green, who devotes an entire chapter to a discussion of "two-ness" in Micheaux's (primarily non-western) films (*Straight Lick*, 41–56).

36. Henry T. Sampson, *Blacks in Black and White: A Source Book on Black Films* (Lanham MD: Scarecrow, 1995), 149; Daniel J. Leab, *From Sambo to Superspade: The Black Experience in Motion Pictures* (Boston: Houghton Mifflin, 1975), 75.

37. Bogle, *Interpretive History*, 110.

38. Quoted in Bowser and Spence, *Writing Himself into History*, 12.

39. Henry Louis Gates Jr., *The Signifying Monkey: A Theory of Afro-American Criticism* (New York: Oxford University Press, 1988), 129.

40. See Bowser and Spence, who discuss the use of dialects and folk idioms in Micheaux's novels and films (*Writing Himself into History*, 206).

41. Eventually, Devereaux marries Agnes when he discovers that she has an African American mother. Micheaux allows the reader to speculate regarding whether Agnes's African ancestry indeed enhances her worth as a heroine, noting early in the novel that Agnes's half brothers are pure white but also "half-witted" (*The Homesteader*, 14).

42. Quoted in Sampson, *Blacks in Black and White*, 158.

43. Oscar Micheaux to the Lincoln Motion Picture Company, June 25, 1918, George P. Johnson Collection, UCLA.

44. VanEpps-Taylor, *Oscar Micheaux*, 97–100.

45. VanEpps-Taylor, *Oscar Micheaux*, 125–26.

46. *The Exile*, directed by Oscar Micheaux, with Eunice Brooks, Nora Newsome, and Stanley Morrell (1931).

47. Leab, *From Sambo to Superspade*, 190.

48. Young, *Black Novelist as White Racist*, 70.

49. VanEpps-Taylor, *Oscar Micheaux*, 7; Leab, *From Sambo to Superspade*, 166.

50. For contemporary reviews of the film see Thomas Cripps, *Making Movies Black: The Hollywood Message Movie from World War II to the Civil Rights Era* (New York: Oxford University Press, 1993), 36, 104.

51. Cathy Caruth, *Unclaimed Experience: Trauma, Narrative, and History* (Baltimore: Johns Hopkins University Press, 1996), 7. Kalí Tal also distinguishes between event and remembrance, noting that the "process of translation of traumatic experience into text is best understood in terms of . . . the dual semiotic and semantic function of language." In narratives dealing with trauma, as in all linguistic accounts, there is a gap between the sign and its referent (*Worlds of Hurt: Reading the Literatures of Trauma* [Cambridge: Cambridge University Press, 1996], 15).

52. Caruth, *Unclaimed Experience*, 2–7.

3. Slavery, Secession, and Uncivil War

1. The nineteenth-century pattern of African American northern migration has been extensively chronicled. See, e.g., Carter G. Woodson, *A Century of Negro Migration* (Washington DC: Association for the Study of Negro Life and History, 1918); Leon F. Litwack, *North of Slavery: The Negro in the Free States, 1790–1860* (Chicago: University of Illinois Press, 1961); Carole Marks, *Farewell—We're Gone: The Great Black Migration* (Bloomington: Indiana University Press, 1989); and Nicholas Lemann, *The Promised Land: The Great Black Migration and How It Changed America* (New York: Knopf, 1991). For a discussion of literary representations of the migration experience, see Farah Jasmine Griffin, *"Who Set You Flowin'?" The African-American Migration Narrative* (New York: Oxford University Press, 1995).

2. For a history of nineteenth-century African American emigration movements, their founders, and leaders, see William H. Pease and Jane H. Pease, *Black Utopia: Negro Communal Experiments in America* (Madison: State Historical Society of Wisconsin, 1963), 3, 8–9; Howard Brotz, introduction to *Negro Social and Political Thought, 1850–1920*, ed. Brotz (New York: Basic Books, 1966), 1–33; Edwin S. Redkey, *Black Exodus: Black Nationalist and Back-to-Africa Movements, 1890–1910* (New Haven: Yale University Press, 1969); George M. Fredrickson, *The Black Image in the White Mind: The Debate on Afro-American Character and Destiny, 1817–1914* (New York: Harper and Row, 1971), 130–64; Sterling Stuckey, introduction to *The Ideological Origins of Black Nationalism*, ed. Stuckey (Boston: Beacon, 1972), 1–29; Wilson Jeremiah Moses, *The Golden Age of Black Nationalism, 1850–1925* (New York: Oxford University Press, 1978), 19–26; Philip S. Foner, *History of Black Americans:*

From the Compromise of 1850 to the End of the Civil War, vol. 3 (Westport CT: Greenwood, 1983), 126–81; and Gary Ashwill, "Emigration," in *The Oxford Companion to African American Literature*, ed. William Andrews, Frances Smith Foster, and Trudier Harris (New York: Oxford University Press, 1997), 256.

3. Oscar Micheaux, *The Conquest: The Story of a Negro Pioneer* (1913; repr., Lincoln: University of Nebraska Press, 1994), 227.

4. Works devoted to the study of African Americans in specific western professions include Philip Durham and Everett L. Jones, *The Negro Cowboys* (1965; repr., Lincoln: University of Nebraska Press, 1983); William H. Leckie, *The Buffalo Soldiers: A Narrative of the Negro Cavalry in the West* (Norman: University of Oklahoma Press, 1967); and Rudolph M. Lapp, *Blacks in Gold Rush California* (New Haven: Yale University Press, 1977). For a survey of various professional roles that African Americans played in the region during this period, see William Loren Katz, *The Black West* (1987; repr., New York: Touchstone, 1996); and Quintard Taylor, *In Search of the Racial Frontier: African Americans in the American West, 1528–1990* (New York: Norton, 1998).

5. The Exoduster movement has been treated most thoroughly by Nell Irvin Painter, *Exodusters: Black Migration to Kansas after Reconstruction* (1977; repr., New York: Norton, 1992); and by Robert G. Athearn, *In Search of Canaan: Black Migration to Kansas, 1879–80* (Lawrence: Regents Press of Kansas, 1978). The following works cover African American migration to Oklahoma in the late nineteenth and early twentieth centuries: August Meier, *Negro Thought in America, 1880–1915: Racial Ideologies in the Age of Booker T. Washington* (Ann Arbor: University of Michigan Press, 1963), 63; Redkey, *Black Exodus*, 99–151; Katz, *The Black West*, 245–64; and Taylor, *Racial Frontier*, 143–51. For case histories of three African American communities in Kansas and Oklahoma, see Kenneth Marvin Hamilton, *Black Towns and Profit: Promotion and Development in the Trans-Appalachian West, 1877–1915* (Urbana: University of Illinois Press, 1991), 5–42, 99–119, 120–37.

6. For accounts of legislation aimed at blacks, and for problems with racism in east Texas specifically, see Weston Joseph McConnell, *Social Cleavages in Texas: A Study of the Proposed Division of the State* (New York: Columbia University Press, 1925), 156–70; Lawrence D. Rice, *The Negro in Texas, 1874–1900* (Baton Rouge: Louisiana State University Press, 1971), 3–5, 13–33; and Arnoldo De León, "Region and Ethnicity: Topographical Identification in Texas," in *Many Wests: Place, Culture, and Regional Identity*, ed. David M. Wrobel and Michael C. Steiner (Lawrence: University of Kansas Press, 1997), 266.

7. James M. SoRelle, "The 'Waco Horror': The Lynching of Jesse Washington," *Southwestern Historical Quarterly* 86 (April 1983): 519.

8. Eugene H. Berwanger, *The Frontier against Slavery: Western Anti-Negro Prejudice and the Slavery Extension Controversy* (Urbana: University of Illinois Press, 1967), 5.

9. "Kansas versus New Jersey," *Colored American Magazine* 2 (February 1901): 314–15.

10. Peter Brooks lists the definitions of "plot": the events that make up a narrative; a "secret plan to accomplish a hostile or illegal purpose"; and a measured area or "small piece of ground" (*Reading for the Plot: Design and Intention in Narrative* [New York: Knopf, 1984], 11–12). The plot of *Imperium in Imperio* illustrates all three definitions. The action centers on a plot, or covert operation, which seeks to establish African American nationalists on their own "piece of ground."

11. Elizabeth Ammons, "Afterword: *Winona*, Bakhtin, and Hopkins in the Twenty-

first Century," in *The Unruly Voice: Rediscovering Pauline Elizabeth Hopkins*, ed. John Cullen Gruesser (Urbana: University of Illinois Press, 1996), 215–16.

12. Pauline Hopkins, *Winona: A Tale of Negro Life in the South and Southwest*, in *The Magazine Novels of Pauline Hopkins*, ed. Hazel V. Carby (1902; repr., New York: Oxford University Press, 1988), 315. Further references to this edition appear in the text.

13. For an account of Griggs's career as a publisher, see Robert Bone, *The Negro Novel in America*, rev. ed. (1958; New Haven: Yale University Press, 1965), 32; and Arlene A. Elder, "Griggs, Sutton E.," in Andrews, Foster, and Harris, *Oxford Companion to African American Literature*, 328. Addison Gayle Jr. suggests that by exercising "control over his material, Griggs was immune to censorship and more prone to honesty than his fellow novelists" (*The Way of the World: The Black Novel in America* [Garden City NY: Anchor, 1975], 60).

14. Moses, *Golden Age of Black Nationalism*, 170.

15. Sutton E. Griggs, *Imperium in Imperio* (1899; repr., New York: AMS, 1975), 126. Further references to this edition appear in the text.

16. Bernard W. Bell, *The Afro-American Novel and Its Tradition* (Amherst: University of Massachusetts Press, 1987), 63.

17. For accounts of the early years of the *Colored American Magazine* and the various positions Hopkins held at the journal, see Abby Arthur Johnson and Ronald Maberry Johnson, *Propaganda and Aesthetics: The Literary Politics of Afro-American Magazines in the Twentieth Century* (Amherst: University of Massachusetts Press, 1979), 1–5; Penelope L. Bullock, *The Afro-American Periodical Press, 1838–1909* (Baton Rouge: Louisiana State University Press, 1981), 65–68, 106–18; Walter C. Daniel, *Black Journals of the United States* (Westport CT: Greenwood, 1982), 123–26; and Hazel V. Carby, *Reconstructing Womanhood: The Emergence of the Afro-American Woman Novelist* (New York: Oxford University Press, 1987), 125–27.

18. "Editorial and Publishers' Announcements," *Colored American Magazine* 1 (May 1900): 60.

19. Ammons, "Afterword," 215–16. Claudia Tate also compares *Winona* with the formula Western in *Domestic Allegories of Political Desire: The Black Heroine's Text at the Turn of the Century* (New York: Oxford University Press, 1992), 200.

20. "If there is a single distinguishing feature of the literature of black women," according to Mary Helen Washington, it is the fact that their writing records "the thoughts, words, feelings, and deeds of black women" (*Invented Lives: Narratives of Black Women, 1860–1960* [New York: Anchor, 1987], xxi). *Winona* would seem to be an exception, since it privileges "the thoughts, words, feelings, and deeds" of white men. For more on this subject, see Claudia Tate, who discusses the way in which Hopkins silences "the discourse of female agency" (*Domestic Allegories of Political Desire*, 208); Elizabeth Ammons, who notes that many of Hopkins's women "suffer terrible silencing" (*Conflicting Stories: American Women Writers at the Turn into the Twentieth Century* [New York: Oxford University Press, 1992], 78); and Rachel Blau DuPlessis, who writes about the marriage plot as a narrative pattern that "muffles the main female character" (*Writing Beyond the Ending: Narrative Strategies of Twentieth-Century Women Writers* [Bloomington: Indiana University Press, 1985], 5).

21. Female cross-dressing was not an uncommon occurrence in the region during this time. For more on the subject see Evelyn A. Schlatter, "Drag's a Life: Women, Gender, and Cross-Dressing in the Nineteenth-Century West," in *Writing the Range: Race, Class, and Culture in the Women's West*, ed. Elizabeth Jameson and Susan Armitage (Norman: University of Oklahoma Press, 1997), 334–53.

22. Michael K. Johnson believes that "Hopkins attempts to rethink constructions of both masculinity and femininity, and she represents the American West as a place where the potential for . . . gender equity exists." Although "rigid gender roles" do collapse, as Johnson suggests, they do so only temporarily. See *Black Masculinity and the Frontier Myth in American Literature* (Norman: University of Oklahoma Press, 2002), 99, 129.

23. Washington argues that female African American writers created chaste heroines in order to counter the perception that African American women were sexually loose (*Invented Lives*, 73). Similarly, cross-dressing enables Winona to manifest her attraction to Maxwell while at the same time representing it as a platonic same-sex affection. What "queers" the relationship is the focus on how Maxwell feels about being kissed by a "man."

24. Moses, *Golden Age of Black Nationalism*, 186. As a poor child, Belton wears hand-me-down clothes, including a man's boot on one foot and a woman's slipper on the other (6). His borrowing of female attire foreshadows his later cross-dressing, and his hand-me-down feminine slipper symbolizes how African American men were emasculated by poverty.

25. Women tend to be disrespected or mistreated on the few occasions when they appear in the novel. Belton abandons his wife because he mistakenly believes that she has committed adultery (136–38), and Bernard is taught to view his wife as mere "property" (98).

26. For biographical information on Griggs, see Arlene A. Elder, *The "Hindered Hand": Cultural Implications of Early African American Fiction* (Westport CT: Greenwood, 1978), 70–71; and Elder, "Griggs, Sutton E.," 328.

27. Alwyn Barr, *Black Texans: A History of Negroes in Texas, 1528–1971* (Austin: Jenkins, 1973), 67–68.

28. For a history of the Baptist Church and of African American congregants in Texas in the mid- and late nineteenth century, see Milton C. Sernett, *Black Religion and American Evangelicalism: White Protestants, Plantation Missions, and the Flowering of Negro Christianity, 1787–1865* (Metuchen NJ: Scarecrow, 1975), 110–15; Edward L. Wheeler, *Uplifting the Race: The Black Minister in the New South, 1865–1902* (Lanham MD: University Press of America, 1986), 8–9, 17, 39, 48; and William C. Montgomery, *Under Their Own Vine and Fig Tree: The African-American Church in the South, 1865–1900* (Baton Rouge: Louisiana State University Press, 1993), 108, 113, 191–252.

In *Imperium in Imperio*, Griggs mentions the Baptist religion just once, in relation to segregation. At the beginning of chapter 2 he notes that Belton and Bernard go to "the colored school," which was formerly "a house of worship for the white Baptists of Winchester" (8).

29. Bone, *Negro Novel in America*, 32.

30. There is little biographical information on Hopkins available. For the best sources see Ann Allen Shockley, "Pauline Elizabeth Hopkins: A Biographical Excursion into Obscurity," *Phylon* 33 (spring 1972): 22–26; Dorothy B. Parker, "Hopkins, Pauline Elizabeth," in *Dictionary of American Negro Biography*, ed. Rayford W. Logan and Michael R. Winston (New York: Norton, 1982), 325–26; Jane Campbell, "Pauline Elizabeth Hopkins," in *Dictionary of Literary Biography*, vol. 50, *African-American Writers before the Harlem Renaissance*, ed. Trudier Harris (Detroit: Gale Research, 1986), 182–89; Jane Campbell, "Hopkins, Pauline Elizabeth," in *Black Women in America: An Historical Encyclopedia*, ed. Darlene Clark Hine (Brooklyn: Carlson, 1993), 577–79; Claudia Tate, "Hopkins, Pauline E.," in Andrews, Foster,

and Harris, *Oxford Companion to African American Literature*, 366–67; and Carby, *Reconstructing Womanhood*, 121–29.

31. W. E. B. DuBois, *John Brown* (Philadelphia: George W. Jacobs, 1909), 140.

32. Hillel Schwartz, *Century's End: A Cultural History of the Fin de Siècle from the 990s through the 1990s* (New York: Doubleday, 1990), 9–10.

33. Tate, "Hopkins, Pauline E.," 366; Parker, "Hopkins, Pauline Elizabeth," 325.

34. Gerald D. Nash investigates the role that the census played in shaping Turner's frontier thesis in "The Census of 1890 and the Closing of the Frontier," *Pacific North-West Quarterly* 71 (July 1980): 99.

35. Bone, *Negro Novel in America*, 33.

36. Jane Campbell, *Mythic Black Fiction: The Transformation of History* (Knoxville: University of Tennessee Press, 1986), 52.

37. Bell, *The Afro-American Novel*, 63.

38. Gayle, *The Way of the World*, 61.

39. Mary V. Dearborn places Hopkins in "the black genteel tradition, in which black writers attempted to show white readers that blacks were fundamentally 'like' whites" (*Pocahontas's Daughters: Gender and Ethnicity in American Culture* [New York: Oxford University Press, 1986], 9). Houston Baker links Hopkins with nineteenth-century African American women writers who pandered to white patriarchal society and to Protestant New England notions of "strict moral rectitude." Writing "courtesy book[s]" for the middle classes, according to Baker, Hopkins depicted African Americans inoffensively in order to win white approval (*Workings of the Spirit: The Poetics of Afro-American Women's Writing* [Chicago: University of Chicago Press, 1991], 25–28).

40. Carby says that Hopkins combined the novel of ideas with "the sensational fiction of dime novels and magazines" (*Reconstructing Womanhood*, 145). Dickson D. Bruce Jr. sees Hopkins as a "sentimental protest writer" who used "romantic plot lines" to advance socially radical themes (*Black American Writing for the Nadir: The Evolution of a Literary Tradition, 1877–1915* [Baton Rouge: Louisiana State University Press, 1989], 146). Tate analyzes one theme in particular, the interracial romance in *Winona* (*Domestic Allegories of Political Desire*, 197).

41. Carby, *Reconstructing Womanhood*, 129.

42. See Lieutenant Braxton, "Company L in the Spanish-American War," *Colored American Magazine* 1 (May 1900): 19–25; and Rienzi B. Lemus, Company K, 25th Infantry, "The Enlisted Man in Action: Or, the Colored American Soldier in the Philippines," *Colored American Magazine* 5 (May 1902): 46–54.

43. For a survey of views on the subject, see Edward A. Johnson, *History of Negro Soldiers in the Spanish-American War* (Raleigh: Capitol Printing, 1899); George P. Marks III, comp. and ed., *The Black Press Views American Imperialism, 1898–1900* (New York: Arno, 1971); Willard B. Gatewood Jr., *"Smoked Yankees" and the Struggle for Empire* (Urbana: University of Illinois Press, 1971); Gatewood, *Black Americans and the White Man's Burden, 1898–1903* (Urbana: University of Illinois Press, 1975); and Nell Irvin Painter, *Standing at Armageddon: The United States, 1877–1919* (New York: Norton, 1987).

44. Quoted in Gatewood, *Black Americans and the White Man's Burden*, 249. A debate over U.S. involvement in the Philippines plays an important role in Griggs's novel *Unfettered* (Nashville: Orion, 1902), 89–96.

4. The Significance of the Frontier

1. Paul U. Kellogg, "The Negro Pioneers," in *The New Negro: Voices of the Harlem Renaissance*, ed. Alain Locke (1925; repr., New York: Touchstone, 1997), 271. An earlier version of the book was published in March 1925 in a special issue of *Survey* magazine, which Kellogg edited. Further references to this edition appear in the text.

In imagining Harlem as a twentieth-century urban manifestation of the U.S. frontier, Kellogg transformed the actual city into metaphorical space. Other critics have also invested Harlem with meanings that extend beyond its spatial perimeters. James De Jongh has argued that "Harlem's appeal to writers lay not in its distinctive details of setting but in its power as a sign," as "a received cultural artifact," or as "a trope" for "the novel idea of a great black city in the very heart of America's premier metropolis" (*Vicious Modernism: Black Harlem and the Literary Imagination* [Cambridge: Cambridge University Press, 1990], 15). Cary D. Wintz claims that Harlem was "a psychology—a state of mind or an attitude. . . . There was no common bond of political or racial ideology, personal experience, background, or literary philosophy that united the various elements in the Renaissance. What [members] held in common was a sense of community," a conviction that Harlem was their "spiritual" rather than their literal home (*Black Culture and the Harlem Renaissance* [Houston: Rice University Press, 1988], 2–3). Like Wintz, Nathan Irvin Huggins defines Harlem as a "spiritual geography" that African American artists explored. During the Renaissance, he maintains, artists produced works that were both "self-consciously national" and "ethnically regional" (*Harlem Renaissance* [New York: Oxford University Press, 1973], 195). Other critics, like Huggins, have identified Harlem as an ethnic geographic pocket, or as a racialized region, and as the headquarters for an African American national or international cultural enterprise. David Levering Lewis has dubbed the early years of the Renaissance "a cultural nationalism of the parlor" in which an elitist group of "mostly second-generation, college-educated, and generally affluent Afro-Americans" sought to achieve civil rights (*When Harlem Was in Vogue* [New York: Penguin, 1997], xxii, xxviii). Houston Baker believes that the goal of the Renaissance movement was the creation of "a national, racial expressivity" and a reconnection with the African "global community" (*Modernism and the Harlem Renaissance* [Chicago: University of Chicago Press, 1987], 81).

2. Frederick Jackson Turner, "The Significance of the Frontier in American History," in *Rereading Frederick Jackson Turner*, ed. John Mack Faragher (1893; repr., New York: Henry Holt, 1995), 38.

3. Houston Baker, *Long Black Song: Essays in Black American Literature and Culture* (Charlottesville: University Press of Virginia, 1972), 3.

4. For differing assessments of Kellogg's essay, see Baker, who writes that the "description of a collective body of people—conjoined in national sentiment and determination—making their way to both the headlands of material success and the peaks of expressive creativity in a single trek is inspiring in the extreme" (*Modernism and the Harlem Renaissance*, 84); versus George Hutchinson, who claims that Kellogg deprives African American experience of its "authority" by subordinating it to an Anglo-Saxon historical paradigm (*The Harlem Renaissance in Black and White* [Cambridge: Cambridge University Press, 1995], 429).

5. Nathan Irvin Huggins, introduction to *Voices from the Harlem Renaissance*, ed. Huggins (New York: Oxford University Press, 1976), 7.

6. Claude McKay, *A Long Way from Home* (New York: Lee Furman, 1937), 95.

7. Wallace Thurman, *The Blacker the Berry . . .* (1929; repr., New York: Scribner, 1996), 214. Further references to this edition appear in the text. The comparison

between residents of modern skyscrapers and high-rise apartments with Native American cliff dwellers extends back at least to 1893, with the publication of Henry Blake Fuller's novel *The Cliff-Dwellers*.

8. James Weldon Johnson, *Black Manhattan* (1930; repr., New York: Arno, 1968), xiv, 155. For an account of the post–World War I black migration to Harlem see Lewis, *When Harlem Was in Vogue*, 3–24.

9. Claude McKay, *Harlem: Negro Metropolis* (New York: Dutton, 1940), 18, 21.

10. Charles S. Johnson, "The New Frontage on American Life," in Locke, *The New Negro*, 297.

11. Eugene Kinckle Jones, "Interracial Frontiers: Extracts from the Annual Report of the National Urban League," *Opportunity* 9 (March 1931): 75.

12. McKay, *A Long Way from Home*, 4. Lewis speculates that Kansas State College was "suitable for agriculture but not ideal for poetry" (*When Harlem Was in Vogue*, 51). Wayne F. Cooper suggests sarcastically that for "a Jamaican countryman with a romantic turn of mind, the Great Plains of distant Kansas must have seemed as foreign as Outer Mongolia" (*Claude McKay: Rebel Sojourner in the Harlem Renaissance* [Baton Rouge: Louisiana State University Press, 1987], 67).

13. Amy Helene Kirschke, *Aaron Douglas: Art, Race, and the Harlem Renaissance* (Jackson: University Press of Mississippi, 1995), xiv.

14. Lizzetta LeFalle-Collins and Judith Wilson, *Sargent Johnson: African American Modernist* (San Francisco: Museum of Modern Art, 1998), 9–10, 27–30.

15. For an analysis of the West and the role that it plays in "Why I Returned," "The Cure," and "Three Pennies for Luck," see Douglas Flamming, "A Westerner in Search of 'Negro-ness': Region and Race in the Writing of Arna Bontemps," in *Over the Edge: Remapping the American West*, ed. Valerie J. Matsumoto and Blake Allmendinger (Berkeley: University of California Press, 1998), 85–104.

16. Taylor Gordon, *Born to Be* (1929; repr., Lincoln: University of Nebraska Press, 1995), 17. Further references to this edition appear in the text.

17. Robert Hemenway, "Introduction to the 1975 Edition," in Taylor Gordon, *Born to Be* (Seattle: University of Washington Press, 1975), x, xxvii–xxviii. Hemenway's close reading of the autobiography and his reconstruction of the author's life is based on his consultation of Gordon's correspondence, unfinished manuscripts, and other archival material.

18. Michael K. Johnson discusses Gordon's ambivalent feelings about his racial identity in "Migration, Masculinity, and Racial Identity in Taylor Gordon's *Born to Be*," in *Moving Stories: Migration and the American West, 1850–2000*, ed. Scott E. Casper and Lucinda M. Long (Reno: Nevada Humanities Committee, 2001). Johnson writes that "Gordon's discovery of 'what it means to be black' alternates between these two opposing positions—an awareness of blackness as a negation of identity, and an awareness of blackness as a source of agency and as the basis for a positive sense of self" (123).

19. Thadious M. Davis, "Introduction to the Bison Books Edition," in Gordon, *Born to Be*, xii; Hemenway, "Introduction," xxiv.

20. Hemenway, "Introduction," xxvi–vii.

21. Review of *Born to Be*, *Crisis* 37 (April 1930): 129.

22. Wallace Thurman, "Quoth Brigham Young: This Is the Place," *Messenger* 8 (August 1926), reprinted in *These "Colored" United States: African American Essays from the 1920s*, ed. Tom Lutz and Susanna Ashton (New Brunswick NJ: Rutgers University Press, 1996), 265–67.

23. For a discussion of other parallels between Thurman and his semi-autobio-

graphical heroine, see Eleanore van Notten, *Wallace Thurman's Harlem Renaissance* (Amsterdam: Rodopi, 1994), 214–23.

24. Eunice Hunton Carter, review of *The Blacker the Berry . . .* , *Opportunity* 7 (May 1929): 162.

25. Gerald Haslam, "Wallace Thurman: A Western Renaissance Man," *Western American Literature* 6 (spring 1971): 59.

26. Thurman, "Quoth Brigham Young," 264.

27. "Flora Belle" first appeared in the *Brooklyn Daily Eagle* in 1935. Hughes reprinted the story in a collection entitled *Something in Common and Other Stories* (1963). Editors Bruce Glasrud and Laurie Champion, in *The African American West: A Century of Short Stories* (Boulder: University Press of Colorado, 2000), have retitled the story "The Gun." Further references to this edition appear in the text.

28. Langston Hughes, *Not without Laughter* (1930; repr., New York: Scribner, 1995), 23, 50. Further references to this edition appear in the text.

29. Carl Van Vechten to Langston Hughes, August 1925, in *Letters of Carl Van Vechten*, ed. Bruce Kellner (New Haven: Yale University Press, 1987), 81.

30. Langston Hughes, *The Big Sea* (New York: Knopf, 1940), 16. Arnold Rampersad discusses this draft, as well as another aborted effort entitled "Scarlet Flowers: The Autobiography of a Young Poet," in *The Life of Langston Hughes*, vol. 1, *"I, Too, Sing America"* (New York: Oxford University Press, 1986), 112, 114.

31. For comparisons between Hughes's relatives and Aunt Hager's family in *Not without Laughter*, see *The Big Sea*, 5–16; Mark Scott, "Langston Hughes of Kansas," *Journal of Negro History* 66 (spring 1981): 1–9; and Faith Berry, *Langston Hughes: Before and Beyond Harlem* (Westport CT: Lawrence Hill, 1983), 95.

32. Hughes, *The Big Sea*, 303.

33. V. F. Calverton, review of *Not without Laughter*, *Nation*, August 6, 1930, 157–58, reprinted in *Critical Essays on Langston Hughes*, ed. Edward J. Mullen (Boston: G. K. Hall, 1986), 59–60.

34. Eric J. Sundquist, "Who Was Langston Hughes?" *Commentary* 102 (December 1997): 57.

35. Lewis, *When Harlem Was in Vogue*, 251.

36. Robert Bone, *Down Home: A History of Afro-American Short Fiction from Its Beginnings to the End of the Harlem Renaissance* (New York: Putnam, 1975), 240.

37. For studies of the Hughes family and its connection to Kansas, see Scott, "Langston Hughes of Kansas," 1–9. Much of the same information appears in another article published by Scott, under the same title, in *Kansas History* 3 (spring 1980): 3–25. See also Cary D. Wintz, "Langston Hughes: A Kansas Poet in the Harlem Renaissance," *Kansas Quarterly* 7 (summer 1975): 58–71.

38. Rampersad, *The Life of Langston Hughes*, 1:8.

39. Frederick Jackson Turner, "The Middle West," *International Monthly*, December 1901, reprinted in Turner, *The Frontier in American History* (New York: Holt, 1920), 129, 154. For related scholarship on the debate over the terms "West" and "Midwest," Turner's purpose in using these terms, and Kansas's role in the reformation of region, see James H. Madison, "Diverging Trails: Why the Midwest Is Not the West," in *Frontier and Region: Essays in Honor of Martin Ridge*, ed. Robert C. Ritchie and Paul Andrew Hutton (Albuquerque and San Marino: University of New Mexico Press and Huntington Library Press, 1997), 45–46; and Walter Nugent, *Into the West: The Story of Its People* (New York: Vintage, 2001), 8–9.

40. Ralph Ellison, *Shadow and Act* (1953; repr., New York: Vintage, 1995), xiii, xvi, 5.

41. Ralph Ellison, *Invisible Man* (1952; repr., New York: Vintage, 1995), 159. Further references to this edition appear in the text.

42. Ellison, *Shadow and Act*, xv–vi.

43. R. W. B. Lewis, "Ellison's Essays," in *Ralph Ellison*, ed. Harold Bloom (New York: Chelsea House, 1986), 9. Jerry Gafio Watts believes that the Tulsa race riot of 1921 may have had a particular effect on Ellison, destroying "whatever lingering . . . belief there was in Oklahoma as a land of opportunity" (*Heroism and the Black Intellectual: Ralph Ellison, Politics, and Afro-American Intellectual Life* [Chapel Hill: University of North Carolina Press, 1994], 34). Similarly, Mark Busby claims that Ellison's boyhood belief in a "free and open territory" was "later contradicted by his oppressive experience." Thus, *Invisible Man* contrasts "a seemingly free world" with one that constrains Negro existence ("Ralph Ellison," in *Updating the Literary West*, ed. Thomas J. Lyon [Fort Worth: Texas Christian University Press, 1997], 521).

44. For an insightful analysis of this scene, see Martin Bucco, "Ellison's Invisible West," *Western American Literature* 10 (fall 1975). Bucco argues that black nationalism, like white westward expansion, springs from "racial arrogance" and misguided idealism. "The Great Migration of the Negro masses . . . is as phantasmagoric as the earlier covered-wagon treks toward a freedom impossible under the old regime" (238).

45. Gregory Stephens, *On Racial Frontiers: The New Culture of Frederick Douglass, Ralph Ellison, and Bob Marley* (Cambridge: Cambridge University Press, 1999), 13–14. Busby concurs, calling Ellison's frontier a borderland where "various forces" meet, interact, and amalgamate ("Ralph Ellison," 521–22).

46. Ralph Ellison, "Going to the Territory" (1980), reprinted in Ellison, *Going to the Territory* (New York: Random House, 1986), 131–33.

47. Ralph Ellison, as quoted in Ishmael Reed, Quincy Troupe, and Steve Cannon, "The Essential Ralph Ellison," in *Conversations with Ralph Ellison*, ed. Maryemma Graham and Amritjit Singh (Jackson: University Press of Mississippi, 1995), 372. Also see Ellison's interview with Hollie West, in which he repeats: "The people who went out there [to Oklahoma Territory] were trying to determine their fate" ("Growing Up Black in Frontier Oklahoma . . . from an Ellison Perspective," in *Speaking For You: The Vision of Ralph Ellison*, ed. Kimberly W. Benston [Washington DC: Howard University Press, 1987], 11).

48. Ralph Ellison, "Remembering Richard Wright" (1971), reprinted in Ellison, *Going to the Territory*, 198.

49. Ellison, "Going to the Territory," 134.

50. Ellison, "Harlem Is Nowhere" (1948), reprinted in *Going to the Territory*, 296–97.

51. For a comparison of the conditions under which each writer worked, see, e.g., Sundquist, "Who Was Langston Hughes?" 56; Huggins, *Voices from the Harlem Renaissance*, 10; and John M. Reilly, introduction to *Twentieth-Century Interpretations of "Invisible Man,"* ed. Reilly (Englewood Cliffs NJ: Prentice-Hall, 1970), 2.

5. Hip Hopalong Cassidy

1. Daryl Jones, *The Dime Novel Western* (Bowling Green: Bowling Green State University Press, 1978), 76, 82.

2. Christine Bold, *Selling the West: Popular Western Fiction, 1860 to 1960* (Bloomington: Indiana University Press, 1987), 13.

3. Edward L. Wheeler, *Deadwood Dick as Detective: A Story of the Great Carbonate Region* (New York: Beadle and Adams, 1879), 10.

4. Edward L. Wheeler, *Deadwood Dick's Doom; or, Calamity Jane's Last Adventure* (New York: Beadle and Adams, 1881), 12.

5. Edward L. Wheeler, *Deadwood Dick's Dream; or, The Rivals of the Road* (New York: Beadle and Adams, 1881), 2.

6. Edward L. Wheeler, *Deadwood Dick's Device; or, The Sign of the Double Cross* (New York: Beadle and Adams, 1879), 6, 10.

7. Michael Denning, *Mechanic Accents: Dime Novels and Working-Class Culture in America* (1987; repr., London: Verso, 1998), 30, 210. On the subject of class politics in the dime novel, see also Henry Nash Smith, *Virgin Land: The American West as Symbol and Myth* (1960; repr., Cambridge: Harvard University Press, 1971), 100; Philip Durham, introduction to Edward L. Wheeler, *Deadwood Dick on Deck; or, Calamity Jane, the Heroine of Whoop-Up* (1878; repr., New York: Odyssey, 1966), x; and Marcus Klein, *Easterns, Westerns, and Private Eyes: American Matters, 1870–1900* (Madison: University of Wisconsin Press, 1994), 100–101.

8. Nat Love, *The Life and Adventures of Nat Love, Better Known in the Cattle Country as "Deadwood Dick"* (1907; repr., Lincoln: University of Nebraska Press, 1995), 1. Subsequent references to this edition appear in the text.

9. Nicole Tonkovich, "Guardian Angels and Missing Mothers: Race and Domesticity in *Winona* and *Deadwood Dick on Deck*," *Western American Literature* 32 (November 1997): 243. I have offered an alternative reading, as well as a lengthy analysis of Love's autobiography, in *Ten Most Wanted: The New Western Literature* (New York: Routledge, 1998), 17–31.

10. For example, see Philip Durham and Everett L. Jones, *The Negro Cowboys* (1965; repr., Lincoln: University of Nebraska Press, 1983), 3.

11. Mary A. Dempsey, "The Bronze Buckaroo Rides Again: Herb Jeffries Is Still Keepin' On," *American Visions* 12 (August–September 1997): 22–26.

12. Dempsey, "Bronze Buckaroo Rides Again," 23.

13. Thomas Cripps, *Slow Fade to Black: The Negro in American Film* (New York: Oxford University Press, 1993), 338.

14. Jim Pines, "Blacks," in *The BFI Companion to the Western*, ed. Edward Buscombe (New York: Atheneum, 1988), 69.

15. *Two-Gun Man from Harlem*, starring Herbert Jeffrey [*sic*], written and directed by Richard C. Kahn (International Studios, 1938).

16. *The Bronze Buckaroo*, starring Herbert Jeffrey [*sic*], written and directed by Richard C. Kahn (Hollywood Productions, 1938).

17. *Harlem Rides the Range*, starring Herbert Jeffrey [*sic*], written by Spencer Williams Jr. and F. E. Miller, directed by Richard C. Kahn (Hollywood Productions, 1939).

18. *Look-Out Sister*, starring Louis Jordan, written by John E. Gordon, directed by Bud Pollard (Astor Pictures, 1946).

19. See Ishmael Reed, *Shrovetide in Old New Orleans* (Garden City NY: Doubleday, 1978), 133–34; and Michel Fabre, "Postmodern Rhetoric in Ishmael Reed's *Yellow Back Radio Broke-Down*," in *The Critical Response to Ishmael Reed*, ed. Bruce Allen Dick (Westport CT: Greenwood, 1999), 22.

20. In *Playing Cowboys: Low Culture and High Art in the Western* (Norman: University of Oklahoma Press, 1992), 127–33, Robert Murray Davis argues that parodies such as *Blazing Saddles* honor the conventions of the Western while mocking them.

In this case, the sheriff confounds expectations because he is a racial minority, but in every other respect he fulfills the role of the hero.

21. Peter Nazareth, "An Interview with Ishmael Reed," reprinted in *Conversations with Ishmael Reed*, ed. Bruce Dick and Amritjit Singh (Jackson: University of Mississippi Press, 1995), 191.

22. Robert Elliot Fox, *Conscientious Sorcerers: The Black Postmodernist Fiction of LeRoi Jones/Amiri Baraka, Ishmael Reed, and Samuel R. Delaney* (Westport CT: Greenwood, 1987), 46.

23. For an analysis of the novel's wide-ranging critique see Todd F. Teichen's "Cowboy Tricksters and Devilish Wangols: Ishmael Reed's HooDoo West" (*Western American Literature* 36 [winter 2002]: 326), which argues that Reed "counters Christian imperialism and its essentializing narratives with HooDoo strategies such as trickster and signifying, and in the process he draws some notable parallels between African American and Native American resistance traditions."

24. Ishmael Reed, *Yellow Back Radio Broke-Down* (1969; repr., New York: Atheneum, 1988), 53. Subsequent references to this edition appear in the text.

25. Reed, *Shrovetide in Old New Orleans*, 134.

26. Keith E. Byerman writes: "In a system where law and order are equated with repression and corruption, the 'good' cowboy must be represented as anarchic and demonic. Thus, the dualistic formula of the western, with its clearly defined categories of good and evil, breaks down." This development leads to "the reconstruction of the formula, through the narrative of its deconstruction, into a new kind of fiction, the hoodoo western," claims Byerman (*Fingering the Jagged Grain: Tradition and Form in Recent Black Fiction* [Athens: University of Georgia Press, 1985], 222).

27. David Anthony Durham, *Gabriel's Story* (New York: Doubleday, 2001), 35. Subsequent references to this edition appear in the text.

28. Todd Boyd argues that gangsta rap, "with its themes of excess, takes the notion of 'gettin' paid' or 'gettin' mine' to its most extreme form." Acquiring "material possessions by any means necessary" is its overriding concern (*Am I Black Enough for You? Popular Culture from the 'Hood and Beyond* [Bloomington: Indiana University Press, 1997], 66). Mike Davis echoes this sentiment, writing that gangsta rappers "disclaim all ideology except the primitive accumulation of wealth by any means necessary. . . . They also offer an uncritical mirror to fantasy power-trips of violence, sexism and greed" (*City of Quartz: Excavating the Future in Los Angeles* [1990; repr., New York: Vintage, 1992], 87).

29. For a history of the evolution of West Coast rap see Nelson George, *Hip Hop America* (New York: Penguin, 1998), 129–30; and Alex Ogg with David Upshal, *The Hip Hop Years: A History of Rap* (1999; repr., New York: Fromm International, 2001), 111–21.

30. *Posse*, starring Mario Van Peebles, written by Sy Richardson and Dario Scardapane, directed by Mario Van Peebles (Gramercy Pictures, 1993).

31. For a defense of the film's conventional characteristics see Tania Modleski, "A Woman's Gotta Do . . . What a Man's Gotta Do? Cross-Dressing in the Western," *Signs* 22 (spring 1997): 520.

32. Donald Hoffman contends that "commercialism, vanity, and a desire for the quick thrill" undermine the film's otherwise admirable qualities ("Whose Home on the Range? Finding Room for Native Americans, African Americans, and Latin Americans in the Revisionist Western," *melus* 22 [summer 1997]: 51).

33. *Wild Wild West*, starring Will Smith, Kevin Kline, and Kenneth Branagh, writ-

ten by S. S. Wilson, Brent Maddock, Jeffrey Price, and Peter S. Seaman, directed by Barry Sonnenfeld (Warner Brothers, 1999).

6. Black Noir

1. Frederick Douglass, *Narrative of the Life of Frederick Douglass, an American Slave* (1845; repr., New York: Penguin, 1987), 47–48.

2. Douglass, *Narrative*, 137.

3. Lydia Maria Child, "Introduction by the Editor," in Linda Brent, *Incidents in the Life of a Slave Girl* (1861; repr., New York: Oxford University Press, 1988), 8.

4. Brent, "Preface by the Author," in *Incidents*, 5.

5. Stephen F. Soitos calls *Hagar's Daughter* "the first African American detective novel" (*The Blues Detective: A Study of African American Detective Fiction* [Amherst: University of Massachusetts Press, 1996], 60), but Paula L. Woods selects *The Conjure-Man Dies* as "the first mystery novel by an African American to feature black characters" (*Spooks, Spies, and Private Eyes: Black Mystery, Crime, and Suspense Fiction* [New York: Doubleday, 1995], 347). Mark Twain's 1894 novel, *The Tragedy of Pudd'nhead Wilson and the Comedy of Those Extraordinary Twins*, the story of a white detective who uses fingerprinting to distinguish between nearly identical white and African American children, precedes both of these works.

6. Rudolph Fisher, *The Conjure-Man Dies: A Mystery Tale of Dark Harlem* (1932; repr., Ann Arbor: University of Michigan Press, 1992), 37.

7. Fisher, *The Conjure-Man Dies*, 3.

8. John A. Williams, "My Man Himes: An Interview with Chester Himes," in *Amistad 1*, ed. Williams and Charles F. Harris (New York: Random House, 1970), 50.

9. Chester Himes, *Cotton Comes to Harlem* (London: Allison and Busby, 1964), 26. Raymond Nelson argues that Himes "recaptures the spirit" of the Renaissance by embracing "the rich folk-traditions of Black American culture," in particular, by reviving the folkloric figure of the "bad nigger" in the form of the mythic detective protagonists, Coffin Ed Johnson and Grave Digger Jones ("Domestic Harlem: The Detective Fiction of Chester Himes," *Virginia Quarterly Review* 48 [spring 1972]: 260–66). However, Sean McCann, focusing on the depiction of the city itself, writes that Himes's "Harlem is not the race capital imagined by writers during the twenties" but a "society reduced by poverty to a surreal state of nature, where . . . everyone must be desperately out for himself" (*Gumshoe America: Hard-Boiled Crime Fiction and the Rise and Fall of New Deal Liberalism* [Durham: Duke University Press, 2000], 284).

10. Chester Himes, *The Quality of Hurt: The Autobiography of Chester Himes; The Early Years* (New York: Paragon, 1971), 63.

11. Williams, "My Man Himes," 49.

12. Chester Himes, *The Real Cool Killers* (1959; repr., New York: Vintage, 1988), 65.

13. Peter J. Rabinowitz, "Chandler Comes to Harlem: Racial Politics in the Thrillers of Chester Himes," in *The Sleuth and the Scholar: Origins, Evolution, and Current Trends in Detective Fiction*, ed. Barbara A. Rader and Howard G. Zettler (Westport CT: Greenwood, 1988), 22. Greg Forter claims that these competing pressures have the representational effect "of cleaving the hero in two," i.e., creating the need for contrasting and complementary heroes in Himes (*Murdering Masculinities: Fan-*

tasies of Gender and Violence in the American Crime Novel [New York: New York University Press, 2000], 193).

14. For an analysis of violence as a form of social protest in Himes, see David Schmid, "Chester Himes and the Institutionalization of Multicultural Detective Fiction," in *Multicultural Detective Fiction: Murder from the "Other" Side*, ed. Adrienne Johnson Gosselin (New York: Garland, 1999), 288; and Lee Horsley, *The Noir Thriller* (Hampshire: Palgrave, 2001), 180.

15. Raymond Chandler, "The Simple Art of Murder," in *The Simple Art of Murder* (New York: Vintage, 1988), 17.

16. Mike Davis, *City of Quartz: Excavating the Future in Los Angeles* (1990; repr., New York: Vintage, 1992), 15.

17. Davis, *City of Quartz*, 43.

18. According to William Marling, critics have failed to notice that most American noir "is set mostly in California, principally Los Angeles" (*The American Roman Noir: Hammett, Cain, and Chandler* [Athens: University of Georgia Press, 1995], 238). However, there is a significant body of scholarship on the relationship between the formula Western and noir. See, e.g., Richard Slotkin, who argues that "the hard-boiled detective story began as an abstraction of essential elements of the Frontier Myth" (*Gunfighter Nation: The Myth of the Frontier in Twentieth-Century America* [1992; repr., New York: Harper Perennial, 1993], 217). Dennis Porter claims that the private eye, like the protagonist of the Western, is a populist hero, formally uneducated, with lower-class origins (*The Pursuit of Crime: Art and Ideology in Detective Fiction* [New Haven: Yale University Press, 1981], 175). Robert Crooks compares the frontier line that distinguishes between "civilization" and "savagery" with the color line that separates whites and African Americans in urban communities ("From the Far Side of the Urban Frontier: The Detective Fiction of Chester Himes and Walter Mosley," *College Literature* 22 [October 1995]: 69). And Cynthia S. Hamilton examines the relationship between the two popular genres in *Westerns and Hard-Boiled Detective Fiction in America: From "High Noon" to "Midnight Cowboy"* (London: MacMillan, 1987).

Even in his Harlem series, Himes alludes to the Western. In *The Crazy Kill* (New York: Avon, 1959), one character refers to Coffin Ed and Grave Digger as "those damned Wild West gunmen" (28). In *All Shot Up* (New York: Avon, 1960) they are described as "two cowboys from Harlem" (31), as "real Western gunmen" (36), and as shootists "in the Hollywood gunslinger's fashion" (148). Frankie Y. Bailey suggests that Himes created a violent world in "his detective novels that makes the Wild West look like a prayer meeting" (*Out of the Woodpile: Black Characters in Crime and Detective Fiction* [Westport CT: Greenwood, 1991], 63).

19. Nathanael West, *The Day of the Locust* (1939; repr., New York: New Directions, 1989), 60.

20. Himes later wrote that there was more racial discrimination in Los Angeles than anywhere else in America (*The Quality of Hurt*, 73).

21. Chester Himes, *If He Hollers Let Him Go* (1945; repr., New York: Thunder's Mouth, 1986), 8–9. Subsequent references to this edition appear in the text.

22. Raymond Chandler, *The Big Sleep* (1939; repr., New York: Vintage, 1988), 139.

23. In this discussion of the car and the concept of spatial mobility I quote from an earlier essay in which I compare Chandler and Himes. See "All About Eden" in *Reading California: Art, Image, and Identity, 1900–2000*, ed. Stephanie Barron, Sheri Bernstein, and Ilene Susan Fort (Berkeley: University of California Press, 2000), 121–22.

24. Himes, *The Real Cool Killers*, 41.

25. For an analysis of the way Marlowe enables the reader to make sense of Los Angeles see William Alexander McClung, *Landscapes of Desire: Anglo Mythologies of Los Angeles* (2000; repr., Berkeley: University of California Press, 2002), 192–93; and Richard Lehan, *The City in Literature: An Intellectual and Cultural History* (Berkeley: University of California Press, 1998), 252. Fredric Jameson suggests that Marlowe provides the reader with a "cognitive map" of Los Angeles in "On Raymond Chandler," *Southern Review* 6 (summer 1970): 629.

26. Chester Himes, *My Life of Absurdity: The Autobiography of Chester Himes*, vol. 2 (New York: Doubleday, 1976), 126. Several critics have disagreed with Himes over the years, including Raymond Nelson, who claims that one of the purposes of the Harlem series is "to envision a particular place at a particular moment in history—its customs, speech, topography, occupations, even its food—and record it for posterity" ("Domestic Harlem," 269). Michael Denning explores the "topographies of this unreal city" in "Topographies of Violence: Chester Himes' Harlem Detective Novels," *Critical Texts* 5 (1988): 11.

27. For example, Gilbert H. Muller argues that representations of the city in Mosley and Himes "are part of the same uniform underworld" in "Double Agent: The Los Angeles Crime Cycle of Walter Mosley," in *Los Angeles in Fiction*, ed. David Fine (Albuquerque: University of New Mexico Press, 1995), 293.

28. Walter Mosley, *Devil in a Blue Dress* (1990; repr., New York: Pocket, 1995), 27. Subsequent references to this edition appear in the text.

29. Roger A. Berger suggests that Mosley repeats Chandler, yet "with a difference," in " 'The Black Dick': Race, Sexuality, and Discourse in the Los Angeles Novels of Walter Mosley," *African American Review* 31 (summer 1997): 8.

30. In "Interview with Walter Mosley," the author acknowledges the influence that Hammett has had on his work. See Samuel Coale, *The Mystery of Mysteries: Cultural Differences and Designs* (Bowling Green: Bowling Green State University Popular Press, 2000), 201–2.

31. John Cullen Gruesser, "An Un-Easy Relationship: Walter Mosley's Signifyin(g) Detective and the Black Community," in Gosselin, *Multicultural Detective Fiction*, 240.

32. Mosley contends that his hero's dilemma is complicated by his "middle-class aspirations" ("The Black Dick," in *Critical Fictions: The Politics of Imaginative Writing*, ed. Philomena Mariani [Seattle: Bay Press, 1991], 132). Madelyn Jablon comments on the way in which the private eye's status as a single father further complicates this dilemma (" 'Making the Faces Black': The African-American Detective Novel," in *Changing Representations of Minorities East and West*, ed. Larry E. Smith and John Reider [Honolulu: University of Hawaii Press, 1996], 27–28). Gruesser considers how the hero's profession affects his relationship with the local African American population ("An Un-Easy Relationship," 244).

33. In addition to speaking to people in different voices, Rawlins also briefly speaks to himself in a private "voice" that he hears in his head. Unlike his speaking voice, which is persuasive and conciliatory, his inaudible voice is aggressive and violent. It "just tells me how it is if I want to survive. Survive like a man" (*Devil in a Blue Dress*, 98). It speaks to Rawlins repeatedly in the first novel but only once in *A Red Death*, and seldom thereafter.

34. Chandler, *The Big Sleep*, 7.

35. Theodore O. Mason Jr., "Walter Mosley's Easy Rawlins: The Detective and Afro-American Fiction," *Kenyon Review* 14 (fall 1992): 179–80. Gruesser describes

the hero "as a signifying detective, adept at juggling linguistic and social codes to deceive and outwit both white and black characters" ("An Un-Easy Relationship," 235).

36. Walter Mosley, *White Butterfly* (1992; repr., New York: Pocket, 1993), 213.

37. Walter Mosley, *A Red Death* (1991; repr., New York: Pocket, 1992), 143.

38. For an extended treatment of this theme see William R. Nash, " 'Maybe I Killed My Own Blood': Doppelgangers and the Death of Double Consciousness in Walter Mosley's *A Little Yellow Dog*," in Gosselin, *Multicultural Detective Fiction*, 303–23.

39. Mosley, *White Butterfly*, 145.

40. Gary Phillips, *Violent Spring* (1994; repr., New York: Berkley, 1996), 59, 86, 104, 118.

41. Gary Phillips, *The Jook* (Los Angeles: Really Great Books, 1999), 79.

42. John Ridley, *Everybody Smokes in Hell* (1999; repr., New York: Ballantine, 2000), 163. Subsequent references to this edition appear in the text.

43. Andrew Pepper, *The Contemporary American Crime Novel: Race, Ethnicity, Gender, Class* (Edinburgh: Edinburgh University Press, 2000), 11.

44. Gar Anthony Haywood, *All the Lucky Ones Are Dead* (1999; repr., New York: Berkley, 2000), 41, 73, 124.

45. Robert Greer, *The Devil's Red Nickel* (1997; repr., New York: Warner, 1998), 161. Subsequent references to this edition appear in the text.

46. Robert Greer, *The Devil's Backbone* (1998; repr., New York: Warner, 1999), 81.

47. Robert Greer, *The Devil's Hatband* (New York: Mysterious Press, 1996), 13, 30.

48. Paula L. Woods, *Inner City Blues* (1999; repr., New York: Ballantine, 2000), 148.

49. In reference to this distinction between African American male and female detectives, see Nicole Décuré, "In Search of Our Sisters' Mean Streets: The Politics of Sex, Race, and Class in Black Women's Crime Fiction," in *Diversity and Detective Fiction*, ed. Kathleen Gregory Klein (Bowling Green: Bowling Green State University Popular Press, 1999), 162–66. For a full-length study see Priscilla L. Walton and Marina Jones, *Detective Agency: Women Rewriting the Hard-Boiled Tradition* (Berkeley: University of California Press, 1999).

50. Terris McMahan Grimes, *Somebody Else's Child* (New York: Onyx, 1996), 31. Subsequent references to this edition appear in the text.

51. Penny Mickelbury, *Where to Choose* (1999; repr., New York: St. Martin's, 2001), 18.

52. Pepper, *Contemporary American Crime Novel*, 90.

53. Williams, "My Man Himes," 48–49.

54. Chandler, *The Big Sleep*, 2.

55. Pepper, *Contemporary American Crime Novel*, 91.

56. Woods, *Spooks, Spies, and Private Eyes*, xv.

7. Everybody Comes to California to Die

1. By 1970, according to the United States census, California had surpassed Texas as the western state with the largest African American population. In 1990 the census reported for the first time that Los Angeles was the most populous city, followed by Houston and Dallas. See Quintard Taylor, *In Search of the Racial Frontier: African Americans in the American West, 1528–1990* (1998; repr., New York: Norton, 1999), 279, 314.

2. Robert Richardson, "Eyewitness Account: 'Get Whitey,' Screams Blood-Hungry Mobs," *Los Angeles Times*, August 14, 1965, 1.

3. Nicolaus Mills, *The Crowd in American Literature* (Baton Rouge: Louisiana State University Press, 1986), 6. Also see Eric J. Hobsbawm, *Primitive Rebels: Studies in Archaic Forms of Social Movement in the Nineteenth and Twentieth Centuries* (Manchester: Manchester University Press, 1959), 111.

4. Gerald Horne, *Fire This Time: The Watts Uprising and the 1960s* (New York: Da Capo, 1997), 329–30.

5. "Dance Company Will Present 'L.A. Riots,'" *Sacramento Observer*, October 21, 1992, F2.

6. Diane Haithman, "Have the Arts Helped Heal L.A.?" *Los Angeles Times*, April 27, 1993, F1.

7. Rowanne Marie Henry, "Performance and the Los Angeles Uprising: Art as Social Change" (master's thesis, University of California, Los Angeles, 1993), 10.

8. Eldridge Cleaver, *Soul on Ice* (New York: McGraw-Hill, 1968), 27.

9. Susan A. Phillips, *Wallbangin': Graffiti and Gangs in L.A.* (Chicago: University of Chicago Press, 1999), 298.

10. U.S. census reports cited in Taylor, *Racial Frontier*, 193, 223, 254, 285.

11. For a history of Watts and its gradual decay see Paul Bullock, *Watts: The Aftermath* (New York: Grove, 1969), 14–15; Nathan Cohen, "The Los Angeles Riot Study," in *The Los Angeles Riots: A Socio-Psychological Study*, ed. Cohen (New York: Praeger, 1970), 5–11; David O. Sears and John B. McConahay, *The Politics of Violence: The New Urban Blacks and the Watts Riot* (Boston: Houghton Mifflin, 1973), 56–60; and Ronald N. Jacobs, *Race, Media, and the Crisis of Civil Society: From Watts to Rodney King* (Cambridge: Cambridge University Press, 2000), 16.

12. "Violence in the City: A Report by the Governor's Commission on the Los Angeles Riots," reprinted in *Mass Violence in America: The Los Angeles Riots*, comp. Robert M. Fogelson (1968; repr., Salem: Ayer, 1988), 4, 85.

13. Robert Conot, *Rivers of Blood, Years of Darkness* (New York: Bantam, 1967), 3.

14. Jerry Cohen and William S. Murphy, *Burn, Baby, Burn! The Los Angeles Race Riot, August, 1965* (New York: Dutton, 1966), 44.

15. Otis O'Solomon, "Understanding the Riots: Part Four; Seeing Ourselves," *Los Angeles Times*, May 14, 1992, T3. Other critics agree that Los Angeles is a metaphorical place where "image" often substitutes for reality. Edward W. Soja claims that it is "more specialized in image production and more prone to be understood through its created imagery" than any other American city ("Los Angeles, 1965–1992: From Crisis-Generated Restructuring to Restructuring-Generated Crisis," in *The City: Los Angeles and Urban Theory at the End of the Twentieth Century*, ed. Allen J. Scott and Soja [Berkeley: University of California Press, 1996], 427). *Los Angeles Times* art critic William Wilson, maintaining that the "myth of Los Angeles . . . is a kind of artwork fashioned by the collective unconscious," nonetheless asked after the 1992 uprising, "How can we go on calling this place Lotusland and Tinseltown or imagining it as a painting by David Hockney after what happened?" ("Year in Review '92: Emergence of Outsider Art throughout L.A.," *Los Angeles Times*, December 28, 1992, F6). Joost van Loon addressed the impact of "race and place" on images of Los Angeles in the aftermath of the 1992 uprising in "Chronotypes: Of/in the Televisualization of the 1992 Los Angeles Riots," *Theory, Culture and Society* 14 (May 1997): 89–101.

16. See, e.g., Julian Hartt, "Guard Force from 40th Armored," *Los Angeles Times*, August 14, 1965, 1, 15; "Anarchy Must End," unsigned editorial, *Los Angeles Times*,

August 14, 1965, 1; and Art Berman, "Negro Riots Rage On; Death Toll 25," *Los Angeles Times*, August 15, 1965, 1.

17. Fogelson, *Mass Violence in America*, 1.

18. Quoted in Horne, *Fire This Time*, 64.

19. Robert M. Fogelson, *Violence as Protest: A Study of Riots and Ghettos* (Garden City NY: Doubleday, 1971), 16.

20. Cohen, "Los Angeles Riot Study," 3.

21. Fogelson, *Violence as Protest*, 16.

22. Budd Schulberg, introduction to *From the Ashes: Voices of Watts*, ed. Schulberg (New York: New American Library, 1967), 2, 5. Subsequent references to this edition appear in the text.

23. Maya Angelou, *A Song Flung Up to Heaven* (New York: Random House, 2002), 80.

24. Quoted in Horne, *Fire This Time*, 331.

25. Milton McFarlane, "To Join or Not to Join," in *Watts Poets: A Book of New Poetry*, ed. Quincy Troupe (Los Angeles: House of Respect, 1968), 3–4. Subsequent references to this edition appear in the text.

26. The Watts Prophets, *Rappin' Black in a White World*, produced by Mike Thorne (Full Frequency Range Recordings, 1971).

27. Robert Epstein, "Watts Writers Workshop: A Blueprint to Fit Today's Needs?" *Los Angeles Times*, May 5, 1992, F1.

28. Susan Anderson, "A City Called Heaven: Black Enchantment and Despair in Los Angeles," in Scott and Soja, *The City*, 357–58.

29. Warren Christopher et al., *Report of the Independent Commission on the Los Angeles Police Department* (Los Angeles: The Commission, 1991), iii–iv, 21–22.

30. Ira Reiner quoted in Marc Lacey and Shawn Hubler, "Rioters Set Fires, Loot Stores, 4 Reported Dead," *Los Angeles Times*, April 30, 1992, A1.

31. Joan Petersilia and Allan Abrahamse, "A Profile of Those Arrested," in *The Los Angeles Riots: Lessons for the Urban Future*, ed. Mark Baldassare (Boulder: Westview, 1994), 140.

32. Peter A. Morrison and Ira S. Lowry, "A Riot of Color: The Demographic Setting," in Baldassare, *The Los Angeles Riots*, 19–20.

33. See, e.g., Victor Merina and John Mitchell, "Opportunists, Criminals Get Blame for Riots," *Los Angeles Times*, May 1, 1992, A1; and Ashley Dunn, "Years of '2-Cent' Insults Added Up to Rampage," *Los Angeles Times*, May 7, 1992, A1; versus Stephen Braun and Ron Russell, "Riots Are Violent Reruns for the Veterans of Watts," *Los Angeles Times*, May 4, 1992, A1.

34. Darnell M. Hunt, *Screening the Los Angeles "Riots": Race, Seeing, and Resistance* (Cambridge: Cambridge University Press, 1997), 166.

35. For an analysis of the video and its interpretation in court see Robert Gooding-Williams, ed., *Reading Rodney King, Reading Urban Uprising* (New York: Routledge, 1993). Houston A. Baker discusses the video's frame-by-frame presentation in "Scene . . . Not Heard" (44). Kimberlé Crenshaw and Gary Peller consider the effects of such presentation in "Reel Time/Real Justice" (58–64). And Judith Butler explains why "there is no simple recourse to the visible, to visual evidence, that it still and always calls to be read," in "Endangered/Endangering: Schematic Racism and White Paranoia" (17).

36. Andrew Goodman, "Truth, Justice, and Videotape," in *Inside the L.A. Riots: What Really Happened—And Why It Will Happen Again*, ed. Don Hazen (New York: Institute for Alternative Journalism, 1992), 122.

37. Lynell George, *No Crystal Stair: African-Americans in the City of Angels* (London: Verso, 1992), 10. Subsequent references to this edition appear in the text.

38. Anna Deavere Smith, *Talk to Me: Listening between the Lines* (New York: Random House, 2000), 36.

39. A number of critics have addressed these aspects of *Twilight: Los Angeles*. Jennifer Drake discusses the play's subjectivity, claiming that "Smith's version of critical ethnography emphasizes the negotiation of meaning, displacing the traditional ethnographer's desire for fixed definitions with the surrealist-ethnographer's exploration of juxtaposition" ("The Theater of the New World (B)orders: Performing Cultural Criticism with Coco Fusco, Guillermo Goméz-Pena and Anna Deavere Smith," in *Women of Color: Defining the Issues, Hearing the Voices*, ed. Diane Long Hoeveler and Janet K. Boks [Westport CT: Greenwood, 2001], 167). Charles R. Lyons and James C. Lyons note that the play's "fragmented and partial speeches . . . constitute representative or emblematic moments that, self-consciously, do not pretend to build to a whole" ("Anna Deavere Smith: Perspectives on Her Performance within the Context of Critical Theory," *Journal of Dramatic Theory and Criticism* 9 [fall 1994]: 44). Robin Bernstein discusses different versions of the text in "Rodney King, Shifting Modes of Vision, and Anna Deavere Smith's *Twilight: Los Angeles, 1992*," *Journal of Dramatic Theory and Criticism* 14 (spring 2000): 123. Reviewer Scott Kraft considers Smith's transformation of prose into free verse in "The Humans within the Events," *Los Angeles Times Book Review*, May 29, 1994, 16.

40. Anna Deavere Smith, *Twilight: Los Angeles, 1992* (New York: Anchor, 1994), 53, 55. Subsequent references to this edition appear in the text.

41. *Twilight: Los Angeles*, starring Anna Deavere Smith, directed by Marc Levin (PBS Pictures, 1999).

42. Frank Clifford and David Ferrell, "L.A. Strongly Condemns King Verdicts, Riots," *Los Angeles Times*, May 6, 1992, A1.

43. For a consideration of some of the play's paradoxical qualities see Lyons and Lyons, who discuss the play's combination of authenticity and artifice ("Anna Deavere Smith," 46). Drake claims that the play "attempts full representation even as it critiques the possibility of full representation" ("The Theater of the New World (B)orders," 166–67). Tania Modleski describes the play as a public event about a public event in "Doing Justice to the Subjects: Mimetic Art in a Multicultural Society: The Works of Anna Deavere Smith," in *Female Subjects in Black and White: Race, Psychoanalysis, Feminism*, ed. Elizabeth Abel, Barbara Christian, and Helene Moglen (Berkeley: University of California Press, 1997), 57. Sandra L. Richards elaborates, claiming that "the provocative nature of [*Twilight: Los Angeles*] threatens to reify the community's fissures, even while it validates the existence of previously marginal or silenced positions" ("Caught in the Act of Social Definition: *On the Road* with Anna Deavere Smith," in *Acting Out: Feminist Performances*, ed. Lynda Hart and Peggy Phelan [Ann Arbor: University of Michigan Press, 1993], 47).

44. Sam Eisenstein, "Riot/art," *High Performance* 12 (summer 1992): 49. Subsequent references to this issue appear in the text.

45. Modleski, "Doing Justice to the Subjects," 71.

8. Women Rewriting History

1. Suzan-Lori Parks, *Getting Mother's Body* (New York: Random House, 2003), 87, 93. Subsequent references to this edition appear in the text.

2. This trend is consistent with recent developments in western American litera-

ture. Krista Comer notes that there has been an "unprecedented boom" in western women's writing since the mid-1970s in "Feminism, Women Writers, and the New Western Regionalism: Revising Critical Paradigms," in *Updating the Literary West*, ed. Thomas J. Lyons (Fort Worth: Texas Christian University Press, 1997), 17. Comer considers works in a variety of genres, written by women of different races, whereas I focus only on historical novels and plays written by African American women. Comer suggests that the writers in her study share an interest in female sexuality and working-class culture, environmental issues, and other concerns, whereas I emphasize the differences as well as the similarities among female African American writers. Comer elaborates on her views in the introduction to *Landscapes of the New West: Gender and Geography in Contemporary Women's Writing* (Chapel Hill: University of North Carolina Press, 1999), 1–16.

3. Pearl Cleage, "Playwright's Note," in *Flyin' West and Other Plays* (New York: Theatre Communications Group, 1999), 6. Subsequent references to this edition appear in the text.

4. Nell Irvin Painter, *Exodusters: Black Migration to Kansas after Reconstruction* (1977; repr., New York: Norton, 1992), vii–viii.

5. Freda Scott Giles, "The Motion of Herstory: Three Plays by Pearl Cleage," *African American Review* 31 (winter 1997): 709.

6. Kenneth Marvin Hamilton, *Black Towns and Profit: Promotion and Development in the Trans-Appalachian West, 1877–1915* (Urbana: University of Illinois Press, 1991), 6.

7. Hamilton, *Black Towns and Profit*, 1.

8. Giles, "The Motion of Herstory," 709.

9. Esther Beth Sullivan, "The Dimensions of Pearl Cleage's *Flyin' West*," *Theatre Topics* 7 (March 1997): 11, 14.

10. J. Brooks Bouson explains that the novel was "based, in part, on [Morrison's] readings about the migration of ex-slaves into Oklahoma in the post–Civil War period" (*Quiet as It's Kept: Shame, Trauma, and Race in the Novels of Toni Morrison* [Albany: State University of New York, 2000], 192). In addition see Paul Gray, "Paradise Found," *Time*, January 19, 1998, 63. In an interview on the *Oprah Winfrey Show* (March 3, 1998), Morrison discusses various influences on the novel in greater detail.

11. Norman L. Crockett, *The Black Towns* (Lawrence: Regents Press of Kansas, 1979), xiv. For more information about the number of African American townships in Oklahoma at the turn of the century, the people who settled there, and their reasons for migrating, see also Hamilton, *Black Towns and Profit*, 102–5; and Jimmie Lewis Franklin, *Journey toward Hope: A History of Blacks in Oklahoma* (Norman: University of Oklahoma Press, 1982), 16–19.

12. Toni Morrison, *Paradise* (New York: Knopf, 1997), 112. Subsequent references to this edition appear in the text.

13. Crockett, *The Black Towns*, 56. Some African American townships advertised that they were safer than other frontier communities. In 1912 one town reported only one rape and one homicide. In 1913 a rival community claimed that no one had ever been murdered there, although one person had died of natural causes in 1907.

14. Crockett, *The Black Towns*, 56, 63–64.

15. Katrine Dalsgard, "The One All-Black Town Worth the Pain: (African) American Exceptionalism, Historical Narrative, and the Critique of Nationhood in Toni Morrison's *Paradise*," *African American Review* 35 (summer 2001): 233. See also Kristin Hunt, who writes that Morrison criticizes the American dream of land acquisition "as a means to an end" ("Paradise Lost: The Destructive Forces of Double Con-

sciousness and Boundaries in Toni Morrison's *Paradise*," in *Reading under the Sign of Nature: New Essays in Ecocriticism*, ed. John Tallmadge and Henry Harrington [Salt Lake City: University of Utah Press, 2000], 123). Evelyn Jaffe Schreiber shares a similar view: "In their re-circulation of patriarchal values, [the men] have embraced materialism and live the American dream" (*Subversive Voices: Eroticizing the Other in William Faulkner and Toni Morrison* [Knoxville: University of Tennessee Press, 2001], 139). Linda J. Krumholz argues that the men in the novel "are associated with phallogocentrism, with fixed authority, unitary meaning, and individual acquisition and control, while the women are associated with movement, multiple meanings, and shared labor and goods" ("Reading and Insight in Toni Morrison's *Paradise*," *African American Review* 36 [spring 2002]: 25). Peter Widdowson sees the problems that beset the African American town (including racial separatism and patriarchal governance) as examples of "all the abuses and failures of the American democratic experiment" ("The American Dream Refashioned: History, Politics and Gender in Toni Morrison's *Paradise*," *Journal of American Studies* 35 [2001]: 324).

16. Philip Page describes this change—from "fragmentation" to "fusion"—in "Furrowing All the Brow: Interpretation and the Transcendent in Toni Morrison's *Paradise*," *African American Review* 35 (winter 2001): 645.

17. Michiko Katukani, "Worthy Women, Unredeemable Men," *New York Times*, January 6, 1998, E8.

18. Geoffrey Brent, "Less Than Divine: Toni Morrison's *Paradise*," *Southern Review* 35 (1999): 146–47.

19. Louis Menand, "The War between Men and Women," *New Yorker*, January 12, 1998, 82.

20. For a statistical account of the damages caused by the riot see Scott Ellsworth, *Death in a Promised Land* (Baton Rouge: Louisiana State University Press, 1982), 65–72; and Tim Madigan, *The Burning: Massacre, Restoration, and the Tulsa Race Riot of 1921* (New York: Thomas Dunne/St. Martin's, 2001), 221.

21. Jewell Parker Rhodes, *Magic City* (1997; repr., New York: Harper Perennial, 1998), 16. Subsequent references to this edition appear in the text.

22. Quoted in Kevin E. Quashie, "Mining Magic, Mining Dreams: A Conversation with Jewell Parker Rhodes," *Callaloo* 20 (spring 1997): 435.

23. Octavia E. Butler, *Parable of the Sower* (1993; repr., New York: Warner, 1995), 9. Subsequent references to this edition appear in the text.

24. Fredric Jameson writes that science fiction "does not seriously attempt to imagine the 'real' future"; rather, it transforms "our own present into the determinate past" ("Progress versus Utopia: or, Can We Imagine the Future?" *Science Fiction Studies* 9 [July 1982]: 152). In a related essay, Jim Miller claims that Butler achieves "historical consciousness" by displacing the past and the present into the future ("Post-Apocalyptic Hoping: Octavia Butler's Dystopian/Utopian Vision," *Science-Fiction Studies* 25 [July 1998]: 347–52).

25. In an essay published the same year as *Paradise*, Morrison complained that paradise was often portrayed as a "protective preserve," located in a "probably nonexistent Eden" or in an "impossible future" ("Home," in *The House That Race Built: Black Americans, U.S. Terrain*, ed. Wahneema Lubiano [New York: Pantheon, 1997], 3–4).

26. Quoted in Frances M. Beal, "Black Women and the Science Fiction Genre," *Black Scholar* 17 (March–April 1986): 14.

27. Octavia E. Butler, *Parable of the Talents* (New York: Seven Stories, 1998), 101. Subsequent references to this edition appear in the text.

28. Quashie, "Mining Magic, Mining Dreams," 431.

29. In the preface to Alfred L. Brophy's *Reconstructing the Dreamland: The Tulsa Riot of 1921; Race, Reparation, and Reconciliation* (New York: Oxford University Press, 2002), Randall Kennedy describes Brophy's attempt to present history from "the Greenwood perspective" (x).

30. Pierre-Damien Mvuyekure, "Jewell Parker Rhodes," in *Contemporary African American Novelists: A Bio-Bibliographical Critical Sourcebook*, ed. Emmanuel S. Nelson (Westport CT: Greenwood, 1999), 402.

31. For a discussion of storytelling as historiography, comparing Morrison's narrative technique with the methodology of Ruby's unofficial historian, see Rob Davidson, "Racial Stock and 8-Rocks: Communal Historiography in Toni Morrison's *Paradise*," *Twentieth-Century Literature* 43 (fall 2001): 355–61.

32. Quoted in Beal, "Black Women and the Science Fiction Genre," 14.

Index